Elements
of Insurance

Fifth Edition

W. A. Dinsdale, Phd, FCII and
D. C. McMurdie, LLB, FCII Barrister

Pitman

PITMAN PUBLISHING LIMITED
39 Parker Street, London WC2B 5PB

Associated Companies
Pitman Publishing Pty Ltd. Melbourne
Pitman Publishing New Zealand Ltd, Wellington
Copp Clark Pitman, Toronto

© Rita M. Dinsdale and D. C. McMurdie 1971, 1973, 1980
Fifth edition published in Great Britain 1980

Text set in 10/11 Times

Printed and bound in Great Britain
at The Pitman Press, Bath

ISBN 0 273 01414 5

The Chartered Insurance Institute

This handbook is issued under the
authority of The Chartered Insurance Institute
and is designed specially for the use of students.

Preface to Fifth Edition

The business of insurance is operating today in a world of intensifying complexity. The factors which contribute to this are many, including new supervisory and control legislation, scientific and technological developments and the new hazards which they bring, extensive law reform with its impact on underwriting, new marketing techniques and economic pressures, not the least of which is the problem of inflation. Added to these are the problems of designing a coherent insurance policy within the framework of the EEC. Although this book is merely an introduction to insurance, a new edition is necessary in order to keep abreast of these changes.

This edition has been written without the invaluable help of my co-author and late colleague, Dr W. A. Dinsdale, who died in 1970. In order to take account of the many changes over the last eight years it has been necessary to revise considerably some of the chapters which we wrote together. However, his influence on the book is still most marked and I trust that his comprehensive knowledge of insurance and lucidity of style will not be entirely lost for some years to come.

Because of the complexity of insurance, it is essential to acquire a general basic knowledge of the business as a whole, and this should certainly be the first step to be taken by new entrants with an insurance career ahead of them. In this way a sense of perspective is obtained, and sound foundations laid for future specialized studies. This is the reason why 'elements of insurance' has been an examination subject since 1954, and this book has been designed to cover the syllabus for this subject in the CII Qualifying Examination and also in the examination for the option module 'elements of insurance' in the Business Education Council National Certificate in Business Studies.

General before specialized studies are desirable. Every insurance student should begin by a study of the risks in life and business with the application of insurance to risk. This necessitates an acquaintance with the development, scope and function of insurance (and re-insurance), the insurance market, the legal principles of insurance—utmost good faith, insurable interest and indemnity—and insurance practice, such as the structure of proposal and policy forms, cover notes, endorsements and renewal procedure. The associations of Insurers and of persons engaged in insurance, the organization of the Companies and of Lloyd's, the ancillary services rendered by Insurers and State regulation of the business also fall within the general introduction to insurance studies. These and other features, including a chapter on claims procedure, are dealt with in this book.

Insurance is so wide in scope that later some degree of specialization is usually necessary. After an initial period of general training, people employed in insurance companies may specialize in one of the many branches of business or even on a narrower basis in one of the principal classes of insurance.

Insurance brokers, however, may not specialize in the same way, although there are often specialists in the larger firms and there are specialist brokers in the Life and Pensions field. One of the dangers of specializing is the development of a narrow outlook, but this is less likely if at the outset a general background is obtained.

In addition to supplying the needs of the examination student, the book is planned for the student at the College of Insurance who follows an introductory course and needs a text book to supplement the oral instruction received. It should be of equal value to new entrants who follow internal office training courses. Then, too, teachers in Business Studies or Economics at institutions of higher education are advised to include in their instruction something about insurance in the same way as they deal with banking, shipping and other services to the community. This book gives the necessary information and can be used by both teachers and students of Business Studies.

In the preparation of previous editions suggestions have been received from various friends and acknowledged with gratitude.

London   D.C.McM.
1979

Preface to First Edition

Insurance covers a very wide field of activity. Its many sections are highly specialized and no man can hope to be master of the whole. Indeed, a considerable period of training in theory with practical experience is necessary in order to obtain a sound knowledge of any one of the main branches of the business—marine, fire, life, or accident insurance. Specialization, however, proceeds farther than this, so that, for example, profits insurance, public liability indemnities, or fidelity guarantee may well be for the specialist the study of a lifetime.

At the same time, there are certain fundamental principles which are common to all classes of insurance, for example, utmost good faith and insurable interest, while in matters of general practice, such as office organization and procedure, reinsurance, and accounting, the underlying method is the same, although there are often differences in detail between the various departments. It is the purpose of this book to deal with the general features of the subject, so that the student may be able to obtain a broad view of insurance as a whole.

There is much truth in the suggestion that one of the dangers of specialization is the development of a narrow outlook. It follows that a general knowledge of insurance, apart from a specialized acquaintance with the features peculiar to one branch, cannot fail to be of value to the student.

It was originally intended to prepare this book jointly with my colleague, Mr H. A. L. Cockerell, B.A., F.C.I.I., but pressure of work made this impossible. I have, however, had the benefit of his advice throughout.

This book is designed primarily for the use of those preparing for The Chartered Insurance Institute Associateship Examination: General Branch, but it can be read with advantage by any insurance man who desires to refresh his knowledge of the fundamental features of the business in which he is engaged.

Valuable help has been received from the suggestions made by various friends, to whom sincere thanks are due, and, in particular.

to Mr S. K. Dunford, F.C.I.I., for his technical criticism of the script, and to Mr G. W. Southgate, B.A., who has checked the proofs.

London   W.A.D.
July, 1948

Contents

(*a*) Marine Collision Liability · (*b*) Employers'
Liability · (*c*) Public Liability · (*d*) Products
Liability · (*e*) Motor Third Party Liability ·
(*f*) Engineering Insurance (Liability) ·
(*g*) Aviation Insurance (Liability)

Table of Statutes

Table of Cases

1 General Approach to Insurance

Insurance is a device for the handling of some of the risks—or chances of loss—to which man is subject. Risks can be classified in various ways. For example, there are business risks and personal risks. Business risks include possible loss of goods by fire or theft or loss by reason of periods of bad trade. Every individual faces risks, so that like the trader his goods may be destroyed while his dependants may suffer loss of income through his death. Another classification is into dynamic or speculative risks, which are uninsurable, and static or pure risks, which are insurable because they are susceptible to the principles on which insurance is based.[1]

Dynamic risks may result in either a profit or a loss, which may be either large or small. There are many risks in the marketing of goods as, for example, changes in fashion making valuable stock unsaleable, variations in trading profit on account of cycles of national prosperity and depression, and labour disputes, which may mean loss of orders on a large scale, both at home and overseas. The marketing of a new product is always risky; it may make a wide appeal or be a complete failure. Political risks, such as the consequences of an outbreak of war or loss of overseas trade by the imposition of currency restrictions, likewise cannot be foreseen. There is no way of measuring these risks and they are therefore uninsurable by commercial Insurers.

Static risks, on the other hand, can result only in loss, such as shipwreck, physical loss of or damage to goods by fire, theft or, say, riot (called perils), the incurring of legal liability to pay damages by negligently causing bodily injury to, or damage to the property of, others, and death, which comes to all sooner or later. These risks are insurable, because they are measurable statistically. For instance, mortality tables extending over a long period and covering hundreds of thousands of lives make it possible to calculate the average number

1 Some writers have used the term uncertainty as a synonym of an ininsurable or dynamic risk, and the word risk for an insurable risk, but today risk and uncertainty are usually regarded as identical.

1

of people who will die in any given year. This is the basis of life assurance. It is thus possible by this law of large numbers or the law of averages to calculate what are the chances of an event or events happening and the amount that will be required to provide the common fund or pool to which the many contribute, and out of which those who suffer losses are compensated.

The risks which can be insured have increased in number and extent owing to the growing complexity of the present-day economic system, and insurance therefore occupies an important place in the modern world. It would be impossible to do without insurance. Moreover, because insurance has over the years been able to offer better service through growing financial strength of Insurers, more reliable statistics, and research within the business itself, it is today impregnable.

Methods of Handling Risk

Because the economic risks faced by businesses and individuals are inevitable concomitants of life, some means of dealing with them have had to be devised. There are the following main possibilities:

Risks may be avoided

Some people may balance the pleasure to be derived from some risky course of action against the degree of risk involved. Thus, for the sake of the short-term gains of cigarette-smoking some people accept a much higher risk of early death. If a man feels that the risk is too great for the pleasure involved, he can stop smoking or not start it. Similarly, it is possible to avoid involvement in an aeroplane accident by not engaging in air travel. Carried to its logical conclusion, however, avoidance of risk would make life very tame and unbearable, if not impossible. Moreover, some risks are inherent in life itself and cannot be avoided. Men are mortal and all must die. The only uncertainty is the date of death, but the fact of death cannot be avoided.

Usually, avoidance is only a satisfactory method of counteracting risk when a choice is available. If a man buys a house he runs the risk of it being destroyed by fire. A house with a thatched roof is a greater fire risk than one with a tiled roof. Most people will avoid the greater risk attaching to the thatch and accept the smaller risk of buying a house of standard construction. In this case the risk has not been avoided so much as reduced.

Risks may be accepted

Because the element of risk is incidental to life and cannot usually be avoided, it may be accepted in the following ways:

a Some risks are accepted in ignorance. For example, the Occupiers' Liability Act, 1957, imposes certain duties upon property owners, but some people may be unaware of the Act and of their legal liability towards visitors who come to their premises. They may make no provision for this liability and run the risk in ignorance.

b Some risks are accepted inadvertently. Exposure to risk is recognized, but the opportunity to transfer it or to minimize it is neglected. A family man may fail to make adequate provision for his family in the event of his premature death or disability through accident. He need not be callously indifferent but merely neglectful.

c Some risks are accepted intentionally. Where the degree of risk is slight or the possible loss is small, a man may be willing to shoulder it without any anxiety. A student may possess a cheap wrist watch which is capable of being lost or damaged. He is prepared to accept this risk and does not seek to secure himself against it by 'all risks' insurance, since the latter would probably cost more than the watch is worth.

Along with the acceptance of risk, provision is sometimes made against the consequences of loss by the creation of a reserve fund. This is a method employed by some large concerns and by some nationalized industries. It can be a dangerous and not very scientific form of self-insurance, especially when the fund has to be built up over a period of years. If a heavy loss occurred during the early years of the scheme, the funds accumulated might well be inadequate to meet the loss. One municipal corporation estimated that it would take 80 years to accumulate a fund sufficient to meet a maximum single risk if its annual fire insurance premiums were paid into the fund and there were no calls upon the fund during the intervening years. Apart from exposure to trifling losses, self-insurance is not an economic method of dealing with risk.

Risks may be averaged

This involves the combination of the risks of many individuals who band together. It does not reduce the aggregate amount of potential loss, but it does achieve a reduction of uncertainty and it spreads the burden for those who are thus banded together. This was the principle on which merchants shared the risks of their seagoing ventures, and was implicit in all partnerships, while from this averaging of risks professional risk-bearing by insurance also developed.

The principle was recognized in marine insurance as long ago as 1601. The preamble to an Act of Parliament of that date states, 'by means of which policies of assurance ... the loss lighteth rather easily upon many, than heavily upon few.' It has been more recently defined as 'a social device for reducing risk by combining a sufficient number of exposure units to make their individual losses collectively predictable. The predictable loss is then shared proportionately by all those in the combination.'

Essential Features for Insurance

Insurance can only cater for risks when the following features are present:

a There must be a sufficient number of risks of a similar class being insured so as to produce an average of loss experience. This is because insurance is based on the operation of the law of large numbers. It would not be possible to administer an insurance portfolio of 30 or 40 cars as such small numbers would make loss prediction impossible. With a large number of risks of a similar kind, however, it is possible to forecast to a degree approaching accuracy the *proportion* of the whole that will sustain loss.

b It must be possible to calculate the chance of loss. The likelihood of an event or loss occurring may be mathematically calculated or it may be based on the statistical results of past experience. If the incidence of loss cannot be calculated statistically, it is impossible to determine the amount of premiums that would be required to accumulate a common fund, or pool, to meet the losses arising.

c The occurrence of loss must be fortuitous. Although it is known that losses will occur and that the frequency of loss can be measured, a specific loss must be unforeseen. A loss which is intentionally brought about or which is expected to happen is not suitable for insurance. In retail shops, for instance, it is known that the incidence of shoplifting is present and therefore it is usual to exclude this from the scope of the cover. Similarly, if it is known that a man is suffering from an incurable disease, life cover is unlikely to be forthcoming. These risks constitute a selection against the Insurers and cannot be offset by reasonable additional premiums.

d There must be an insurable interest to protect. It has been suggested that insurance is really a form of gambling, in that both transactions contemplate the risk of loss. Essentially, however, they differ in that a wager creates the risk of loss, while an insurance contract provides security against the consequences of a loss. A contract of insurance is fundamentally concerned with preserving the interest of the Insured, whereas the interest in a wager is confined to the stake money which is put at risk.

e The possible loss must not be catastrophic. When large numbers of people are subject to the same kind of losses at the same time, it is an obvious deviation from the principle that the losses of the few are borne by the contributions of the many who do not suffer loss. Thus it is usual to exclude political and war risks from most insurance policies, although these risks may sometimes be shouldered by the State.

Technical Terms

In the study of insurance many technical terms will be met, and the student will find his studies easier if he masters definitions of those terms. The following are basic:

Insurance a device for the transfer of risks of individual entities to an Insurer, who agrees, for a consideration (called the premium), to assume to a specified extent losses suffered by the Insured.
Peril a contingency which may cause a loss.
Risk the chance of loss.
Hazard a condition which may create, decrease or increase the chance of loss from a given peril.

In practice, terms are sometimes given more than one meaning, which is unfortunate. Risk may be used when what is in mind is peril or degrees of hazard, while a risk may refer to the subject-matter of insurance. Thus, one is said to be insured against fire risks, and a risk (meaning a building) which is slated or tiled is a better risk than one which is thatched.

Assurance or Insurance

There is no difference between the terms *assurance* and *insurance*. In Great Britain *assurance* is usually applied to life assurance and *insurance* to the other classes of business, but one large life Company uses the term Insurance in its title (the Norwich Union Life Insurance Society) and life insurance is the normal term in the USA. There are the corresponding terms Assurer, Assured, and Insurer, Insured.

Branches of Insurance

Insurance for practical and study purposes is divisible into various branches. It has been customary to use a fourfold classification—marine, fire, life and accident insurance. On this basis, the branches may differ in some details of practice, but they have many features in common.[1]

The Insurance Companies Act, 1974, adopted a classification which divided insurance into two main categories, (1) General Business, and (2) Long-term Business.

1 *General Business.* This comprises:

a Liability insurance, e.g., public liability, namely, liability incurred for bodily injuries or damage to the property of others.

b Marine, aviation and transport insurance, e.g., insurance of ships, aircraft and goods in transit.

c Motor vehicle insurance, which includes third party liability and loss of or damage to the Insured's own vehicles.

d Pecuniary loss insurance, e.g., fidelity guarantee (such as loss to an employer by the dishonesty of staff).

1 These branches cover insurance as conducted by private enterprise. National or social insurance is undertaken by the State through the Department of Health and Social Security.

e Personal accident insurance to cover death, loss of limbs or eyesight or temporary disablement by accident.

f Property insurance, e.g., loss of or damage to material property by fire.

2 *Long-term Business*, comprising:

a Ordinary long-term insurance, which includes life assurance and annuities.

b Industrial assurance, which is life assurance the premiums for which are paid in small instalments collected at the homes of the policyholders by industrial assurance agents.

Yet another classification which is now widely used is as follows:

1 *Insurances of the person.* Life assurance and personal accident insurance come under this heading.

2 *Insurances of property and pecuniary insurances.* The former include fire, special perils, theft, 'all risks' and motor insurance, while the latter relate to consequential loss, money, credit and fidelity insurance.

3 *Insurances of liability.* Indemnities in respect of legal liability are provided by employers' liability, public liability, motor and fire insurances. They also arise in marine insurance, e.g., collisions at sea.

The industrial life Offices use yet a further classification: I.B. (Industrial (life assurance) Branch), OB (Ordinary (life assurance) Branch), and GB (General Branch) to cover fire and accident business.

Lloyd's Underwriters divide their business into marine and non-marine. The latter relates to fire and accident insurance; they do not transact life insurance as such.

Functions of Insurance

The functions of insurance, irrespective of those of its separate branches, are set out below.

Principal Function

The main function of insurance is risk-bearing. The financial losses of the individual entity are equitably distributed over the many. In fire insurance, for example, the policyholders pay premiums into a common pool, out of which those who suffer loss are compensated. The amount of the premium or contribution is fixed according to individual circumstances; thus risks are assessed and rates of premium graduated so that if one type of risk is likely to involve more frequent or costly calls on the pool than another, the rate of premium will be higher and special requirements may be imposed. In life assurance every policy which does not lapse eventually becomes a claim, but there is the same principle of spreading of risk.

Insurance must be offered to the public on terms attractive enough to encourage them to insure and yet sufficient to offer a reasonable margin of profit.

Subsidiary Functions

The following functions, although subsidiary to the main function, are not insignificant.

a Insurance stimulates business enterprise. Insurance has made possible, and helps to maintain, the present-day large-scale industrial and commercial organization. No large-scale enterprise could function in the modern world without the transference of many of its risks to Insurers. Vast amounts of capital equipment, such as premises, expensive machinery and plant are at risk in industrial undertakings, and new risks have been created by technological developments especially in this nuclear age with the use in industry of various radioactive substances. Legal liabilities, too, have become more onerous by changes in the law made necessary because of mechanization with increased risk of accidents to employees and members of the public, whilst any goods sold or supplied can at times involve claims for damages of thousands of pounds.

Bankers and other financial houses require the security of marine insurance in financing home and overseas trade; fire insurance makes it possible for property to change hands and for mortgages to be granted without fear of loss by fire; life assurance encourages saving; and accident insurance provides against many contingencies which individuals and firms should not bear themselves.

Insurance safeguards capital and at the same time it avoids the necessity on the part of industrialists and others of freezing capital to guard against various contingencies. Instead, they can pay a fixed contribution by way of premium and obtain financial security against the insured risks. They are therefore free to use their capital as may seem best in the development of their business.

b Insurance encourages executive efficiency. Underwriters, by the nature of their specialized training and experience, learn how to assess risks and the bases on which various insurable risks can be undertaken. Industrial and commercial executives are adept in many aspects of managing a business, but they are not necessarily equipped to measure the types of insurable risks to which their businesses are exposed. The worry and uncertainty of such risks could seriously diminish their personal efficiency but for the way in which insurance relieves them of these strains. The availability of this relief is no less real because corporations are now tending to employ risk managers whose function is to determine what risks should be insured and what risks the business can afford to carry.

In personal forms of insurance not only executives but members of the community generally are relieved of hardship and anxiety so that insurance contributes to the efficiency and well-being of countless people.

c Insurance promotes loss-prevention. The community would suffer much greater economic impoverishment through material losses if it were not for the loss-prevention measures of Insurers. The extent to which loss-prevention is encouraged is particularly evident in property insurance. For instance, regular inspections of steam boilers, engines and other equipment carried out by the engineering departments of Insurers with the making of recommendations for the efficient and economic working of the plant reduce explosions and breakdowns to the minimum. Similarly, Insurers place their knowledge and experience at the disposal of their policyholders through the work of fire and accident insurance surveyors (see p. 228). The system of rating encourages loss-prevention because Insurers often allow discounts for good features and load premiums or impose special conditions where the risk is unsatisfactory.

Various associations which are maintained wholly or in part by Insurers help to achieve the same aims. Thus, the Fire Protection Association seeks to educate the public in methods of reducing fire waste, while the Fire Insurers Testing and Research Organization conducts research into fire protection equipment and appliances. There are also voluntary insurance organizations whose activities have a beneficial influence on the community. An example is the Association of Burglary Insurance Surveyors, whose object is to disseminate up-to-date technical knowledge and so help to combat the development of the incidence of crime.

d Insurance solves social problems. Some of the social problems which beset a modern civilized community are taken care of through insurance. Many of the measures are provided through the system of National Insurance, while others are provided through free enterprise insurance. Moreover, since some of the benefits of National Insurance are of necessity modest in amount, they may be supplemented by private insurance schemes. The effect, however, of the concurrent operation of free enterprise and National Insurance is that compensation is available to victims of industrial injuries and road accidents, while the financial difficulties arising from old age, disability or death are mitigated.

Indirect Functions

There are also various indirect functions some of which may be regarded as benefits rather than functions proper. They are as follows:

a Investment of funds. By reason of their principal function, Insurers accumulate large funds which they hold as custodians and out of which claims and losses are met. These funds themselves are invested so that not only do they earn interest to be added to the funds but they also benefit government, municipal and public authorities and industry among whose securities the investments are spread. The 1978 figures show the investments of British Insurance Companies totalling £11,612m. for general business and £39,319m. for long-term business. These amounts represent increases of 8.5 per cent and 11.4 per cent respectively over the 1977 investments. The proportion of these sums invested in equities is 24.4 per cent for general business and 29.9 per cent for long-term business which is only marginally different from 1976 in both instances, whereas there is now the beginning of a trend to record them at market value.

b Invisible exports. British Insurers operate in many parts of the world and earn vast sums in overseas markets in terms of underwriting profit and investment income. By this means insurance forms a considerable part of the country's invisible exports (i.e., services such as shipping, air transport, tourism, banking and insurance facilities, as distinct from the sale of material goods overseas, which are 'visible' exports. Overseas premium income for the year 1978 in fire, accident and motor insurance alone was in the region of £3,800m. This, in turn, means that a substantial contribution is made to Great Britain's 'balance of trade,' namely, the difference between exports and imports. Insurance activities, comprising companies, Lloyd's and brokers, produced invisible earnings of £909m. in 1977.

c Use of reserve funds. Because of the investment policy of Insurers, their reserve funds are not static, but are used productively. This results in a reduction of the cost of insurance to the insuring public. If the reserve funds were not so used, the income they now earn would have to be obtained through higher premiums.

d Effect on prices. The cost of insurance to industrialists is passed on to consumers, along with other production costs, but, paradoxically, the existence of insurance benefits the consumer public in terms of reduced prices. This is because the cost of insurance is less than would be the cost of risk without insurance.

Subject-matter of Insurance

No insurance can prevent loss by fire, theft or other perils or the creation of legal liability. It can merely provide financial assistance in such circumstances. An insurance, therefore, does not protect, for instance, the material property which is the subject-matter of the insurance, but the pecuniary *interest*[1] of the Insured.

The following are examples of the subject-matter of insurance, using the following classifications:

Insurances of the person. The person of the Life Assured, the policy moneys being payable under a whole life contract at his death, or under an endowment assurance at maturity or death, whichever first occurs. (The Assured and the Life Assured may be different persons.) The person of the policyholder under a personal accident insurance.

Insurances of property. Buildings, goods, vehicles and machinery.

Insurances against pecuniary loss. Money which may be the subject of a fidelity guarantee or money in transit insurance. Consequential losses, such as are insured under a profits policy.

Insurances of liability. A legal liability, such as is insured under a third party indemnity.

Marine, aviation and transport insurances. Here the subject-matter may be the ship, aircraft, freight, cargo, or legal liability.

1 This interest is the subject-matter of the *contract*, and should be distinguished from the subject-matter of the insurance.

Physical and Moral Hazards

In all classes of business, the Insurers carefully assess the physical and moral hazards associated with the risks proposed for insurance.

Physical Hazard

Physical hazard relates to the subject-matter of insurance, and the following are examples of unfavourable physical hazard:

Insurances of the person. A proposer in a poor state of health or one who intends to reside abroad in an area known to be unhealthy. A proposer for personal accident insurance suffering from defective vision or loss of a limb.

Insurances of property. A thatched dwelling, hazardous processes, jewellers' stock.

Insurances of liability. Premises in bad repair proposed for public liability insurance.

Marine. Stowage of cargo on deck; bad packing.

It is often possible to improve the physical hazard as, for instance, by the fixing of additional locks and bolts for the better security of premises against burglary. There are, nevertheless, limits beyond which it is not practicable to make recommendations; a proposer would hardly be likely to remove thatching in favour of slates or tiles in order to reduce the fire risk.

Moral Hazard

Moral hazard mainly concerns the *bona fides* of the proposer and is therefore dependent upon his character and business integrity. It is essential that the Insured be scrupulously honest in all his dealings with his Insurers so that he will act with the same prudence as he would do if uninsured. An extreme illustration of bad moral hazard is the person who effects a policy of insurance in order to make a profit by means of false and exaggerated claims.

Moral hazard does not always imply fraud or dishonesty. There can be bad moral hazard where a person is careless about the safety and welfare of his employees, where he fails to take reasonable care of his property or where his habits increase the risk of injury or disease. There is also the type of claimant who is 'awkward' in the sense that no reasonable offer in settlement appears to satisfy him. Moral hazard, too, is connected with the general course of events, so that when times are good and trade brisk, there is not the same tendency, for instance, to malinger or to have a fire as during a trade depression.

Parties to the Contract

Insurance contracts concern two parties—the Insured and the Insurers.[1]

Insured. This term refers to the party effecting the insurance, either direct or through an agent or broker, and may consist of an individual, several individuals, such as trustees or legal personal representatives, or a corporate body. The party effecting an insurance is known as the proposer throughout the negotiations and until the contract is in force, when the proposer becomes the Insured.

Insurers. The term Insurers refers to the party providing the protection to be afforded by the policy. Insurers is a general term and covers all the types of Insurers set out below. An Underwriter is an Insurer, all insurances at Lloyd's being effected (through brokers, as explained below) with Underwriters who are members of Lloyd's. The term Underwriter also refers to a senior official of an Insurance Company whose duties are concerned with the acceptance of new business as, for instance, a Marine Underwriter.

The Insurance Market

Insurance is not a material commodity but a service of availability, and the market in which it is dealt embraces the insuring public on the one hand and Insurers on the other with the various insurance intermediaries, as described later in this chapter.

The market is represented diagrammatically for the convenience of the reader.

1 A fidelity guarantee involves three parties, as in a commercial fidelity guarantee where there are the employee, the employer, and the Insurers.

i The Insuring Public

The insuring public can be divided into two sections. There are the private individuals, to some of whom industrial life assurance makes its appeal, and also those who buy household insurances, holiday travel insurances, and other personal insurances. The rest of the buyers comprise associations, clubs, companies, corporations, societies and similar organizations.

ii Insurers

Insurers may be divided into several groups, according to their constitution. The principal groups are (1) Proprietary Companies, (2) Lloyd's Underwriters, (3) Mutual Insurers, and (4) Collecting Friendly Societies, as follows:

1 *Proprietary Companies*. Insurance Companies are incorporated under the Companies Acts, by Royal Charter (e.g., *The London Assurance*), private Act of Parliament (e.g., *Railway Passengers Assurance Co.*), or Deed of Settlement. The Companies originally incorporated by Deed of Settlement have as a rule now reconstituted themselves under the Companies Acts.

The proprietors of a Company are the shareholders who have supplied the capital.

2 *Lloyd's Underwriters*. These Underwriters are individuals who personally insure risks, and they are members of the Corporation of Lloyd's. In practice, they usually transact business as members of Syndicates.

All persons elected as Underwriting Members of Lloyd's must furnish substantial security in respect of their underwriting liabilities as the Committee of Lloyd's may require. The security must be in cash and/or approved securities.

3 *Mutual Insurers*. These are organizations which transact business on a mutual basis, that is, the profits go to the policyholders, there being no shareholders. The policyholders are the members, often of some particular trade. The members make contributions to the funds and are liable to additional calls if the contributions received are not sufficient to cover claims and expenses. At the present time, however, many Mutual Insurers are organized as Companies limited by guarantee.

DIAGRAM OF THE INSURANCE MARKET

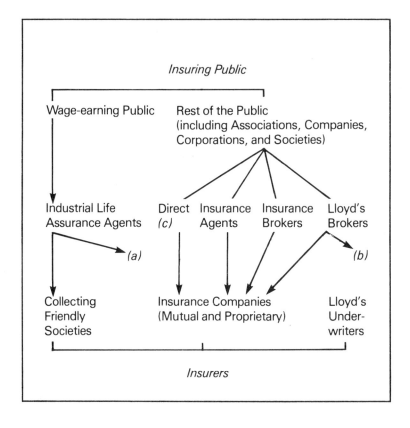

(*a*) Some industrial life assurance agents are permitted to place general branch business with outside Companies.

(*b*) Insurances at Lloyd's can be arranged only through Lloyd's brokers. Such brokers also place a considerable amount of business with the Companies.

(*c*) An own case agent is one who receives commission on his own insurances only, and who introduces no other business. Australasian and Canadian Life Offices and some of the newer British Life Offices sell direct to the public.

In practice, the mutual principle is departed from in various ways and some Companies have the word 'mutual' as part of their name although they do not differ from an ordinary Insurance Company constituted under the Companies Acts.

4 *Collecting Friendly Societies.*[1] These Societies, registered under the Friendly Societies Act, 1974 (consolidating the Friendly Societies Acts, 1896 to 1971), transact life assurance business. This is mainly industrial life assurance, but the larger societies transact tax exempt ordinary life or endowment assurances up to £1,000 any one life.

Specialist and Composite Insurers

This is a classification of Insurers according to the type of business transacted. A specialist Insurer carries on one class of business only, for example, life assurance, whereas a composite Office transacts all or the majority of the various kinds of insurance business.

Business at Lloyd's is classified into marine and non-marine, and an Underwriter (or Syndicate) normally transacts either marine or non-marine business, not both.

iii Insurance Intermediaries

A proposer can himself negotiate an insurance (except at Lloyd's) with an Insurer of his choice, but he may, if he wishes, arrange the insurance through an agent. The agent may be a full-time agent,[2] or a part-time agent such as an accountant, shopkeeper, garage proprietor or solicitor. The majority of full-time agents are insurance brokers; they are specialists who hold themselves out as competent to give professional advice to their clients on insurance matters. Insurance with Lloyd's Underwriters may be effected only through Lloyd's brokers, because Underwriters at Lloyd's do not deal directly with the public.

Some insurance brokers are concerned not only with direct insurance but also with reinsurance business (see p. 169). There are also a number of very large and well-established firms of reinsurance brokers who do no direct business at all.

---

1 The Friendly Societies, other than Collecting Friendly Societies, receive contributions at specified places and not by means of collectors; they usually specialize in the provision of sickness benefits.

2 An industrial agent or representative is engaged full time in industrial life assurance (and other classes of business) but he is an agent in a different sense. He is an employee under an ordinary contract of service with an industrial life assurance company or collecting friendly society (see p. 41).

Brokers and Agents: Their Duties and Responsibilities

The term 'agent' has a wider application than the meaning used loosely in insurance practice to describe one who introduces business to the Insurer. Agency is 'the relationship that exists between two persons one of whom, the principal, expressly or impliedly consents that the other, the agent, similarly consenting, should represent him or act on his behalf' (*Bowstead on Agency*, 13th ed., p. 1 (Sweet & Maxwell, 1968)).

In insurance transactions an agent is a person who acts as an intermediary between the Insurer and the proposer or Insured; he may act in the negotiations leading up to the contract, in the renewal or alteration of the contract, or in the negotiation of claims. Agents are intermediaries through whom Insurers and Insured come into agreement. They may be appointed by the Insurer or by the Insured; it is even possible for a single agent to be, in one part of the negotiations, the agent of the Insured and, in the other part, the agent of the Insurer.[1] In *Newsholme Brothers* v. *Road Transport & General Insurance Company* (1929), 2 KB 356, a partner in Newsholme Brothers made a proposal for motor insurance to an agent of the Insurers. The form was completed by the agent and, although he was given correct information by the partner, it was discovered, when a claim was made, that the agent had incorrectly filled in the answers to three questions. The form contained a warranty that the answers were true, and the Court decided that the Insurers were able to avoid liability because, in completing the form, the agent was for that purpose the agent of the proposer.

Agents of the Insured

Where negotiations are carried on by an agent of the proposer or Insured, for example, by a director on behalf of a limited company, the principal is bound by the agent's acts, as if the principal had done them himself, provided the agent is acting within the scope of his authority. If, therefore, an agent fails to exhibit the utmost good faith in arranging the insurance, the effect is the same as if the proposer himself had failed to disclose material information.

1 But see footnote on p.198.

Agents of the Insurer

Insurers usually transact much of their business through agents, and their agents may be divided into four classes:

a General agents who stand in the place of Insurers; these include directors, managers, underwriters, and salaried staffs. Their authority, however, is limited by the ordinary rules of business and by the powers of the undertaking that they represent.

b Agents employed to introduce business to the Insurer, who have a limited authority to bind their principals, for example, agents (including brokers) who are permitted to give cover within limits set by the Insurer, or who have authority to collect premiums and issue renewal receipts.

c Agents who merely receive commission on business they introduce to the Insurer, with no authority to give cover or otherwise to bind the Insurer.

d Agents employed by Insurers for a particular task, for example, an adjuster instructed to deal with a claim. The authority of such an agent depends on the instructions given to him in each particular claim.

Authority of the Agent

The scope of the authority of an agent depends on his terms of appointment, and on instructions given to him by the principal. Authority may be implied as well as express. In *Murfitt* v. *Royal Insurance Co. Ltd.* (1922), 38 TLR 334, the plaintiff, who owned an orchard near a railway, approached an agent of the Insurers. The agent said the risk would be held covered pending the Insurer's decision. A fire occurred but, before the Insurers knew of it, they declined the risk. They pleaded that the agent had no authority to give cover; the plaintiff, however, showed that the agent had previously given him cover for insurances of another class, and that on each occasion the cover had been ratified by the Insurers. The Court held that the Insurers were bound, because the agent had implied authority.

Rights and Duties

The agent must act with reasonable care and skill and must comply exactly with any instructions given to him. If he cannot comply with any instructions, he must promptly inform his principal.

The agent is entitled to the agreed payment (in insurance usually by commission) for his services; he may also be entitled to receive reimbursement of any payment properly made on behalf of his principal, e.g., some Insurers allow agents a sum for postages and similar out-of-pocket expenses.

Insurance Brokers

An insurance broker is a special class of agent. He commonly acts, not only for his client, but also for the Insurer.[1] When he issues cover notes or collects premiums he acts on behalf of the Insurer; when he negotiates the terms of an insurance with the Insurer, he is acting on behalf of his client. A client is entitled to expect a high standard of professional skill and conduct from the insurance broker, and if the broker fails to maintain this standard, he may become liable in damages to his client.

By custom, a broker usually receives his remuneration from the Insurer with whom he places the insurance on behalf of his client.

Termination of Agency Appointments

When Insurers wish to put an end to an agent's authority, they must ensure that they notify not only the agent but also all persons who have dealt with him. *Murfitt* v. *Royal Insurance Co. Ltd. (supra)* shows that authority may be implied, and, unless persons who have dealt with the agent are notified, acts done by the agent after his agency has been terminated may bind the Insurers.

Statutory Control

In recent years, the State has tended to exercise an increasing control over private enterprise. Indeed, today some industries have been nationalized. Insurance is essential to the well-being of the country, and Insurers themselves accept the view that a certain measure of State control is all to the good, if only because it eliminates any risk of unsound undertakings entering or continuing in the business. For many years Insurers were left completely unfettered to transact their own business, and during that period they built up a first-class reputation for sound dealing and the honouring of obligations. State

1 But see footnote on p. 198.

supervision in this country was minimal and was described as a policy of 'freedom with publicity'—freedom to provide insurance on the Insurer's own terms and conditions, subject to the publicity of published accounts and other returns in statutory form. However, this freedom has been steadily eroded in recent years partly as a result of the collapse of a large motor insurance company in 1971, the development of new and highly publicized forms of life assurance, linked with equities or property, and partly because of the closer involvement of British insurance in the EEC and the need to think in terms of reconciling UK legislation with the more restrictive supervisory systems in Europe.

The 1967 Companies Act had given the Department of Trade wider powers of supervision and investigation although the Department had failed to take advantage of these powers before the failure of the Vehicle and General in 1971. The Department was subsequently strengthened and reorganized and more extensive powers were conferred upon it by the Insurance Companies Amendment Act, 1973. The following year saw the consolidation of the provisions of the Insurance Companies Acts, 1958 to 1973 and Part II of the Companies Act, 1967, by the passing of the Insurance Companies Act, 1974.

The main features of the 1974 Act are:

1 All kinds of insurance are covered, and insurance is divided into the classes shown on p. 6.

2 The Act applies to all insurance companies whether established within or outside Great Britain, which carry on insurance business within Great Britain, but Lloyd's underwriters are excluded provided they comply with Section 73 which prescribes rules more appropriate to their requirements.

3 A company which was carrying on insurance of any class before 3 November 1966 is authorized to continue doing so. A company wishing to transact a class of insurance which it has not previously done requires an authority from the Department of Trade.

4 An authorization will not be issued to any company which has a share capital unless the amount paid up thereon is £100,000 or more.

5 If a Company has not completed its first financial year it must have a paid-up share capital of not less than £100,000 and at all times during the year assets must exceed liabilities by not less than £50,000. If a Company has completed its first financial year and transacts 'general business' (see p. 6) it must likewise have a paid-

up capital of not less than £100,000 and assets must exceed liabilities by the 'relevant amount' as below:

General Premium Income	Excess of Assets over Liabilities (Margin of Solvency)
Not exceeding £250,000	£50,000
Exceeding £250,000 but not exceeding £2,500,000	One-fifth of income
Exceeding £2,500,000	The aggregate of £500,000 and one-tenth of the amount by which income exceeds £2,500,000

6 The Secretary of State for Trade may by order vary the foregoing financial requirements and it is likely that they may be amended in due course to harmonize the margins of solvency with those being proposed for insurers operating in the EEC.

7 An authorization will not be issued to any company unless the Secretary of State is satisfied that adequate reinsurance arrangements are in force in respect of each class of insurance to be transacted or that it is justifiable not to make such arrangements.

8 The Secretary of State will not issue an authorization to any company if it appears to him that any director, controller or manager of that company is not a fit and proper person in relation to the particular office to be occupied.

9 The Secretary of State is empowered to make regulations requiring companies to submit periodic statements of their business, in addition to annual accounts and balance sheets, and to prescribe the form, contents and frequency of such statements.

10 Companies undertaking long-term business are required to maintain a separate account for each class of long-term business, a separate fund with an appropriate name and books of account which clearly identify the assets and the liabilities attributable to long-term business. An actuary must be appointed for long-term business and is required to make an investigation into the company's financial condition at least once every three years and a special investigation if called for by the Secretary of State at any time.

11 The Secretary of State is given residual powers which enable him to require a company to take such action as appears to him to be appropriate for the purpose of protecting policyholders against the risk that the company may be unable to meet its liabilities.

12 The Secretary of State is empowered to apply to the court to wind up unsound companies and there are special provisions in the Act for the continuation of long-term business wherever possible and for the insulation of long-term funds from those of any other business if it is necessary to terminate the long-term contracts.

National Insurance

National Insurance began in a modest way at the beginning of this century with the Old Age Pensions Act, 1908, which provided a small pension for persons over the age of 70. The first National Insurance Act was passed in 1911 and provided some limited unemployment benefits for certain trades and health insurance for employed persons. A full programme of national insurance based on the Beveridge report of 1942 was enacted by the National Insurance Act, 1946, and the National Insurance (Industrial Injuries) Act, 1946. These Acts, which came into operation in 1948, created the 'Welfare State'.

There has been a number of amending Acts but the current scheme, which replaces the former National Insurance Scheme 1948–1975, is derived from the Social Security Act, 1975, and the Social Security Pensions Act, 1975, and is administered by the Department of Health and Social Security.

1 The new social security scheme like its predecessor is *not funded* for assured pension provision, except to the extent that it has taken over the Industrial Injuries Fund and the assets of the National Insurance Scheme. (Funded contributions are those which are actuarially calculated so that they accumulate in a fund specifically intended to provide the contributors with the benefits for which they were calculated.) The new scheme is financed on a pay-as-you-go basis mainly by contributions but in part out of Exchequer funds. However, the contributions under the new scheme are earnings-related to a greater extent than the former National Insurance contributions.

2 The scheme is compulsory for all employed and self-employed persons in Great Britain while non-employed persons may become voluntary contributors. Rates of contribution are standard for all persons in a particular class except that those 'contracted-out' (*see* 3 below) pay at a lower rate. Contributions are of four classes:

Class 1, earnings related

    a primary Class 1 contributions payable by employed earners;

b secondary Class 1 contributions payable by employers and other persons paying earnings;

Class 2, flat-rate, payable weekly by self-employed earners;

Class 3, flat-rate, payable by earners and others voluntarily with a view to providing entitlement to benefit, or making up entitlement; and

Class 4, payable by self-employed persons in respect of the profits or gains of a trade, profession or vocation, or in respect of equivalent earnings.

No differentiation is made within each class according to the degree of risk so that there is no scope for selective underwriting as in commercial insurance.

3 When employed persons are 'contracted out' both primary Class 1 and secondary Class 1 contributors pay the standard rates of contribution up to a lower earnings limit (at present £17.50 a week). The rates are reduced on earnings above the lower limit up to an upper earnings limit (currently £120). This is to take account of the fact that the employer's occupational pension scheme is taking over from the state responsibility for the additional pensions of his employees. The latter may, of course, have to contribute to their occupational pension scheme.

4 Contribution of the insured person *covers those* of his family who are *not insured persons*, in so far as dependants' benefits are payable for wives and children under school-leaving age. This is different from commercial insurance generally, although the property of members of the family is included under a household policy, and drivers other than the Insured may be indemnified under a motor policy.

5 The Secretary of State for Social Services is empowered by the Social Security Acts to alter certain rates of contribution by order approved by both Houses of Parliament and to make annual reviews of the general level of earnings to determine whether such an order should be made. Similarly, he is empowered to increase certain rates of benefit if an annual review shows that they have not retained their value in relation to the general level of earnings and prices obtaining in Great Britain.

6 Benefits payable under the Social Security Acts are as follows:

a Contributory Benefits:
Unemployment benefit

Sickness benefit

Invalidity pension and allowance

Maternity benefit, comprising maternity grant and maternity allowance

Widow's benefit, comprising widow's allowance, widowed mother's allowance and widow's pension

Child's special allowance

Retirement pensions payable to men and women on their own contributions (*a*) if they are over 65 for men and 60 for women and (*b*) have retired from regular employment. Men aged 70 and over and women 65 and over are not required to satisfy condition (*b*). Under certain circumstances pensions are also payable to a woman on her husband's contributions.

b Non-contributory Benefits:

Guardian's allowance

Attendance allowance

Non-contributory invalidity pension

Mobility allowance

Some non-contributory pensions may also be paid, for example to very elderly people aged 80 or to those who were over pensionable age in 1948.

c Benefits for Industrial Injuries and Diseases.

7 There are no policies of insurance. The Class 1 contributions are deducted from earnings by the employer and are paid, together with the employer's contribution, to the Inland Revenue along with income tax collected under the PAYE system, so dispensing with contribution cards for employed earners. Classes 2 and 3 contributions may be paid by direct debit of a bank or National Giro account or by stamping a contribution card. Class 4 contributions are generally assessed and collected by the Inland Revenue along with Schedule D income tax.

8 There is one system of adjudication on all claims for benefit under the Social Security Acts. With certain exceptions, questions as to the right to benefit are decided by independent statutory tribunals and not by the ordinary law courts.

Method of Study

There are two methods of approach to the study of insurance. The student may begin the specialized study of one branch of insurance—probably the branch which he enters as a junior—and later acquire a general knowledge of the business of insurance as a whole. Alternatively, he may commence his studies on broad and general lines and subsequently specialize according to the career which he eventually finds marked out for him by personal aptitude or force of circumstances. There is much to be said for the latter method, because it enables the student from the start to obtain a wide view and to understand something of the problems with which his colleagues in other branches are faced. Moreover, there is considerable specialization within each branch, for example, underwriting, claims negotiation, surveying, and new-business getting, all of which will be better undertaken if the necessary technical knowledge is built upon a general foundation.

Examination students are now required at the outset to gain some knowledge of insurance generally, and in dealing with the fundamentals of insurance, therefore, reference is made throughout this book to all branches of the business.

2 Outline Development of Insurance

As this chapter deals with the development of insurance it has been divided into marine, fire, life and accident insurance, which has until recently been the usual way of classifying insurance. In the succeeding chapters concerned with the present and future position of the business the modern division into insurance of the person, of property and pecuniary loss, and of liability is followed.

Early Schemes

Bottomry bonds[1] were known to merchants in the times of classical Greece in the fourth century B.C., and the wording of one of them is given by Demosthenes in a court action in which he delivered one of his 'Private Orations.' (An English translation is available in the Loeb Classics—*Demosthenes*, Vol. 1, p. 283.)

In Roman times the value of a life annuity was assessed for legal purposes; it was an estimate, however, and was not based on statistics, so far as is known. There were also burial clubs, but contributions to them were not assessed actuarially.

Many of the early guilds in England were religious associations. They were encouraged by the Church in view of their religious objects and their charitable activities. At a later stage there were guilds merchant under whose charters the commercial interests of their members were protected, although the religious element was retained, and the succour of members who had met with misfortune

---

1 A loan on bottomry was an advance of money on a ship during the period of a voyage. If the ship arrived safely, the loan was repaid with the agreed rate of interest (which corresponded to the modern premium), but if the ship was lost, the borrower was freed from the obligation to repay the loan. Loans on bottomry were used by the mediaeval Mediterranean traders—see p. 5 *A History of British Insurance* (Raynes). An alternative to pledging the ship itself as collateral was the pledging of cargo, in which case the contract was known as one of *respondentia*.

was included in their objects. The craft guilds were of later date; in general, they were subordinate to the guild merchant, though some craft guilds obtained charters from the Crown which ensured their independence of merchant guild supervision. A craft guild in a town included all who followed the craft; all members were bound to obey the regulations of the guild and were entitled to its protection. (From these the present livery companies in our cities have come into existence.) The wealthier guilds exercised charity towards their poorer members in many ways—payments following loss by fire or theft, or in time of sickness or in old age, burial payments, and the care of widows and orphans of members.

Friendly Societies appeared early in the eighteenth century and were concerned with sickness insurance. They were not derived from craft guilds but organized the relief of their members as an alternative to the harshness of the administration of the Poor Law.

Commercial insurance based on contract (as distinct from custom, which predominated in the mediaeval guilds) had a different origin. It began with marine insurance, probably among the Florentine and other Italian merchants about the end of the thirteenth century.

Marine Insurance

It follows that marine insurance is the oldest branch of insurance business transacted in Great Britain. In the Middle Ages trade was mainly centred on the Mediterranean, with well-known trade routes to the east (to Constantinople and India) and to the north (over the Brenner Pass to Bruges or by sea to Flanders). The northern Italian cities—Florence, Genoa, and Venice—became centres for banking, commerce, and insurance.

The large commercial firms had representatives in the majority of the important cities of north-western Europe, including England. The connection between Lombardy and Lombard Street, London, is not accidental, and it is on record that the famous firm of *Bardi* had a lease of premises in Lombard Street as early as 1318. The word 'policy' is derived from the Italian *polizza*.

In his book, *A History of British Insurance*, Mr Harold E. Raynes states that the earliest marine policy relating to this country is dated 20 September, 1547—a short document of fourteen lines relating to a marine insurance from Cadiz to London. Interesting information bearing upon some of the early contracts has been preserved among the documents of the Admiralty Court of Tudor times. They were known as Bills of Surance or Bills of Assurance, and it appears that the word 'policy' was not used until after the setting up of the Chamber or Office of Assurances in 1575, when the documents became longer and more formal. The influence of Lombard Street is evident by the phrase found in the early marine assurances:

> 'This writing of assurance shall be of as much force and effect as the surest policy or writing of assurance heretofore made in Lombard Street.'

Chamber of Assurances

The Tudors (1485–1603), particularly Elizabeth I, were very much interested in mercantile matters, and the Tudor Privy Council from time to time received complaints from merchants who could not collect assurance moneys from Underwriters. This resulted in the setting up of the Chamber of Assurances, in London, in the year 1575.

Richard Candler, an associate of Sir Thomas Gresham, was the first Registrar, and he was required to draw and enter in his books of record all policies effected in the City of London, and, on request and payment of a prescribed fee, to give information relating to such policies. He procured a patent on 21 February, 1575, and this enabled him to offer material advantages to those who effected policies. Registration was evidence of the contract and this was very useful if the policy was subsequently lost.

One of the main functions of the Chamber was the settlement of disputes, but the Commissioners of the Chamber had no legal powers, and merchants submitted a petition stating that the orders and regulations were not being carried out. This was referred by the Privy Council to the Lord Chief Justice and resulted in the setting up of a Court of Commissioners. The decisions of that Court were subject to a right of appeal to the Court of Chancery.

In the course of time, it appeared that all policies were not registered with the Chamber of Assurances, and although Candler's monopoly was renewed, his successors found that the brokers, who had been unfriendly from the outset, began to give a service not inferior to that offered by the Chamber. On its legal side the Chamber likewise declined because the Law Merchant became absorbed into the Common Law of the country. The Chamber ceased to exist before the middle of the eighteenth century, after having been the means of standardizing the marine insurance policy and giving permanence to merchants' customs in marine insurance.

Two Chartered Companies Formed

Events began in 1716 which eventually led to the formation of two Companies by Royal Charter—the *Royal Exchange Assurance* and *The London Assurance*—with a monopoly for the transaction of marine insurance business. There must have been some collaboration between the petitioners because they took similar steps and each offered £300,000 for the use of His Majesty's Government in order to secure the Charter. The Government was in need of money; this was the time of wild speculation of the South Sea Bubble period. By the Act which granted the Charters, there was also a prohibition after 24 June, 1720, of:

'all undertakings tending to the prejudice of trade, and all subscription thereto or presuming to act as corporate bodies, or raising transferable stock without legal authority, and all action under obsolete charters shall be deemed illegal and void.'

The monopoly was against all other Corporations, Societies, and Partnerships 'as now or hereafter shall be entered into by any persons for assuring ships or merchandise at sea or for lending money on bottomry.' The South Sea Bubble burst and the promises of the subscribers to the two Companies for payment of the shareholding could not be fulfilled. Both Companies eventually paid or gave security for one-half (£150,000), and this was accepted instead of the original sum.

As the monopoly precluded only all other Corporations, Societies, and Partnerships from transacting marine insurance, it left individual Underwriters unfettered. Gradually, marine underwriting by individuals became a specialized business, a market developed, and this led to the formation of Lloyd's, as it is known today.

Lloyd's Underwriters

The individual merchants who underwrote marine risks met in the coffee house of Edward Lloyd in Tower Street. The coffee houses of that time were the centres of much of the business life of the City of London and the subscription list of *The London Assurance* was arranged at Garraway's coffee house. Each coffee house catered for a specialized type of customer, and Edward Lloyd attracted merchants, seafaring men and Underwriters. In 1691 this coffee house moved to Lombard Street, and brokers got into the habit of giving their address as Lloyd's.

The growth of Lloyd's coffee house as a home of marine

insurance, however, was apparently slow, for no mention is made of it when brokers opposed the granting of Charters to the *Royal Exchange Assurance* and *The London Assurance* in 1720. By about 1760 a Register of Shipping was maintained and issued by a 'society of Underwriters at Lloyd's coffee house.' This Society formed the nucleus of Lloyd's. The coffee house could not provide rooms for the exclusive use of Underwriters and brokers, hence a new coffee house was set up at Pope's Head Alley. This was not suitable, and eventually a lease of premises in the Royal Exchange was taken. The tremendous growth in trade by reason of the industrial and commercial revolutions meant that there was more than enough business for the two Companies and also for the individual Underwriters at Lloyd's. The history of Lloyd's was one of continual expansion, and in 1928 Lloyd's moved to its own building in Leadenhall Street, London. In 1957 a new building was opened in Lime Street with marine Underwriters housed on the ground floor and non-marine Underwriters in the gallery. Such has been the expansion of Lloyd's business over the last twenty years that even this building is now proving inadequate to house the underwriters and their staffs.

The Monopoly Repealed in 1824

In the early part of the 19th century various attempts were made to oppose the monopoly of the two Chartered Companies. Although the attempts were not immediately successful, they paved the way for the successful application of the *Alliance British and Foreign Fire and Life Assurance Co.* in 1824. This Company had very strong banking interests, and as there was no real defence against the petition, the monopoly was withdrawn by an Act of Parliament which received the Royal Assent on 24 June, 1824.

This did not operate to the detriment of the two Corporations because expansion of trade at home and overseas together with the advent of the steamship provided enough business for all. Other Companies gradually entered the marine insurance market, until today it comprises many Companies and also Lloyd's Underwriters together transacting a huge volume of business.

Marine Insurance Organizations

Marine Insurers found it desirable to associate together for the protection of their common interests. The three main bodies are the Liverpool Underwriters' Association (established 1802), the Institute of London Underwriters (established 1884), and Lloyd's Underwriters' Association (established 1909). An important function of the Institute of London Underwriters is the framing and revision of standard clauses for use in marine insurance policies by the whole market, and this work is entrusted to the Technical and Clauses Committee. It is carried on in collaboration with the other two Associations. (For further details, see p. 210)

Fire Insurance

Fire insurance began, for all practical purposes, after the Great Fire of 1666. Before that time a few of the guilds provided some measure of relief where the fire was not the result of a member's own fault, and in the seventeenth century the main system of relief was by means of 'briefs.'[1] In 1638, however, a petition was made to the King for a patent under which it was proposed that an annual payment should be made by house owners in return for which they were to have the right to have their premises rebuilt in case of destruction by fire. The scheme, however, did not materialize.

According to tradition, Nicolas Barbon set up an Office for insuring houses against fire in 1667, but there is no proof of this; in fact, it appears that no Office was established until 1680.

Four Early Fire Insurers

The first undertaking was the *Fire Office*, later termed the *Phenix*. It appears that the scheme began in 1680 and the insurance ran for a term of seven years. It applied to houses, and double rates were charged for timber-built houses. In its 'proposals' in 1712 it was stated that the Office had been in existence for 31 years and had met claims for over £50,000, all of which had been punctually paid.

The next scheme arose out of a petition to the Common Council of the City of London in 1669. Nothing came of it until 1674 when a member of the Corporation presented a petition which embodied the features of the earlier petition. He was persistent and the Common Council of the City eventually recommended that the scheme should be adopted by the Corporation, 'any surplus from the contributions of the assured to go to the Chamberlain and not to be divided among the adventurers.' There was opposition to the scheme,

---

1 'Briefs' were authoritative letters distributed to each parish to be read in churches, and collections were made by churchwardens. The system was abused and the amount subscribed bore little relation to needs.

mainly because of the impropriety of citizens who managed the revenues of the City venturing those revenues on such a project. The scheme was abandoned.

In 1683 *The Friendly Society* became a competitor of the *Fire Office*. On joining, members paid a deposit and entered into an undertaking to subscribe, if called upon, up to a specified sum for each £100 insured, towards any claim arising under any one fire and also to pay an annual subscription per £100 insured. The deposit was returned at the termination of the insurance. Contributions were doubled for timber-built houses.

Lastly, the *Amicable Contributors for Insuring from Loss by Fire*, better known as the *Hand-in-Hand*, was formed in 1696. This was also a mutual scheme and there were no guarantors other than the members themselves.

Other Offices Formed

The early history of the *Sun Fire Office* was associated with Charles Povey, who founded the *Traders' Exchange House* in Hatton Garden, London, in the year 1708 for insuring moveable goods, merchandises, and wares against loss or damage by fire. On the buildings in which the property was insured there was nailed a token of the sun and from this sign the Office became known as the *Sun Fire Office*. Povey went some way towards starting a scheme for insuring houses and goods against fire outside the London area and in 1709, before the scheme had reached fruition, he entered into an arrangement with a group known as the *Company of London Underwriters*, by which he sold the fire business of the *Exchange House Fire Office* (referred to in early advertisements as the *Traders' Exchange Fire Office*) and the projected scheme for insurance outside London. In the deed by which the transaction was carried through, the *Exchange House Fire Office* is referred to as 'alias the *Sun Fire Office*.' The new undertaking was constituted by a deed of settlement dated 7 April, 1710, and, with various constitutional changes, this Office is in existence today.

By arrangement with the *Hand-in-Hand*, the *Union Fire Office* was formed in 1714 to insure goods and merchandise on somewhat similar terms to those on which the *Hand-in-Hand* insured buildings. It was, therefore, a mutual Office, and the *Union* undertook not to insure houses and buildings. This undertaking lasted until 1805 when the *Hand-in-Hand* began to insure goods and the *Union* began to insure buildings. The *Westminster Fire Office* was established by deed of settlement in 1717 and it is today a subsidiary of the Sun

Alliance London Group. In the provinces the first Office to be established was the *Bristol Crown* in the year 1718. In Edinburgh the *Friendly Society* was formed in 1719 on a mutual basis and existed as an independent undertaking until 1847 when the business was taken over by the *Sun Fire Office.*

The early Offices were successful, partly on account of the form in which insurance was offered. One only of the schemes gave an absolute guarantee in exchange for a fixed premium. The other Offices made no definite estimate of the cost of insurance beforehand, but required their Insured to contribute rateably within specified limits to the claims experienced, and bound their Insured for a term of years, usually seven, by taking a deposit returnable only at the end of the period.

Later Developments

The Industrial Revolution resulted in the building of factories and in considerable expansion in plant and equipment generally. As the simplicity of the early manufacturing processes was replaced by a complicated system, so fire insurance rating likewise became complicated. In the eighteenth century there was merely a simple system of threefold classification—common, hazardous, and extra-hazardous risks.

Before 1782, every fire policy issued was subject to a stamp duty, but in that year an annual duty, according to the sum insured, was also payable. The amount of this duty varied from time to time, and it was not removed until as late as 1869.

In the early nineteenth century there was a rapidly-increasing demand for fire insurance and various joint-stock Companies were formed for the transaction of this class of business. Several Offices were established in London, and among those founded in the provinces were the *Essex & Suffolk*, the *Kent*, the *Liverpool*, the *Birmingham*, the *West of England*, and the *Sheffield* Insurance Companies. There were corresponding developments in Scotland. A large fire insurance market also developed at Lloyd's.

The repeal of the fire insurance duty gave an impetus to fire insurance, and, at the same time, many of the old-time policy restrictions were gradually removed. In later years, new classes of insurance have been introduced, such as loss of profits following fire and insurance against various extra or 'special' perils, for example, riot and civil commotion, storm and tempest and flood, bursting or overflowing of water tanks, apparatus, or pipes, and impact damage by road vehicles, horses, or cattle.

Fire Offices' Committee

The Scottish fire managers met regularly from 1829 onwards. In England, however, there was no similar association, but there were attempts from time to time to secure agreement on rates. Eventually, a meeting of Offices was called in London towards the end of 1858, and two representatives of the Scottish Offices were invited to attend. There was another meeting in 1860, as a result of which the fire Offices were divided into three Committees. The Scottish Offices constituted one, and the other Committees met one in London and the other either in Liverpool or Manchester. The whole of the association does not appear to have been called the Fire Offices' Committee until 1868 (see also p. 212).

The early history of the Committee was profoundly affected by the famous Tooley Street fire which broke out on the 22 June, 1861, and caused damage variously estimated at between £1,000,000 and £2,000,000. Following the fire, rates were materially increased and this resulted in a protest from City merchants, with an appeal to the Lord Mayor. There was a meeting at the Mansion House and, as a result, the Offices modified the early schedule of rates, two new Companies were formed, and the London Fire Engine Establishment (the fire brigade formed and supported by the fire Insurance Offices) was taken over by the Metropolitan Board of Works, a relief from responsibility which was welcomed by the Offices.

Fire Research Station

The Testing Station erected by the Fire Offices' Committee at Boreham Wood, Elstree, and opened by His Royal Highness the Duke of Kent on 26 November, 1935, was designed to undertake technical research into all features of the science of fire prevention. Highly-skilled industrial chemists and scientists were engaged to conduct the work of testing timber, concrete, reinforced and pre-stressed concrete, building boards, and other building materials (including raw materials either before or after they are put on the market) from the standpoint of fire resistance, and also to test all types of fire-extinguishing equipment.

The results obtained were published as a guide to builders and architects as well as to Insurers, and from this research were developed many of the solutions to problems connected with the reduction of fire waste. The FOC thus became the recognized authority on the testing and grading of fire-fighting appliances, and its standards were adopted throughout the greater part of the then British Empire as well as in many other places abroad. The Station was taken over in 1946 by the Joint Fire Research Organization then established. This was done by the creation of a Joint Fire Research Board consisting of the Department of Scientific and Industrial Research and the Fire Offices' Committee, thus constituting the unusual arrangement of joint research by a Government Department and a commercial interest, at a cost shared equally by the Department of Scientific and Industrial Research and the Fire Offices' Committee.

In more recent years there has been an increasing emphasis on research while demands for routine testing have also grown. In 1976, following a Government enquiry, it was decided to dissolve the Joint Fire Research Organization and in its place two separate bodies were formed, the responsibility for the conduct of fire tests passing to a newly-formed body, the Fire Insurers' Research and Testing Organization (FIRTO). The FRS continues as a research station financed entirely by the Government. It is primarily concerned with 'research into all aspects of fire with the object of preventing loss of life and injury by fires and of mitigating material damage.' The FRS is one of three Government research activities, the others being concerned with building and with forest products. Together they form part of the Building Research Establishment which, in turn, is part of the Department of the Environment.

Fire Insurers' Research and Testing Organization

This body is a company limited by guarantee and is financed by subscriptions from the fire insurance industry. As its name implies it is designed to meet the needs of fire insurers in respect of the research and testing which are required to maintain their approvals procedure for fire protection equipment. FIRTO has an Appliances Division which has taken over all routine testing previously conducted by JFRO whether or not such work is in connection with acceptance for insurance purposes. A major part of its work is concerned with the evaluation of automatic sprinkler and ancillary equipment, automatic fire alarm systems and portable fire extinguishers.

The Sprinkler Technical Secretariat of the Comité Européen des Assurances (CEA) is entrusted to FIRTO so that it is also closely involved in all technical matters relating to the preparation of test specifications and rules for the installation of automatic sprinkler systems internationally as well as nationally.

FIRTO also has a Construction Division which is mainly concerned with research and testing related to the behaviour in fires of elements of construction and building materials. This Division, as is the Appliances Division, is closely involved in the drafting, development and revision of relevant national and international standards.

Fire Protection Association

The war-time Fire Waste Campaign, which was introduced to assist the Ministry of Aircraft Production in reducing fire waste in aircraft factories and was then developed on a national basis, demonstrated what could be done to educate the public in methods of reducing destruction or damage by fire. In consequence, in 1946 the Fire Offices' Committee formed the Fire Protection Association, which is controlled by representatives of the fire Insurance Offices and of commerce and industry.

The Association is backed by years of experience, and close liaison is maintained with the Fire Research Station and with the Fire Insurers' Research and Testing Organization, the Fire Offices' Committee and the Fire Services Section of the Home Office.

Salvage Corps

There are Salvage Corps maintained by Insurers in Glasgow, Liverpool and London. The Glasgow Rate and Salvage Association[1] was formed in 1892, the Fire Salvage Association of Liverpool, Ltd., in 1842 and the London Salvage Corps in 1866.

The Corps work in close collaboration with the fire brigades (for details of their activities see p. 226).

Ordinary Life Assurance

Life assurance can be traced back to the sixteenth century, when short-term assurances were usually effected as collateral security for loans. The earliest policy which has been located was an assurance

1 The Glasgow Insurance Committee—to deal only with rating—was formed in 1847, and the Glasgow Salvage Corps came into existence in 1873. The two Committees, i.e., the 'Glasgow Insurance Committee' and the 'Glasgow Salvage Corps Committee' were combined in 1876 as the Glasgow Rate and Salvage Committee, being reconstituted under the present title in 1892.

for twelve months on the life of William Gibbons, and dated 18 June, 1583.

In the seventeenth and eighteenth centuries, notwithstanding the absence of mortality tables, Associations of members were formed in order to subscribe to a fund out of which payments were made at the death of a member, dependent on the amount in the fund. Sometimes these Associations were restricted to those of a particular class, such as the clergy. All these early schemes, with one exception—the *Amicable Society for a Perpetual Assurance Office*—disappeared in the period of the South Sea Bubble.

The Amicable Society

This Society devised by Hartley, a London bookseller, was supported by a number of influential persons, and a Royal Charter was granted in 1706. The scheme was organized on a mutual basis, but the amount payable at death was not certain, as it depended (*a*) on the number of nominees who had died during the year, and (*b*) on the contributions received in that year. The fluctuating sum payable at death was unsatisfactory, and in 1757 the Society guaranteed a minimum payment on death of £125: this was raised in 1770 to £150. A fresh Charter was obtained in 1807 and life assurance was then transacted on a sound actuarial basis.

The problem of the mortality table was being solved by mathematicians of the day. Halley read a paper before the Royal Society in 1693 in which he deduced a mortality table from the deaths recorded at Breslau. In the following decades there were important actuarial developments. Methods were devised for the calculation of life annuities without the vast amount of arithmetical labour which Halley had found to be necessary. A table of mortality was deduced from bills of mortality of London and conditions generally became ripe for the application of this actuarial knowledge so as to make it possible to transact life assurance on a scientific foundation.

Church of Scotland Fund

The Church of Scotland received favourably proposals laid before it for providing for the families of its deceased ministers, and in 1744 an Act of Parliament was obtained. The Fund is still in a flourishing condition and it is now the oldest surviving Society for life contingencies in the world. It offered fixed benefits from the outset and in this respect differed from the *Amicable* Society. The *Scottish Widows' Fund*, established in 1815, was the first Scottish life Office and it was inspired by the desire to 'extend to all ranks' benefits similar to those available to ministers of the Church of Scotland.

The Equitable

In 1756 preliminary steps were taken for the establishment of the *Society for Equitable Assurances on Lives and Survivorship.* It was to be a mutual Society and in 1757 application was made for a Royal Charter. This was opposed, and the report of the Attorney General was adverse. The report concluded, however, with the suggestion that if the petitioners were so sure of success, they could enter into voluntary partnership. This was a clear indication that an association for the purpose in mind would not, in the opinion of the legal advisers to the Crown, be contrary to the provisions of the Bubble Act. It was therefore decided to proceed with the undertaking under a deed of settlement, which was executed in 1762. The Society transacted life assurance as a permanent contract, with level premiums according to the age at entry.

Life Assurance Act, 1774

During the eighteenth century there was an extraordinary wave of gambling, as explained on p. 88. As Francis explains, 'This mode of speculation is one of the strangest by-ways in the annals of insurance ... policies being opened on the lives of public men, with a recklessness at once disgraceful and injurious to the morals of the country ... When George II fought at Dettingen, 25 per cent was paid against his return.'[1]

In order to put an end to these practices, the Life Assurance Act, 1774 (known as the Gambling Act), was passed by which insurances on lives were prohibited, except 'where persons insuring shall have an interest in the life or death of the person insured.' The Act also provided that no policy should be issued without the insertion of the name of the person interested or for whose use the policy was made. Also, the amount to be recoverable was not to exceed the value of the interest of the Assured in such life or lives.

Two Further Offices

Before the end of the eighteenth century two other Offices were established. The *Westminster Society* applied for a Charter, but it

1 *Annals, Anecdotes and Legends: A Chronicle of Life Assurance* (Francis), p. 140.

was opposed and eventually the promoters established themselves in 1792 under a deed of settlement.[1] The *Westminster Society* did not transact a great deal of business, but the undertaking is of interest because it was the first of the proprietary Companies with share capital established under deed of settlement for the carrying on of life assurance business. In 1797 the *Pelican Life* Office was established as a proprietary Office under a deed of settlement, as a sister Office to the *Phoenix Fire* Office. By the end of the century there were thus several Offices in existence which transacted life assurance according to the principles of actuarial science.

Nineteenth Century

In the first phase of the Industrial Revolution there were three forms of institution: (*a*) the joint-stock Companies formed under deeds of settlement, with transferable shares and not associated with any fire Office, as, for instance, the *Rock Life* Insurance Office (1806); (*b*) the joint-stock Companies formed separately but associated with a fire Office and having common directors, such as the *Pelican Life* Office, associated with the *Phoenix*, and the *Sun Life*, associated with the *Sun Fire*; and (*c*) the mutual life Offices, as, for example, the *London Life* (1805) and the *Scottish Widows' Fund*, formed in Edinburgh (1815).

Throughout the century, whole life assurance was the main type of business underwritten, but towards the end of the century the comparatively new endowment assurance increased rapidly in popularity. This class provided for the payment of a fixed sum of money, with or without participation in profits, if the Assured reached a certain age or died before reaching that age, and it was attractive because the Assured himself could look forward to benefit from the policy. At the present time, the endowment assurance is in greater demand than the whole life contract, and is used for various purposes such as for retirement, house purchase, and education of children. Among other special schemes of recent years are group life assurance, and group pension schemes, while a large volume of annuity business is written.

In the 1880s a type of non-forfeiture clause was introduced so that the benefit of assurance was not entirely lost if the renewal premium was not paid. Since then, keen competition has resulted in

---

1 Before 1 November, 1844, joint stock Companies were usually formed by a deed of settlement as distinct from an Act of Parliament, a Royal Charter or letters patent. The deed constituted certain persons trustees of the Company property and contained regulations for the management of the Company's affairs.

the inclusion of various such privileges in life assurance policies (see also p. 62).

Associated Action

The first recorded minutes of a meeting among the Scottish Offices were dated 10 July, 1835, and in 1841 an Association was formed with rules embodied in printed resolutions.

In London, association was originally on a less formal basis. The actuaries of the chief Offices met, either at the office or private house of one of them, with the primary object of securing reliable data and the preparation of a mortality table. It was not until 1889 that the Life Offices' Association was established, working in collaboration with the Association of Managers of Life Assurance Offices in Scotland, now known as the Associated Scottish Life Offices (see also p. 214).

Industrial Life Assurance

Burial Clubs and Friendly Societies

Industrial life assurance originated in the Burial Clubs formed to provide for the payment of funeral expenses. Later Friendly Societies were formed, mainly to provide sickness benefits and also the payment of a sum of money at death. The Friendly Societies date from the late seventeenth century and they made rapid progress in the succeeding century. The working men and women who formed these Societies, however, were ignorant of actuarial science, and the benefits payable were sometimes not forthcoming when required, but, with facilities for registration, the Societies gradually put their affairs in order.

Later Developments

The rapid development of the Industrial Revolution in the nineteenth century led to the industrial assurance Companies being formed in the middle of the nineteenth century, and the bulk of the business is now transacted by a relatively small number of industrial assurance Companies and Friendly Societies.

They met a widespread demand for insurance from the rapidly-rising industrial population under the factory system. Collection of the premiums at weekly or four-weekly intervals at the homes of the policyholders became an essential feature of industrial life assurance. The offices decided to transact ordinary life assurance as well, and the agents frequently secured fire and accident new business when collecting premiums from the industrial life policyholders (see p. 15).

Far-reaching legislative control was imposed by the Industrial Assurance Act, 1923, notably by the creation of the office of the Industrial Assurance Commissioner (who is also the Registrar of Friendly Societies). He has wide powers, including power to inspect the affairs of a Company or Society in certain circumstances and to hear disputes and make awards.

Section 72 of the Friendly Societies Act, 1974, reproducing provisions in the Industrial Assurance and Friendly Societies Act, 1948 (as amended by the Industrial Assurance and Friendly Societies Act, 1948 (Amendment) Act, 1958), restricted 'life of another' business, other than husband and wife, to parents, step-parents, and grand-parents, and to not more than £30; hence at the present time the chief tables of industrial life assurance are those shown on p. 65 where the scope of the business is considered.

Today, the industrial life Offices secure about one-third of their total income from ordinary life assurance and fire and accident business. The Friendly Societies are empowered to transact ordinary life business up to £1,000 only. The Companies are not so restricted.

There have from time to time been criticisms of this business, but it is clear that the Offices enjoy the confidence of their Assured, if only because of the millions of policies in force.

Associated Action

The industrial Offices formed the Industrial Life Offices' Association in 1901 (see p. 214).

Accident Insurance

Accident insurance consists of a number of different sections. It is the youngest of the four main branches of insurance and provides for protection against all those risks outside the scope of the marine, fire, and life departments.

There were various experimental schemes before the nineteenth century. In 1720 an attempt was made to establish a fidelity guarantee

Society. Schemes were devised from time to time to provide livestock insurance, but they were usually operated by small clubs, on a mutual basis, and they broke down when cattle plague or some other scourge developed. In 1787 William Weller opened the *General Insurance Office* 'to Insure Persons from Loss of Property by Burglaries, Highway and Footpad Robberies, Public and Private Thefts, together with the Expense of Prosecution.' The Office lasted for two years. In 1814 a curious system was proposed to increase the police, abolish the 'nightly watch,' and offer rewards to the police and others so that they would be so keen to detect robbers that 'such a united body would soon triumph over the unorganized bands of depredators.'

Accident insurance on a stable basis began a little more than a century ago as a result of the changed conditions of life for which the Industrial Revolution was responsible. This Revolution made possible the manufacture of goods on a large scale by means of machinery. The consequent growth in trade led to a commercial revolution, and the goods sold had to be transported, thereby opening up the transport revolution by the railway, the steamship, and later the mechanically-propelled road vehicle. The immediate effect was a marked increase in the number and seriousness of accidents of all kinds. This created a demand for accident insurance, which was the term first applied to insurance against accidents to the person while travelling by the railways which were being built in the middle of the nineteenth century. The other departments—marine, fire, and life—were firmly established and the scope of their operations clearly defined; hence accident business grew up separately. In the course of time demand arose for other new types of insurance and these were assigned to, and developed by, the newly-formed accident branch. Indeed, it brought within its scope fidelity guarantee, which began to be transacted a few years before personal accident insurance.

Personal Accident and Sickness Insurance

The early railways were experimental and more dangerous than the stage coaches, so that by 1849 *The Times* stated 'railway accidents are almost of daily occurrence, generally ending in loss of limb—often of life.' It is not surprising, therefore, that there was a demand for accident insurance, and in 1848 the *Railway Passengers Assurance Co.* was formed to insure railway passengers only against accident as follows:

Fatal Injury
  £200 third-class passengers
  £500 second-class passengers
  £1,000 first-class passengers

Non-fatal Injury
  Such sum (not exceeding the fatal benefit) 'as shall be deemed
  a reasonable and liberal Compensation for such Injury, as well
  as for the Pain of Mind and Body and the Loss of Time and
  Money consequent thereon.'

The insurance tickets (single journey and also periodical ones)
were printed in the same size and style as the travel tickets, and
were issued by the booking clerks, who received a commission.

The *Accidental Death Insurance Co. No. 1* issued general accident
policies from 1850 but the *Railway Passengers Assurance Co.* did
not do so until 1855. In the succeeding years many other Companies
entered the field.

Permanent sickness and accident insurance began in 1885 when
the *Sickness and Accident Assurance Association Ltd.* was formed
(the name was altered to the *Century Insurance Co., Ltd.* in 1901),
and the new Association computed its early tables on the experience
of the Friendly Societies.

The Infectious Diseases (Notification) Act, 1889, introduced compulsory notification where a person was suffering from certain zym-
otic diseases, and the statistics which became available enabled the
Law Accident Insurance Society, Ltd. to offer in 1893 a combination
policy to provide double benefits for railway accidents and weekly
benefits for scarlet fever, smallpox, typhoid, and typhus. Other
Offices followed this lead and added various specified diseases.

In 1900 the *Preferred Accident Insurance Co.* of New York opened
an office in London and offered accident and all sickness insurance
without medical examination.

Personal accident insurance was initiated because of travel risks,
and this has again become an important feature of the business
because of the development of aviation. As from January, 1946,
Offices decided to include flying risks under their ordinary annual
policies, so that a reasonable amount of flying is now covered without
extra premium.

Group schemes have their roots as far back as 1851, when the
Railway Passengers Assurance Co. issued a collective policy for the
employees of the Lancashire and Yorkshire Railway. The recent
developments are dealt with on p. 66.

Fidelity Guarantee

Private suretyship goes back to Old Testament days, but it was not until 1840 that a workable scheme of corporate suretyship was devised by the founders of the *Guarantee Society*. There was some opposition to the new idea because the so-called 'moral security' was thought to be lacking, but in course of time it was found that a Company's guarantee did not make the guaranteed person a rogue, although it relieved him of being under obligation to friends.

The *Guarantee Society* soon met competition. Many of the early Companies combined fidelity guarantee with life assurance. A fidelity claim meant the forfeiture of the life assurance, while the life policy proceeds could be utilized towards any such fidelity claim. The scheme ceased for all practical purposes with the failure of the *European* in 1872. Some Offices specialized in the granting of guarantees to Government departments.

It was not until the 1870s that corporate suretyship extended to Court bonds (see p. 77). The Probate Court has always required security, but as far as can be traced it was not until 1878 that the *Guarantee Society's* bonds were accepted. Corporate suretyship for Court of Protection bonds for receivers of the estates of mental patients goes back, at least, to 1889.

Government bonds are also entered into by surety Companies. Since the passing of the Bankruptcy Act, 1883, it has been customary for trustees in bankruptcy to seek a Company's bond. Deeds of Arrangement bonds date from the Bankruptcy and Deeds of Arrangement Act, 1913. Customs and Excise bonds were entered into by the *Guarantee Society* from 1842, and in 1849 the Lords of the Treasury authorized acceptance of bonds given by the *British Guarantee Association*.

The fidelity department undertakes various subsidiary types of business. Insurance against drawings was devised by the *London Guarantee and Accident* in 1913, but there was no marked progress until Victory Bonds were widely purchased. Building society indemnities date from 1924 (see also p. 78).

Employers' Liability Insurance

At Common Law it was not easy for an injured workman to recover damages against his employer, because the latter had several defences. Many accidents occurred, however, with the use of machinery to which workpeople were unaccustomed and there were demands for an alteration to the law. There was a minor change in 1846 when the Fatal Accidents Act was passed, which enabled dependants of a deceased person to recover damages to the extent of financial loss if the death was caused by the negligence of another. Some more far-reaching change was required and this came, after much opposition, by the Employers' Liability Act, 1880. Even then, it was still necessary to prove negligence to be able to recover damages. In that year the *Employers' Liability Assurance Corporation, Ltd.*, was established.

The Act applied to certain classes of employment only, and Joseph Chamberlain was largely responsible for further agitation in order to ensure the payment of compensation merely by reason of occupational injury, whether or not the employer was negligent. This step forward was taken in the Workmen's Compensation Act, 1897; it was followed by others until the Act of 1906 included almost all employees. This opened a new chapter in accident insurance history because all the older fire Offices then had to transact accident insurance to preserve their connections, and in this way the modern composite Office became a general feature of British insurance.

The Holman Gregory Report, 1920, recommended very close supervision of the business, but all the recommendations were not carried out. In 1925 a consolidating Act was passed, and in 1934 compulsory workmen's compensation insurance for the coal mining industry became operative by the Workmen's Compensation (Coal Mines) Act of that year. Compensation was increased during World War Two (as had been done by the War Addition Acts in World War One), while on and from 5 July, 1948, the workmen's compensation section of the business was lost by private enterprise, on being merged in the extended scheme of National Insurance.

In the meantime, the number of Common Law claims was increasing because high damages were more attractive than the comparatively small amounts of weekly compensation provided by the Workmen's Compensation Acts. Many of the claims were based on breach of statutory duty, more particularly after the passing of the Factories Act, 1937 (now the Factories Act, 1961). The business has reverted to its original name—employers' liability insurance—to provide an indemnity for what was left of an employer's liability for occupational accidents (and diseases) after the repeal of the Employers' Liability Act, 1880, and the Workmen's Compensation Acts. The Common Law claims are today very costly to Insurers. In 1969 the Employers' Liability (Compulsory Insurance) Act was passed making it compulsory for employers to have insurance covering their liability to employees for injury or illness sustained at work. The new Act remained inoperative for two years but was brought into force by a Statutory Instrument on 1 January, 1972.

Public Liability Insurance

Public liability insurance was not encouraged because it was thought to be against public policy. This attitude gradually disappeared and the business received its initial impetus with the passing of the Employers' Liability Act, 1880. A few years before that time policies for horse-drawn vehicles were available.

Any one accident may cause injuries to employees and also to members of the public, and the latter became aware of the possibility of damages until today there is a general litigation-complex, assisted by the publicity given to motor vehicle accidents with large awards of damages. This, in turn, encouraged the growth of public liability insurance. During the 1880s engineering Insurers began to include under their policies a public liability indemnity. At this time, too, public liability (general) indemnities were sought by builders and contractors.

The *Northern Accident* offered property owners' indemnities in 1897. The demand for this class of protection—and this is true of all kinds of public liability policies—arose out of case law.

Scholars' indemnities began after the case *Ching* v. *Surrey County Council* (1909) in which an education authority was held responsible to a boy scholar who was injured by catching his foot in a defective asphalt pavement.

The *Prudential* offered golfers' policies in 1919 and the *Sun Fire* devised a comprehensive type of contract for golfers, such as is usual today. The case *Castle* v. *Augustine's Links, Ltd.* (1922), in which the plaintiff lost an eye through a golf ball striking a taxi-cab windscreen, encouraged the business. Clubs, as well as individuals, began to insure.

Personal liability insurance began in 1927, and the policy can be arranged to include cycling. The revival of cycling because of petrol restrictions during World War Two resulted in many new personal liability policies being issued. The case of *Eames* v. *Capps* (1948), in which damages of £2,500 were awarded against a jay-walker, also showed the value of a personal liability contract, and subsequent cases include *Challen* v. *Bell* (1954) and *Cotton* v. *Sherridan and Gabanski* (1959).

Other kinds of policies, designed to meet the needs of different undertakings, include innkeepers' indemnities, offered about 1914, estate owners' and farmers' indemnities following the case of *Stratton*

v. *Huleatt* (1925), in which a boy lost a leg through the fall of a defective tree, and radio and television insurances. Professional indemnities began with druggists' indemnities which were granted by the *Northern Accident* in 1896, and today accountants, architects, solicitors, and all kinds of professional men seek protection against the consequences of neglect, omission, or error in the course of their professional work.

A modern development within the field of public liability insurance concerns insurance in respect of liabilities which may be incurred to third parties by anyone who is engaged in the sale or supply of goods of all kinds, and is generally referred to in the market as products liability insurance. Cover may be provided by an extension to a general public liability policy or by the issue of a separate policy.

Theft (or Burglary) Insurance

Theft is given a place in the Mosaic Law, but it was not until the 1880s that a satisfactory scheme of burglary insurance was formulated. At the request of a broker, a *Lloyd's* Underwriter extended a fire policy to cover burglary, but the first Company to issue separate policies, renewable annually, with a full statement of the risks covered and the conditions applicable, was the *Mercantile Accident and Guarantee* of Glasgow. The scheme was based on one devised by a police constable. The *National Burglary Insurance Corporation* was founded in London in 1892, and this new undertaking purchased the burglary portfolio of the *Mercantile Accident and Guarantee*. Other Companies were established: the *Fine Art and General* in 1890, the *Goldsmiths' and General* in 1891, and the *Ocean* began burglary business in 1893. By 1900 there were some thirty Offices interested.

Private dwellings policies were followed by those for business premises, and in 1893 the *Fine Art and General* offered a combined 'burglary fire and damage' policy which was the forerunner of the householder's comprehensive policy, usually termed householder's policy. The *British Dominions* (now the *Eagle Star*) offered such a policy in 1915 and called it an 'all-in' policy.

'All risks' insurance was preceded by special insurances on packages sent by post. The *Parcels Post Insurance Co., Ltd.*, founded in 1883 and dissolved in 1891, issued policies of this type. The business, as it is known today, began about 1896 with the insurance of valuables belonging to private individuals, and Insurers have gradually extended their operations so that now many kinds of 'all risks' policies are issued, even to cover furniture in course of removal.

Cash-in-transit (now termed money) insurance began about 1909, and baggage insurance in 1912 with the *Railway Passengers'* scheme.

Motor Vehicle Insurance

The motor industry dates from the inventions of Benz and Daimler in 1883–4, and progress was made on the Continent in the next decade. The first 'patent motor velocipede' to enter this country was a two-seated Benz car in 1894. Development was impossible because of restrictive legislation, but the restrictions were removed by the Locomotives on Highways Act, 1896, and the famous emancipation run from London to Brighton took place on the day when the Act became operative—14 November, 1896. Two small and short-lived Companies tried to transact motor insurance, but the real pioneer was the *Law Accident*, with the *General Accident* also in the field. The late Mr Frederick Thoresby devised the *Law Accident* schemes from 1898 until he left to form the first Company specializing in motor insurance—the *Car and General* founded in 1903. Another similar office, the *Motor Union*, began business in 1906.

World War One showed the usefulness of the motor vehicle, many men learned to drive while in the Forces, and hire-purchase facilities made it easy to acquire the mass-produced vehicles which came on the market in the post-war years. There was, therefore, a tremendous extension of road transport, and many road accidents occurred, following some of which injured third parties could not secure the damages to which they were entitled. There were agitations for compulsory third party motor insurance and this eventually became law by the Road Traffic Act, 1930, with many changes in practice necessitated by the issue of certificates of insurance, withdrawal of days of grace, and revision of policies to comply with the Act so that an indemnity unlimited in amount was afforded against liability for death of, or bodily injuries to, third parties. The 1933 and 1934 Acts went further, and the latter introduced 'emergency treatment' payments to doctors and hospitals. There were several subsequent Acts affecting motor insurance, but all of this legislation has been consolidated in the Road Traffic Act, 1972. The current Act also incorporates in s.148(3) the provisions of the Motor Vehicles (Passenger Insurance) Act, 1971, whereby compulsory insurance is extended so that users of motor vehicles are now required to be insured in respect of liability for death of or bodily injury to passengers. Similar provisions apply in Northern Ireland under the Road Traffic Act (Northern Ireland), 1970. Contracting out of liability is not permissible, but there is no compulsion to insure against liability for damage to the *property* of third parties.

As from 1 January, 1974, all motor insurance policies issued in the UK include cover against such liabilities as are compulsorily insurable under the national laws of each of the other Member States of the European Economic Community.

The Cassel Committee on Compulsory Insurance was appointed, and reported in 1937. The recommendations were not carried out because of World War Two, but the recommendation for the establishment of a Central Fund to compensate injured parties who could not, for one reason or another, obtain the damages to which they were entitled, was implemented by the voluntary action of all motor Insurers. They set up the Motor Insurers' Bureau to look after any cases where third parties would otherwise be prejudiced by the absence of insurance or by ineffective insurance.

Motor insurance today produces a premium income larger than that of fire insurance. For many years the business was subject to tariff regulations, but these were discontinued as from 1 January, 1969.

Engineering Insurance

When steam boilers were first used, there were no safety regulations, and calamitous accidents frequently caused loss of life, serious injuries, and damage to property. Riders were added to verdicts at coroners' inquests about the need for periodical inspection of plant.

Eventually, the *Manchester Steam Users' Association* was formed in 1854 to provide periodical inspection services, but the Association would have nothing to do with insurance. The first boiler insurance Company was the *Steam Boiler Assurance Co.*, founded in 1858, followed by the *National Boiler Insurance Co., Ltd.* in 1864. These Companies provided inspections and insurance, thereby creating difficulties for the pioneer Association. The latter maintained its attitude but adopted a system of guarantees, so that 'we do not insure for explosions; but we do propose to guarantee that explosions shall not take place.' Eventually the *MSUA* was absorbed by the *British Engine* in 1932.

In 1872, the Company today known as the *Vulcan* began insurance and inspection of steam engines, and this led to the formation of a new Company, the *British Engine*, in 1878. This latter Company was the pioneer of electrical plant insurance in 1897–8 when the 'steam men' had contempt for the new motive power. Lift insurance and inspection also came to the fore towards the end of the century.

Legislation has had much to do with the growth of engineering insurance. The Boiler Explosions Act, 1882 (followed by another Act in 1890), was sponsored by the *MSUA*, and it provided for investigations into boiler explosions by the Board of Trade. Owners found it cheaper to have their plant inspected than to be held to blame with consequent liability for costs of the inquiry. The Factory and Workshop Act, 1901, went further by providing for compulsory inspections by a 'competent person,' and the principle of expert periodical inspections was considerably extended by the Factories Act, 1937. Much new business was brought to the engineering insurance Companies because their inspections met statutory requirements, and if any recommendations made are at once carried out, it is an answer to any charge of negligence. The current Act is the Factories Act, 1961, but this is gradually to be replaced by regulations and non-statutory codes of practice by virtue of the powers contained in the Health & Safety At Work, etc. Act, 1974.

In recent years there has been a substantial increase in the demand for consequential loss cover whereby the Insured is indemnified against financial loss arising when production stops following the failure of plant.

Accident Offices' Association

Accident Insurers found it desirable to associate together, and the first attempt was the formation of the Accident Offices' Committee. This was not successful by reason of the fierce competition in the years immediately following the passing of the Workmen's Compensation Act, 1897. In 1906, however, the principal Offices formed the Accident Offices' Association and it is impossible to overestimate the far-reaching benefits of, and enormous volume of work carried through by, the Association since it first came into existence.

The Future

Despite the phenomenal growth of accident insurance during the last 50 years, there is still scope for further development. Some business men do not recognize the desirability, for example, of effecting public liability indemnities, and others rely upon the out-of-date system of private bondsmen instead of taking advantage of corporate suretyship.

Accident Insurers find it necessary to devise new types of policies from time to time as law cases and other developments reveal hitherto unsuspected liabilities for which it is prudent to secure insurance protection.

Aviation Insurance

Aviation was in the experimental stage before World War One. There were a few third party and crash risks insurances effected from 1909–10, and the so-called *White Wings* policy was issued by a Lloyd's syndicate from 1911 onwards. World War One stimulated development of heavier-than-air dirigibles and the first regular civil aviation service began in 1919, but nothing more is known of a printed form of policy until 1923 when the *British Aviation Insurance Group* was formed by the *Union of Canton Insurance Co.* and the *White Cross Insurance Co.*

This Group method was adopted because of the unknown nature of the risks involved. The Group gathered strength, other Insurance Companies joined the Group, and in 1931 the name was changed to the *British Aviation Insurance Co., Ltd.* In 1935 another Company, similarly constituted, was formed by some leading Insurers and it was called the *Aviation and General Insurance Co., Ltd.*

There were two types of development: (1) the building up of commercial air lines engaged in the international carriage of passengers and goods, and (2) the growth of a light-aeroplane movement as a result of which enthusiasts gained experience. The insurance market affected both these features of aviation by acting as a restraining influence where unnecessary risks were being run, and also as an encouraging influence in allowing reductions of rates where any new development justified this.

World War Two accelerated aeronautical progress and today the insurance market comprises the two Groups, a number of Lloyd's Underwriters working in syndicates, and several Companies which opened aviation departments after 1945.

Aviation is now brought within the statutory control applicable to other main classes of insurance by virtue of the provisions of the Insurance Companies Act, 1974. Compulsory third party aviation insurance is included within the Civil Aviation Act, 1949, but this provision has never been implemented.

Associated Action

Insurers engaged in aviation insurance found it desirable to form central organizations to deal with problems of common interest. In

1949 the Aviation Insurance Offices' Association was formed and a corresponding Association at Lloyd's has been in existence since October, 1935 (see p. 216).

War Risks Insurance

The widespread destruction of property during a modern war has made it impossible for the risk of war damage to property on land to be insured other than by the Government. Life and marine risks are in a different category.

World War One

An Aircraft Insurance Scheme was drafted by the Government under which buildings and their contents were insured. Insurers undertook the operation of the Scheme on behalf of the Government.

In the marine market, war risk insurance on cargo was available from Insurers generally and also from the War Risks Insurance Office, which was set up by the Government.

As regards British hulls, these were entered in the Mutual War Risks Associations and reinsured by the Government to the extent of 70 per cent. From 1917 onwards, the Associations continued to give cover, but they obtained full reinsurance from the Government, by reason of the heavy incidence of loss.

World War Two

The war risks exclusion clause was standardized in 1937 and applied to the insurance of property on land. However, the War Damage Acts, 1941 and 1943, made provision for the insurance of land and buildings and in respect of business equipment and private chattels against war risks. Except for land and buildings, these arrangements were undertaken by Insurers as agents for the Government.

In the marine market, ships and cargoes were insured by Underwriters against war risks, the latter being subject to qualifications as provided by the Waterborne Agreement,[1] but practically all such insurances in respect of cargoes to and from the United Kingdom

1 The effect of the Waterborne Agreement, 1937, was to exclude from the marine policy cover in respect of war risks on land, and in this way the marine policy was brought into line, as far as possible, with non-marine policies. The Agreement has from time to time been modified in various ways.

were placed through the War Risks Insurance Office, leaving other voyages to be insured by the market. British hulls entered for war risks in the War Risks Associations were heavily reinsured with the Government. Life Assurers were prepared to grant cover for war risks on terms according to circumstances.

Atomic Energy and Insurance

The use of atomic energy in World War Two led to the development in the post-war years of practical applications of atomic energy in industrial, agricultural, medical and other processes, with the result that Insurers found themselves facing new types of risk, some of which might give rise to catastrophic losses. The position of Insurers was complicated by the pressure of public demand for cover combined with the difficulty in measuring the risks involved in the absence of any experience.

Advisory Committee

Insurers considered that a concerted study by the market as a whole was obviously the most satisfactory way of approaching the problems involved in insuring the new types of risks with which they were faced. Hence, the British Insurance (Atomic Energy) Advisory Committee was set up for the purpose. This Committee reported in 1957 and identified two principal types of problems confronting Insurers:

1 those relating to the risks emanating from nuclear reactor installations, comprising both material damage to the property of the reactor operator and injury to persons and damage to property belonging to the general public;

2 those relating to risks arising from the use, outside reactor installations, of other sources of radiation such as radioactive isotopes, particle accelerators and X-ray machines.

Market Pools

To handle the risks in group (1) the Committee recommended a market pool for property risks and a separate pool for liability risks in order to provide maximum cover without overlapping of liabilities. It was considered essential that each Insurer should know the precise extent of his liability, but it was recognized that the normal method of scheduling risks would not be appropriate. Under this method Insurers make their own reinsurance arrangements and clearly this could lead to accumulation of risks incapable of precise quantification. Accordingly, the Committee recommended and Insurers have accepted a system of net lines from the pool without recourse to reinsurance. However, reinsurance Companies also share in the pool by direct lines.

The total liability of the property pool in respect of any one reactor installation depends on the value of the installation and can amount to many millions of pounds. The maximum possible loss to the liability pool is governed by the Nuclear Installations Act, 1965, which limits the amount of compensation which any person is liable to pay to £5m. in respect of any one occurrence.

The Committee considered that risks in group (2) could be dealt with in the ordinary course of business under material damage or third party policies. Radioisotopes are radioactive forms of well-known substances, and their use in industry, medicine and research is subject to very stringent safety precautions. There is usually no difficulty in obtaining insurance cover for these risks.

Radioactive Contamination Exclusion Clause

Apart from the pools and the insurance cover given for risks in group (2), the Committee considered that nuclear energy risks should not properly be covered under ordinary material damage and liability insurance policies. Accordingly, it was decided that such policies (which do not include life, pensions, personal accident and sickness policies) should be subject to a clause which excludes risks arising from radioactive contamination. The clause has been extended in recent years following the accidental release of nuclear bombs over Spain and Greenland, occurrences the consequences of which it was generally agreed ought not to be within the scope of normal insurance policies.

The following is the full wording of the clause currently in use:

'The Insurers shall not be liable in respect of:
a loss or destruction of or damage to any property whatsoever or any loss or expense whatsoever resulting or arising therefrom or any consequential loss;

b any legal liability of whatsoever nature directly or indirectly caused by or contributed to by or arising from—

i ionising radiations or contamination by radioactivity from any nuclear fuel or from any nuclear waste from the combustion of nuclear fuel;

ii the radioactive, toxic, explosive or other hazardous properties of any explosive nuclear assembly or nuclear component thereof.'

No alteration in insurance policies is necessary to provide against the contingency that nuclear devices might be used in time of war, since this contingency is covered by the war risks exclusion clause referred to above.

Sonic Bangs

Another class of risk which is invariably excluded from insurance policies is 'sonic bangs'. It is usual to endorse material damage policies to exclude this risk with wording such as: 'loss, destruction, or damage, occasioned by pressure waves caused by aircraft and other aerial devices travelling at sonic or supersonic speeds.' In 1970 the British Government undertook to compensate for this type of damage arising out of Concorde's test flights.

3 General Scope of Insurance

Insurance provides protection against a wide variety of risks, and the scope of the business is here considered according to the three-fold classification—insurances of the person, of property and pecuniary loss, and of liability.

1 Insurances of the Person

A LIFE ASSURANCE

Many different kinds of life assurance contracts can be obtained. These contracts have been devised to meet the varying needs of individuals in their endeavours to provide for the future, either for themselves or for their dependants.

The business is divisible into two main sections—ordinary life assurance and industrial life assurance. The main distinction is that under industrial life policies the premiums are usually payable at more frequent intervals than under ordinary life policies, and the sums assured are smaller.

ORDINARY LIFE ASSURANCE

There have been considerable extensions and specialization in recent years, and the main sections of ordinary life assurance are detailed below.

Whole Life Assurance

A whole life assurance contract provides for the payment of the sum assured on the death of the Life Assured. Premiums may be payable throughout life, or, for a little extra, they can cease at a specified age, say, 60 or 65. The method of 'limited payments' is desirable because the premiums will then cease to be payable after retirement, when income will normally be less than in the years of full working capacity. Single premium contracts are also available for those who wish to put down a lump sum with a Company.

The family man should ideally seek this class of contract because his main concern should be to make the best possible provision for his dependants, in the event of his death.

Endowment Assurance

The endowment assurance contract provides for payment of the sum assured when the Life Assured reaches a specified age or at his death, whichever occurs first.

Endowment assurances are arranged for varying terms from, say, 10 up to 40 years, and the premium is naturally higher the shorter the term. As the Life Assured himself obtains the policy moneys if he survives until maturity date, the endowment assurance contract is a useful form of saving, quite apart from the life cover provided. Under a whole life policy the Life Assured can never receive the policy proceeds; they are payable only on his death.

Term Assurance

As the name implies, this is an assurance for a specified period, and the contract is so arranged for the sum assured to be payable on the death of the Life Assured only in the event of that happening during the specified term, say, five years. The sum assured may be constant or it may decrease with each year of the term. A contract of the latter type is called a decreasing term assurance.

When a substantial temporary loan is granted, the creditor may effect a term assurance on the life of the debtor. Business men who find it necessary to make trips abroad, whether or not by air, may seek term assurance for the periods of those trips.

Convertible Term Assurance

This form of assurance is exactly the same as term assurance during the term concerned, but it provides for a valuable option to convert the assurance into one of another type during the term, say, during the first five years of a seven-year term assurance. A young professional man who is making his way may not have sufficient income to permit him to effect forthwith a substantial whole life or endowment assurance, so he enters into a term assurance to afford him some protection in the early years of his career, with the privilege of conversion later without any further medical examination.

If the option is not exercised within the period specified in the policy, the assurance lapses at the end of the term.

Family Income Assurance

This type of assurance is offered under different names according to the Company concerned, but the basic principles of the schemes are identical, namely, the provision of income benefits as well as payment of a capital sum.

According to the policy terms, if death occurs at any time within the first 20 or 25 years of the date on which the assurance is effected, then a fixed sum is payable per annum during the remainder of the period and a capital sum at the end. (Sometimes the capital sum is paid on death instead of at the end of the income payments, or part on death and the remainder at the end of the term.) A family man who dies, say, two years after such an assurance has been effected knows that his widow will receive an annual income for the next 18 (or 23) years and then a lump sum at the end of that time.

A family income assurance exemplifies the way in which actuaries have been able to adapt existing schemes to meet special requirements. A family income assurance is simply a decreasing term assurance (a decreasing sum assured that is payable in annual instalments) and whole life or endowment assurance.

House Purchase Assurance

Most people purchase their houses by means of mortgage facilities provided by private individuals, building societies, or Insurance Companies. The person who borrows is called the mortgagor, and the individual or company who lends is termed the mortgagee. The mortgagee has the deeds of the property as security for the loan, and with building societies the mortgagor covenants to make periodical payments which represent interest on the sum advanced and gradual repayment of the capital. If the breadwinner dies before the mortgage has been redeemed, his widow may be unable to continue the payments, whereupon the mortgagee will foreclose. This means that the mortgagee will sell the property to repay the balance of the loan. So long as the price realized covers the outstanding mortgage, that is all that matters to the mortgagee, and there may be little or nothing left over for the widow.

Insurance Companies are able to remove this unfortunate possibility by means of house purchase assurance, under which any outstanding mortgage at the date of death is discharged and the house belongs to the widow free of encumbrance. There are two ways of doing this.

1 A decreasing term assurance is effected to repay, in the event of death during the term of a mortgage, the sum outstanding at the date of death under the type of mortgage where agreed periodical repayments are made.

2 An endowment assurance is arranged for the amount and period of the mortgage. No periodical repayments are made, so that it is not a reducing mortgage, but when the mortgage is due to be redeemed the sum assured under the endowment policy is available for this purpose. If the mortgagor should die before the mortgage is due for repayment, then the policy moneys will likewise be available to extinguish the mortgage. (Interest payments are made on the full amount of the loan while the mortgage remains.)

Children's Assurance

This is a useful type of provision for children and can be arranged in one of several ways.

1 An assurance is effected at the birth of a child or during the early years at, say, a modest annual premium and the sum accumulated is a so-called pure endowment, that is to say, there is no 'life' cover. If, therefore, the child dies before age 21 or 25 (known as the 'vesting age'), the premiums are repaid with or without interest. If, however, the child is alive at the vesting age, there are valuable options which it is possible to exercise. A lump sum can be taken, which then forms a very useful birthday present for the child, or a whole life or endowment assurance can be effected at the same annual premium. In the ordinary way, the premium for such an assurance at the substantial amount offered would be much higher, but this low premium is possible because the parent has, in effect, subsidized the assurance by the payments made during the 'deferred' period. Moreover, no medical examination is required, hence the Office cannot refuse to grant the assurance even to a child who is in failing health.

2 An assurance can be arranged in exactly similar terms to those under (1), save that for a small extra premium the Company is prepared to undertake that no further premiums are to be payable if the parent should die during the period of deferment, i.e., before

the child reaches 21 or 25 years of age. The child is thus assured of a good financial start in life, either by means of a cash option or a useful life assurance.

3 A still more popular way of arranging the assurance is for an endowment assurance to be effected on the parent's life for the amount of the cash option at vesting age because Income Tax allowance is then granted within the statutory limits on the whole of the premium. In the event of the death of the parent or his survival to maturity date, the same options as mentioned above are available for the child at vesting age.

4 Some children's policies are known as educational assurances because the proceeds can be used for the education of children. These policies are, in fact, endowment assurances effected on the life of the parent and payable in instalments, so that there is money available when the child is, say, aged 14, 16, and 18. Sometimes, the same object is attained by effecting several endowment assurances to mature at regular intervals over a set period.

Group Schemes

Group assurance schemes are today very popular with large and small firms alike, and they are closely bound up with general staff welfare. They are divisible into two sections: (*a*) group life schemes, and (*b*) group pensions schemes.

a Group life schemes. The assurance is arranged for all the employees of a firm by means of group one-year term assurances or by endowment assurances effected under the group pensions schemes mentioned below. Contributions are normally made by the employer only, under the group life term policy, and by both employer and employees under the group endowment assurance scheme. All employees of a firm are usually included at inception and a single policy is issued with a certificate to each individual, but there is always the problem of transferability. If a man leaves the firm he can as a rule convert his certificate into an individual life assurance, although he will not get the benefit of the low premium available to the group.

b Group pensions schemes. Many employers seek to provide pensions for staff who have given long and good service. This provision can be made by the purchase of deferred annuities, or by the effecting of endowment assurances, the proceeds from which may be used to purchase immediate annuities on maturity at pension age. However, it is more usual nowadays, when more than two or three employees are concerned, to arrange a composite group or master policy, and pensions for quite large groups of employees are often provided in this way. Sometimes the schemes are fully insured but in some cases insurance in the strict sense may not be present at all, the insurance company acting merely in the role of an investment manager or unit trust. Some employers pay the whole cost of the pension while others may require the employees to contribute to the cost. If the employer's contributions are to rank as allowable business expenses for income tax purposes the scheme must satisfy certain requirements of the Inland Revenue in order to be approved by them. Modern schemes usually provide a wide range of benefits including pensions, lump sum benefits on retirement, lump sum benefits on death in service and, to an increasing extent, widows' and dependants' pensions on death in service or after retirement.

Other Life Contracts

Among the other types of contracts offered by the life department are double endowment assurances and joint life policies. Under the former twice the sum assured is payable if the Life Assured survives to maturity date, while the latter may provide for the sum assured to be payable on the death of the first life or on the death of the last survivor.

Yet another variation is the contingent life assurance contract which secures the payment of the sum assured if the death of one person occurs during the lifetime of another.

Many Offices are now issuing equity-linked and property-linked policies. These combine life cover with investment in unit trusts.

Annuity Contracts

Life Offices transact a large volume of annuity business and many of these annuities are, in effect, pensions provided by the annuitants from their own savings. Although there are various kinds of annuities, the majority ensure the payment of amounts periodically during the lifetime of the annuitant in consideration of the payment of an agreed sum to the Insurance Company. The principal kinds of annuities are:

1 *Immediate annuity.* An immediate annuity is purchased by a single payment, and it is payable usually once every six months. The

first payment is made six months after the capital sum has been received by the Insurance Company, and the annuity then continues until the death of the annuitant.

2 *Deferred annuity.* A deferred annuity may likewise be secured by a single payment, but periodical payments are as a rule made. The annuity does not begin until a fixed future date, say, fifteen years after payment of the single amount or at the end of the payment of fifteen periodical instalments. Once the annuity begins, it continues until the death of the annuitant. It is ideal for a person who wishes to secure for himself a 'pension' from, say, age 55 or 60.

3 *Annuity certain.* An annuity certain may be either an immediate or a deferred annuity. It is secured in one or other of the respective ways described above, the only difference being that instead of payment ceasing on the death of the annuitant, it is made for a fixed or certain period in no way connected with the duration of the life of the annuitant. It ensures that no part of the capital sum is lost on the death of the annuitant.

4 *Self-employed pension annuity.* This is a special deferred annuity carrying certain tax concessions permitted by the Inland Revenue to persons who are not in pensionable employment. It is a condition that such an annuity shall be non-assignable and its value non-commutable for a cash payment. In these restrictions it differs from an ordinary deferred annuity.

5 *Reversionary annuity.* On the death of another life, a person's income may be seriously diminished, and to guard against that a reversionary annuity can be arranged, under which an annuity for the rest of life is payable if the annuitant survives the other life concerned.

Participating and Non-participating Policies

Life assurance policies are in the nature of permanent contracts and the premiums paid gradually accumulate in the life assurance fund, in readiness for claim payments as they arise. The funds are held by the Companies as custodians and those funds are invested, so that the maximum yield compatible with security is obtained. A life policy which merely guarantees the payment of the sum assured on the occurrence of the assured event is known as a non-participating or non-profit policy. For a slightly higher premium, however, many people prefer to effect a participating or with-profits policy, under which bonuses are payable. There is no guaranteed bonus. Life Offices make periodical valuations of their assets and liabilities—there may be annual, triennial, or quinquennial valuations according to the practice of the Company concerned—and the bonus declared depends upon the surplus available in the life fund at the time of the valuation.

Rates of interest, the general state of the money market and many other factors are also taken into account, but, despite the uncertainty of our times, people have such faith in the stability of life Assurance Companies that the majority of proposers prefer with-profits contracts. During the war years most Companies did not declare any bonuses, but that would be unusual in normal times.

The kind of bonus varies as between Assurers. The main types are as follows:

1 *Simple reversionary bonus.* This type of bonus is a percentage addition to the sum assured and it is payable at the same time as the sum assured. For example, if an endowment assurance is effected for 20 years in 1978 and the first bonus declaration is in 1980, then, assuming a quinquennial bonus basis, bonuses will be declared again in 1985, 1990, and 1995. If the Life Assured survives to the maturity date, then for the last three years there will be an interim bonus and the position can be

Sum assured payable in 1998	£1,000·00
Bonus 1980 £1·8%	36·00
Bonus 1985 £2%	100·00
Bonus 1990 £2.25%	112·50
Bonus 1995 £2.5%	125·00
Interim bonus 1998 £2·4%	72·00
Total sum payable	£1,445·50

2 *Compound reversionary bonus.* By this method the bonus is added to the sum assured, so that each succeeding bonus is computed on the sum assured plus accrued bonuses. The distinction between the two methods may be compared with simple interest and compound interest. A compound reversionary bonus usually gives a better return to the policyholder.

Both of these types of bonus may be surrendered for a (smaller)

cash payment forthwith, instead of allowing the bonus to accumulate until the sum assured is payable.

3 *Cash bonus*. By this method a cash payment is made to each with-profits policyholder at each bonus distribution. (This must not be confused with a cash surrender of a bonus under (1) or (2).)

4 *Discounted bonus*. This is a bonus which is 'anticipated' and used to reduce premiums payable. If bonuses declared exceed those anticipated, the excess is credited to the sum assured; if they fall short, the sum assured is reduced or a cash payment is required from the policyholder.

5 *Contribution bonus*. This depends on a system which attempts a scientific calculation of bonus according to the contribution each policy has made to the surplus divisible. (Although the method is equitable, it is complicated, difficult to explain to the public, and therefore little used.)

6 *Guaranteed bonus*. The guaranteed bonus is, in reality, the grant-ing of a non-profit assurance with an increasing sum assured—increasing each year by the amount guaranteed.

7 *Terminal bonus*. This is a bonus which is paid by some life Assurance Companies in addition to normal reversionary bonus when a policy becomes a claim. This is done because it is difficult otherwise to give policyholders a full share in the capital gains made by the life fund. Some Companies pay terminal bonus only on a claim by maturity or death and others pay it also on surrender. The amount of terminal bonus may vary considerably according to the Company concerned and the year in which the claim occurs, and no Company guarantees its terminal bonus so it is not of very much significance for quotation purposes.

Where a claim arises between two bonus declarations, the sum assured is allocated its share of bonus for the period since the previous valuation. This is at a special rate and is known as an interim bonus.

INDUSTRIAL LIFE ASSURANCE

The scope of industrial life assurance has been limited to some extent by the Industrial Assurance and Friendly Societies Acts, 1948 and

1958, and the Friendly Societies Act, 1974 (see p. 41), so that today the main sections are:

Whole life assurance, to provide a sum payable at death in return for a weekly premium payable throughout life. (The policies are often freed from premium payments under profit-sharing declarations after a policy has been in force for a certain number of years and the Life Assured has reached a certain age.)

Endowment assurance, to provide a sum payable at the end of a selected term of years or on previous death.

A Friendly Society is also permitted to grant ordinary life assurance contracts up to £1,000 per person, but there is no limit applicable to the other Assurers.

Provision for funeral expenses is no longer the main purpose of industrial life assurance; a rising proportion of the new business is endowment assurance, but the need for collection of premiums at the homes of the policyholders at regular intervals still dominates. In this feature lies the value and basis of the success of industrial life assurance. These policies are, on the whole, effected by people in the socio-economic groups C2 and D.

B PERSONAL ACCIDENT AND SICKNESS INSURANCE

This type of business began with personal accident insurance, and the standard scale of benefits for this class of policy is as follows:

	£	
Death	1,000·00	
Permanent total disablement (loss of two limbs or loss of one limb and sight of one eye) . .	1,000·00	
Permanent partial disablement (loss of one limb or sight of one eye)	500·00	
Temporary total disablement .	6·00 }	limited
Temporary partial disablement .	1·25 }	to 52 weeks

These events must be caused by 'accident,' as defined in the policy.

When specified diseases[1] were added, temporary total disablement benefit at the rate given above was available. The same applied when the accidents and all sickness contract was devised. (Sometimes, temporary partial disablement benefit is also included.)

Permanent contracts were drafted on similar lines but there are usually two kinds[2] of policies—those with immediate benefits and those under which benefits are not payable until after the first six months of disability. The premium under the latter type of policy is much smaller than under the former, and the contracts are intended to guard against lengthy periods of disablement only.

In recent years, there have been many departures from the standard scale. Some Insurers offer 100 weeks instead of 52 as the maximum period under the temporary total and partial disablement sections. There are also selective schemes, so that the proposer can choose the benefits he requires, e.g., temporary total and partial disablement only or fatal accident cover only. The benefits differ as between Insurers, so that one may add a lump sum for blindness or for paralysis by disease, and another an annuity therefor for ten years.

Group schemes are in demand not only for the employees of firms but also for members of sports clubs and other associations. Some of the group schemes are designed to provide for payment of the difference between National Insurance (Industrial Injury) Disablement Benefit and full wages, so that there is no diminution in the family income during a period of disablement.

Personal accident aviation insurance is available freely, and in view of comparatively low rates of premium proposers often seek substantial sums insured.

Group personal accident insurance is often arranged by firms for their employees who fly in the course of business and policies are also effected in respect of civilian air crew.

Individual passengers effect personal accident insurances, often on the airfield immediately before flight. Rates are unremunerative and there is a catastrophe hazard because a crash usually results in the death of all on board.

1 The specified diseases policy is now obsolescent; accidents only or accidents and all sickness is usual.
2 The two kinds of policies are not limited to permanent contracts but can be obtained in other classes of personal accident business.

C PERMANENT HEALTH INSURANCE

This is a class of insurance which has been developed in the UK in recent years, although it has been widely available in the USA for much longer. The insurance is designed to replace earned income for disability arising out of sickness or accident on a longer term basis than that offered under (b) above. Disability in this context means that the Insured is completely unable by reason of sickness or accident to perform any part whatever of the duties of his occupation. The insurance is permanent in the sense that it cannot be cancelled by the Insurer before the normal terminating age which is usually 65 for males and 60 for females. There is normally a deferred period of 4, 13, 26 or 52 weeks before the benefit commences to accrue. The premium payable depends upon the deferred period selected. On expiry of that period the benefit is payable so long as disability lasts, up to the stated terminating age. Generally premium is not payable for those periods when insured benefit is being received. Premiums for this type of insurance do not qualify for any rebate of income tax. Benefits payable to a disabled Insured, although legally taxable, normally enjoy a tax concession in that they are not assessed to tax unless and until they have been paid for a full fiscal year. Thereafter, they are assessed to tax as unearned income.

Proposals for this type of insurance can usually be considered without medical examination when the age at entry does not exceed 50 years and the amount of benefit does not exceed £25 per week. The policy usually contains some restrictions on foreign travel and residence.

D SOCIAL SECURITY

Although private Insurers are not involved, social security is, strictly speaking, covered by this classification. An outline of the system is described in Chapter 1.

2 Insurances of Property and Pecuniary Loss

A MARINE INSURANCE

Goods are not as a rule sold on cash terms, if only because of the distances which intervene and the large sums involved. Some crops are sold before they are harvested, and, on a futures system, even before they are sown, and many merchants at times need more capital than they can themselves immediately provide. For these and other reasons, banks and similar financial institutions—all parts of the complicated Money Market—are involved, and they require security for loans and other financial arrangements into which they enter. An essential part of that security is protection against loss or damage by perils of the sea or through the hazards of transit generally. Such protection is afforded by marine insurance. The same is true of ships, and insurance on hulls and machinery is an important part of the security provided for mortgagees.

Ship Insurance

As the word 'ship' implies, this section of marine insurance relates to the insurance of the ship itself, namely, the hull and the ship's machinery. Such an insurance is effected by the shipowner to protect him against loss by the operation of the perils of the sea, such as heavy weather, stranding or collision, fire and similar perils of a fortuitous nature. War risks can also be insured on special terms, but, generally speaking, as far as British vessels are concerned, war risks are insured by the Protection and Indemnity Clubs or Associations wherein the vessel is entered (see p. 81). A ship insurance is usually arranged for twelve months, and while policies are issued on single vessels, many vessels are owned and operated in fleets, hence the insurance is arranged on a fleet basis.

Ships may be insured against 'all risks' or against total loss or partial damage. Total loss may be actual or constructive. The former includes the destruction of the ship or a missing ship which is presumed to be lost when there is no information about her after the lapse of a reasonable period. A constructive total loss arises when the cost of repairing a vessel exceeds its value after repair, or when the insured is irretrievably deprived of the vessel. If an assured claims for a constructive total loss he must give notice of abandonment to the underwriters so that they may protect their interests. Partial loss or damage is known in marine insurance as particular average which must be accidental or fortuitous unlike general average which is voluntary and intentional.

The type of cover can be varied according to requirements by sundry clauses which are used to bring the time-honoured marine policy forms up to date. The many clauses currently in use are drafted by the Institute of London Underwriters, the market representative body for companies transacting marine insurance, in conjunction with Lloyd's.

Cargo Insurance

It is necessary not merely to insure the ship but also the valuable goods carried; hence cargo insurance relates to cover in respect of goods, produce and/or merchandise imported from, or exported to, various parts of the world. Here again, there are various types of policies:

a FPA (Free from Particular Average) according to the Institute Cargo Clauses which confine the cover to partial loss or damage by major perils, such as strandings, collisions, sinkings and fire, with the addition of general average and total losses. But the breaking of the warranty by one of the named casualties can convert the policy to 'With Average' (see (*b*)).

b WA (With Average) in accordance with the Institute Cargo Clauses which, in addition to cover as in (*a*), also cover partial loss through the perils of the sea, such as sea water damage.

c All Risks cover in accordance with the special Institute Clause. This cover does not extend to loss, damage or expense proximately caused by delay or inherent vice or nature of the subject-matter insured. In other words, fortuitous losses of every description are covered, which would include the risks of theft and pilferage.

d In conjunction with the above types of policies, war and strikes risks are usually insured in accordance with the special Institute Clauses.

The geographical scope of the cover is guided by the Institute Clauses, e.g., the Institute Cargo Clauses grant warehouse to warehouse cover, but with a limit of 60 days cover after discharge at final port. The insurance remains in force although there may be deviation or transhipment or if there is delay beyond the control of the Assured. The Extended Cover Clause, which was attached to all cargo policies, was included from 1 January, 1958, as part of the Clauses. This protects the cargo owner where, by circumstances beyond his control, the adventure is terminated before delivery of the goods into final warehouse. Cover is continued until final disposal.

For certain produce there are what are known as Trade Clauses, e.g., for grain, jute, rubber, and sugar. The conditions of these Trade Clauses are agreed between Underwriters and merchants.

Freight Insurance

Considerable sums are involved in freight, which may be defined, for present purposes, as a sum paid for the transporting of goods (or for the hire of a ship), and if the adventure is lost, freight will likewise be lost. Freight is 'at the risk' of shipowners, i.e., freight or hire money in process of being earned, or of the charterers who have hired the vessel wholly or in part. There are special Freight Clauses to cater for these types of insurance. Chartered freight may be for voyage or for a period of time.

Where freight is paid in advance, it is usually added to the value of the goods and the total insurable value computed accordingly. In this event, the freight amount ranks as a part of the cargo value. At times, however, freight is not payable until the goods reach their destination, when it is, of course, at the risk of the shipowner who stands to lose if the cargo is not delivered. Even if the cargo is damaged, provided it arrives with value, freight is still payable, but this would not be so if it was a constructive total loss.

B FIRE INSURANCE

In the last sixty years the scope of insurance normally written in the fire department has been considerably extended by:

1 the granting of wider cover under the ordinary material damage fire policy (e.g., special perils);

2 the undertaking of new classes of business (e.g., loss of profits insurance); and

3 the introduction of various concessions and general improvements (e.g., declaration policies, and the reinstatement extension).

Generally speaking, the various types of cover now granted by the fire department can be divided into four main sections, viz.:

1 Ordinary fire insurance.

2 Special perils.

3 Household insurance (sometimes written in the accident department).

4 Other types of insurance not included in the foregoing.

Ordinary Fire Insurance

This is the oldest and most common form of cover given. Policies are issued to indemnify owners of property, whether buildings or contents, against destruction or damage caused by fire and lightning. Two forms of policy are in general use. One is for private houses and their contents (household goods and personal effects), the cover being extended to include loss or damage by explosion and some other minor contingencies; and the other, known as the 'standard' policy form, is normally used for everything else, e.g., factories, shops, warehouses, and their contents consisting of machinery, stock- and materials-in-trade, and fixtures and fittings. The cover granted by the standard policy does not extend to include destruction or damage by explosion, except to a very limited degree.

Loss of rent, whether payable or receivable, consequent upon the insured premises being rendered partly or wholly uninhabitable by any of the perils covered, may be insured by a separate item. Architects' and surveyors' fees necessarily incurred in supervising the reinstatement of a building following destruction or damage by any of the perils covered may also be insured either as a separate item or as an extension of the item covering the building, care being taken in this event to make sure that the sum insured is adequate.

Fire policies cover a very wide range of property, varying from small buildings and their contents to huge factories extending over many acres of ground and insured for millions of pounds sterling. These large insurances are often 'scheduled,' i.e., divided among various Offices,[1] each one taking a percentage or proportion of the total schedule. The Office with the largest share is known as the leading Office, and is usually responsible for carrying out surveys of the premises insured and for preparing the policy (including the schedule of amounts covered, description of buildings, and various additional clauses and extensions).

Special Perils Insurance

Special perils are known also as extra or additional perils, and this form of cover was first introduced by fire Insurers to meet a demand for protection against those perils normally excluded from the cover granted by the ordinary fire policy. Many additional perils, however, have since been added, and the field has widened considerably, even to the extent of granting cover against what is termed 'water damage' (other than damage caused by water used in fire extinguishment,

1 Such Offices are known as Co-insurers.

which is always treated as 'fire damage'), e.g., storm, tempest, flood, and bursting or overflowing of water tanks, apparatus, or pipes.

Special perils can be classified under four general headings:

1 *Perils of a Chemical Nature:*
Explosion
Spontaneous combustion, heating, or fermentation.

2 *Social Perils:*
Riot, civil commotion, strikers, locked-out workers, or persons taking part in labour disturbances or malicious persons *acting on behalf of or in connection with any political organization.* (Malicious damage can be provided for with the qualification embodied in the words italicized.)

3 *Perils of Nature:*
Earthquake.
Flood.
Hail, thunderbolt.
Storm or tempest.
Subsidence and landslip.
Subterranean fire.

4 *Miscellaneous Perils:*
Aircraft and other aerial devices or articles dropped therefrom.
Breakage of household mirrors.
Accidental damage to underground water and gas pipes or electricity cables.
Bursting or overflowing of water tanks, apparatus, or pipes.
Impact by road vehicles, horses, or cattle.

Many of these perils are automatically included in the cover granted by household policies (see later) and the popularity of this type of contract for private dwellings has undoubtedly created a demand for special perils insurance for trade premises.

Household Insurance

Household policies were first issued in 1915, and they fulfil the private individual's need for a single policy to cover the majority of perils to which he, as householder or house owner, is normally subject. These include fire, various special perils (including storm, tempest, flood, and burst pipes), theft, and various legal liabilities to the public. Loss of rent is also covered and there are generous extensions, particularly for insurances on contents (e.g., temporary removals), liability for accidents to servants, and a capital sum for fatal injury to the Insured caused by fire or burglars.

Household policies are issued for buildings or contents or both buildings and contents, and they are also issued to cover blocks of residential flats. 'All risks' cover in respect of valuable and other personal property is included in some household policies, provided contents are also insured. Some Offices may also include cover in respect of loss or damage to caravans, their equipment and third party liability.

A recent development in household insurance designed to encourage policyholders to keep their insured values up to date in times of inflation is the provision of an automatic increase clause in the policy. By this method the sum insured is increased by a small percentage at the end of each month subject to an increase in premium at each following renewal date. Some policies also provide that claims in respect of total loss or destruction of any household appliance, carpet or article of furniture up to five years old will be settled on the basis of the cost of the article as new. This is a modification of the principle of indemnity (see p. 108).

Insurers also provide a type of comprehensive (preferably called combined or traders') insurance for trade premises. The policy, although comprising one contract only, is made up of a facing sheet incorporating the proposal form and detailing the general terms and conditions followed by several sections for each of the various risks covered, e.g., fire and special perils, profits, public liability, employers' liability, and burglary. Each section sets out the terms and conditions applicable to the particular risks covered.

Other Types of Insurance

These normally comprise:

a Sprinkler leakage policies, covering damage by water accidentally discharged from, or leakage of water from, an automatic sprinkler installation, whether from the sprinkler heads themselves or other parts of the installation.
(N.B. If the sprinkler heads discharge water in the course of fire extinguishment, the resultant damage is, of course, treated as 'fire' damage.)

b Policies covering destruction or damage caused by *hail*. There are two types of policy, one covering agricultural crops in the open and the other covering glass in glasshouses. The practice of Offices varies in the way in which these insurances are handled. Some Offices write the business in the fire department, some in the accident department, and some even have an entirely separate department.

c Policies covering *farming stock*. While these insurances are written on a standard form, there are many special conditions and extensions which make them different from those of the ordinary fire policy, e.g., cover applies to livestock away from the Insured's farm, grain removed to other premises for drying, and live and dead stock in transit.

Other Features of Fire Insurance

The need to meet:

1 competition,

2 particular circumstances,

3 the increasing demands of industry for improved cover, and

4 Offices' desire for simplification, wherever possible,

has led Insurers in recent years to introduce many new features. Examples are as follows:

a Declaration policies. Instead of having to maintain for stock-in-trade insurances a high sum insured to cover all eventualities, or, alternatively, to make constant alterations to the sum insured to follow fluctuations in value, Insured are allowed to effect cover for the maximum value likely to be at risk during the year. Seventy-five per cent of the full premium applicable is paid in advance and periodical declarations are made at fixed dates throughout the year of the actual values at risk, the 'real' premium earned being calculated at the end of the year by charging the rate applicable to the average of the declarations made. Comparison is made between this earned premium and that actually paid, and a suitable adjustment effected.

b Reinstatement insurances. These were introduced after World War One, mainly for machinery, when the rapid increase in prices meant that normal provision for depreciation was not sufficient to make up the difference between the cost of a new machine and the market value of a used machine.

To meet the resultant difficulties, *reinstatement insurance* was devised by which an Insured, by insuring on the basis of replacement or reinstatement value *as new*, could, in effect, obtain 'new for old.' Two important conditions were, and still are, attached, viz.:

1 Reinstatement value is paid only if the property is reinstated, and

2 The amount payable is assessed by comparing the cost of reinstatement *at the time of reinstatement* with the sum insured in force *at the time of the loss.*

Although the conditions which brought about reinstatement insurances largely disappeared between the two World Wars, the concession was never withdrawn and is now a permanent feature of fire insurance. The extension can also be applied to buildings.

c Blanket policies. To avoid the constant necessity of keeping close watch on hundreds or even thousands of sums insured on numerous buildings and contents, industrial firms having very large premises, with total sums insured involving many millions of pounds sterling, are allowed to arrange their insurance so that one sum only is applied to buildings, a second to plant, machinery and the like, and a third to stock-in-trade. Each item is, of course, subject to the *pro rata* condition of average (see p. 184).

d Collective policies. Until World War Two, each Office used to issue its own policy, even for scheduled insurances, so that a firm owning a large factory insured by, say, twenty Offices would receive twenty policies, each incorporating a copy of the schedule. For reasons of economy, it was agreed that only the policy issued by the leading Office should incorporate a schedule, although each of the following Offices still issued a policy. This was generally known as the 'Economy' method. Soon after, Offices agreed to the issue of one policy only by the leading Office, in which the names of all the Co-insurers and their individual proportions were shown. This, known as the 'Collective' policy method, is usually adopted today.

C THEFT INSURANCE

The Theft Act, 1968, which came into operation on 1 January, 1969, was designed to alter the criminal law, but it affects crime loss policies since the term 'burglary' has been widened, 'theft' has been given a statutory definition, while the terms 'housebreaking' and 'larceny' disappear from the statutory vocabulary. Insurers, however, have amended the wording of their policies so as to give substantially the same cover as was available before the 1968 Act came into operation.

The business is divided into several sections as follows:

Private dwellings. Although cover is available for the contents of private dwellings, separate theft policies are rarely issued nowadays in view of the popularity of the household policy.

Business premises. This section covers a wide variety of risks—retail shops, offices, warehouses, sports clubs; indeed, any type of premises not within the first category.

'*All risks.*' This class of insurance is designed to cover specified valuables against almost all risks while the property is anywhere in the UK (and, sometimes, while overseas). Today, there is a growing tendency to offer 'all risks' cover for many other kinds of property, even for furniture in transit, because of the demand for the widest cover possible.

Money. Hold-ups have illustrated the value of money insurance and the cover is on 'all risks' lines. The insurance can be arranged in respect of money drawn from, or paid into, the bank, while in transit, or it can be provided on a wider basis so that, for example, a rent collector's money is insured as he goes from house to house and until he pays in.

Miscellaneous. There are various other types of insurances. Baggage is often marine department business, but it is dealt with at times by the accident department. Here again, the cover is on 'all risks' lines and insures personal baggage on a floating basis according to a traveller's requirements. Special theft (and fire) policies are issued to persons who own clothes and personal effects but no general furniture.

D MOTOR VEHICLE INSURANCE

As noted on p. 85 'own damage' is insured under a comprehensive policy and it cannot be insured apart from third party liability. Sometimes fire and theft risks only are insured, as an addition to a third party policy (see p. 85).

E LIVESTOCK INSURANCE

Animals are insured against death by accident or disease, and other special policies are issued as in (*d*), (*e*), and (*f*) below. The main sections are:

a Horses.
b Cattle.
c Pigs.
d Anthrax.
e Consequential loss following foot and mouth disease.
f Transit risks.

F FIDELITY GUARANTEE AND CONTINGENCY

This business is divided into four main sections, with other miscellaneous types of policies also dealt with by the fidelity department.

Commercial guarantees are designed to provide an employer with an indemnity against loss of moneys (and frequently loss of stock also) by the default of his employee(s). Policies are issued in respect of one employee, or a collective guarantee can be arranged to relate to a number of persons specified in the contract, with a separate amount of guarantee against each. Yet again, a floating policy refers to all the employees by name, but there is one amount of guarantee over the whole. The 'positions' policy is one in which the position is guaranteed and not the individual by name. The 'blanket' policy goes even further and gives protection against the dishonesty of the staff generally.

Local government guarantees are similar to ordinary commercial guarantees, but the cover is wider. They protect the local authority not merely against dishonesty but also against any loss arising through mistake, intentional or otherwise. Collective or floating policies are almost always required, and there may be an excess floater to cover any unusually heavy defalcation.

Court guarantees relate to Court of Protection bonds, Queen's Bench and Chancery guarantees. Positions of trust to which individuals are appointed by the Court, whether as receiver or manager, involve the handling of money and other assets; hence the Court requires security, and this is best secured by obtaining a bond from Insurers.

Government bonds are required in somewhat similar circumstances for special managers in bankruptcy, trustees under deeds of arrangement, liquidators, and those concerned with dutiable goods. These are but a few of many of such guarantees required from persons who are in positions of trust. A customs and excise bond, for example, ensures that no loss will be sustained by the authorities if those responsible for the payment of duties should fail to meet their obligations.

Miscellaneous business includes insurance against drawings and building society indemnities. Under the former, if bonds are liable to be drawn for repayment at par, insurance can be effected to provide for payment of the difference between the purchase price and par value in the event of their being drawn. The latter class of insurance enables a building society to advance beyond its usual limit on private dwellings occupied by the borrowers—say, up to 95 per cent of the purchase price—and if there is a default before repayment has reduced the advance to the normal limit, say, 75 per cent, the Insurers pay the difference between 75 per cent and the amount outstanding.

Contingency indemnities. This highly specialized section provides protection against loss in such unusual circumstances as, for example, enforcement of a restrictive covenant which has not been observed for many years, and losses that may arise when estates are distributed where there are missing beneficiaries who may subsequently come to light, or losses connected with the issue of duplicate documents, such as share certificates, because the originals are apparently lost.

G CONSEQUENTIAL LOSS INSURANCE

Many business men are still content with an ordinary material damage fire policy on the buildings and contents of their premises because they do not realize the heavy uninsured loss they would sustain in the event of fire by reason of the interruption or complete stoppage of business. While the fire policy will, in time, and if adequate, provide the money necessary to reinstate the material damage, the Insured is faced with two serious financial problems until his premises are completely rebuilt and re-equipped and his trading activities return to normal. These problems are:

1 The temporary loss, partial or complete, of normal revenue; and

2 The necessity of maintaining various payments, e.g., rates, mortgage interest, salaries or wages to certain of his employees, while revenue has ceased or diminished.

In addition, he may incur heavy extra expenditure in an attempt to carry on the business by renting other premises, having work done elsewhere, and adopting other similar expedients.

These financial problems can be overcome by means of a loss of profits policy which covers:

1 Loss of net profit (from revenue).
2 Continuing (or standing) charges which do not vary with the turnover.
3 Extra expenditure incurred to reduce the loss of revenue to a minimum.

If a business man has a properly-drafted profits policy, with an adequate indemnity period (the period during which the shortage in turnover is dealt with under the terms of the policy), he should be indemnified for his loss of trading during reinstatement following fire, in addition to indemnification under his material damage fire insurance for the loss of, or damage to, the buildings and contents.

Various special perils, mainly similar to those detailed above, can be insured, and there is also an extension peculiar to profits insurance, covering loss of profits following upon suicide at an hotel or boarding house causing the guests to seek accommodation elsewhere; or loss of trade at such establishments because of the outbreak of an infectious disease.

Consequential loss, or 'time loss,' cover is also available in respect of financial loss resulting from breakdown of plant.

H AVIATION INSURANCE

As explained on p. 86, 'own damage' is insured with third party liability whether aeroplanes, gliders or helicopters are concerned. There is also cargo insurance for which provision has to be made. Despite the heavy charges, considerable quantities of goods are sent by air and there is a demand for insurance, more particularly because such goods are usually of small bulk and high value. The property is not insured for a period of time but until it has reached its destination, hence cover continues after a forced landing or a crash. 'All risks' insurance is as a rule provided.

I MISCELLANEOUS RISKS

Property and pecuniary loss departments also provide the following covers:

Glass insurance. Accidental breakage of glass is insured usually at business premises. The main attraction is the speedy replacement service provided by Insurers.

Hailstorm insurance. Crops and also glass in greenhouses are insured against damage by hail (see also p. 73).

Contract guarantee. This relates to guarantees for the fulfilment of contracts, mainly those of the public works kind.

Credit insurance. This is designed to protect merchants and manufacturers against financial loss by reason of the insolvency or protracted default of their customers, and may include transactions in both home and overseas trade. There are various 'political risks' associated with overseas trade, such as government restrictions on remittances or local wars. Commercial Insurers exclude these risks from their policies, but cover is obtainable from the Export Credits Guarantee Department which is a government department.

Licence insurance. The object of this section is to give protection against loss by the forfeiture or non-renewal of a licence for the sale of intoxicating liquor.

J WAR RISKS INSURANCE

The war risks exclusions clause continues to apply in fire and accident contracts, but marine Underwriters now freely insure ships and cargoes against war risks, although the restrictions of the Waterborne Agreement still apply. In practice, British hulls are usually insured against war risks with the P & I Clubs or Associations in which they are entered.

In life assurance there has been a tendency to issue unrestricted policies, unless a proposer declares his intention of going to a war zone.

3 Insurances of Liability

Liability policies have traditionally been issued in the accident, motor, engineering, marine and aviation departments. However, liability arises from many causes and in consequence claims sometimes relate to the policies of more than one department. There has been a recent movement away from the issue of departmental policies to the issue of one contract covering employers' liability and public liability risks, and a specimen proposal form appears on page 152. In some Offices the liability risks dealt with in the accident, motor and engineering departments are now combined in one policy.

The features of each particular class of liability insurance are considered separately in the following paragraphs.

A MARINE COLLISION LIABILITY

London is the centre of the world marine insurance market, and the huge volume of business transacted is dealt with by the marine departments of the Companies, and by Lloyd's Underwriters operating as syndicates. There is another large market at Liverpool, and at Glasgow there is to be found a number of private marine Underwriters acting as agents on behalf of the Companies. The Companies transact business on a world-wide basis through branch offices and agencies, and Lloyd's Underwriters do likewise through the mediation of Lloyd's brokers.

Marine insurance is an essential feature of trade, particularly overseas trade, and as Great Britain has always been connected with seafaring interests as a carrying nation, it is not surprising that she is in the forefront of marine insurance business.

So far as liability cover is concerned, however, marine policies are usually limited to collision liability. This is not to say that a shipowner is unable to cover other liabilities, such as those which arise under contract in connection with cargo or liabilities to passengers or employer's liability in respect of the crew. Most of these risks, however, are insured by shipowners mutually in Protection and Indemnity Clubs or Associations, although Insurers do sometimes grant cover in respect of such risks.

In the case *De Vaux* v. *Salvador* (1836), it was decided that an Underwriter was not liable under the ordinary marine policy for shipowner's liability for damage caused to another ship in collision. After that Underwriters inserted the Running Down Clause in hull policies, under which they were liable for three-fourths of collision liability. This was at a time when public liability insurance was thought to be against public policy, hence the co-insurance up to one-fourth. This one-fourth was insured by shipowners mutually in Protection and Indemnity Clubs or Associations.

B EMPLOYERS' LIABILITY

This class of insurance provides an indemnity to employers against their liability to employees for personal injuries or disease sustained in the course of their employment. This requirement arises out of the Employers' Liability (Compulsory Insurance) Act, 1969, which came into operation on 1 January 1972 and made it compulsory for all employers to effect an approved insurance and obtain from their insurers a certificate. Copies of the certificate must be displayed at all the insured's premises for the information of employees while the original must be available for inspection when required.

The 1969 Act and the statutory regulations made thereunder have virtually deprived an employer and his insurers of any defence against claims for indemnity for personal injury or disease sustained at work. It is no longer necessary for an employee to establish his claim by proving one or more alternative faults or omissions by his employer such as personal negligence, failure to take reasonable care to provide safe plant, machinery and conditions of work, or breach of statutory duty. An employer can no longer avoid liability at common law if the injury is caused by a fellow employee.

Other legislation which has enlarged the scope of employees' claims includes the Employers' Liability (Defective Equipment) Act, 1969, which increases the liability of an employer for injuries to his work force which are attributable to defective equipment provided by the employer for the purpose of his business.

Another relevant statute is the Health and Safety at Work etc. Act, 1974, the main purpose of which is to secure the health, safety and welfare of persons at work and to protect persons other than persons at work against risks to health or safety arising out of the activities of people at work.

C PUBLIC LIABILITY

Public liability indemnities may be classified as follows:

1 Shops, warehouses, offices, and other premises risks.

2 Tradesmen, contractors, and others working away from own premises.

3 Builders and other erection undertakings.

4 Public works and other contracts.

5 Public authorities.

6 Estate owners and farmers.

7 Hospitals[1] and nursing homes.

1 Hospitals in England, Wales and Scotland within the National Health Service do not insure.

8 Inns, hotels, and boarding-houses.

9 Cinemas and theatres.

10 Personal liability.

11 Property owners' indemnities.

12 Lifts.

13 Golf, cricket, tennis, racquets, and similar sports.

14 Sporting guns.

15 Radio and television.

16 Horse-drawn vehicles.

17 Pedal cycles.

18 Products liability.

19 Professional indemnities.

The cover is similar in each group of risks (an indemnity in respect of legal liability for accidental death or bodily injury or accidental damage to property), but there are special risks associated with some undertakings. Under (8) the strict liability of an innkeeper for the safety of guests' property is insured; under (10) the indemnity relates to liability for accidents caused in the capacity of a private citizen, not arising out of any trade or business or the ownership or occupation of land or buildings; under (11) the indemnity concerns liability for accidents caused only by defects in buildings. Professional indemnities (19) are different from the others because they provide protection against any neglect, omission or error which may cause financial or personal injury to clients.

Under some of these types of policies other risks are incorporated. For example, under (13) a golfers' policy often includes limited fire and theft cover on personal effects, accidental breakage of clubs in the course of play, and limited personal accident benefits. Under (16) it is optional to insure loss or damage to own vehicles and theft of horses; also fatal injury to horses.

D PRODUCTS LIABILITY

Products liability insurance grew out of public liability insurance but is now an important class of insurance in its own right. For many years it has been possible to insure liability to another for death, bodily injury or illness, or damage to property, arising out of poison or other deleterious matter contained in food or drink. In *Donoghue v. Stevenson* (1932), A.C. 562 a claim was made because a person drank a glass of ginger beer only to find the remains of a decomposed snail in the dark-coloured bottle. This case, which went to the House of Lords, drew attention to the liabilities of sellers and suppliers of goods but it also established that where there is no reasonable possibility of intermediate examination, as happens when goods are sold in a sealed container, then the manufacturer is directly liable to the consumer.

Far wider cover is available nowadays and it is possible to insure against claims arising out of goods sold, or supplied or installed, erected, altered or treated by the insured elsewhere than at his own premises. The insured may be the manufacturer, repairer, importer, exporter, wholesaler, or retailer. The risk may be heavier still where the manufacturer gives written guarantees or where the goods are to be sold overseas. If goods have been brought from another country it may not be possible to obtain any recovery from the overseas supplier.

Premiums are generally based on turnover and have to take into account the fact that while the insurance covers claims arising during the period of the policy, the goods may have been produced and sold some years previously. Claims can prove complicated as there may be more than one defendant. For example, in a case where fur trimming caused dermatitis, the retailers, the wholesalers, the manufacturers of the trimming, the dyers and the manufacturers of the dye were all involved, i.e. five parties, and the legal costs were out of all proportion to the amount of damages.

E MOTOR THIRD PARTY LIABILITY

Motor insurance business is the largest single section of accident insurance, if judged by premium income, but this relates to motor business as a whole. Under a comprehensive policy liability insurance is combined with 'own damage' (property insurance) while under a private car policy there is an injury to owner section (insurance of the person). The business is therefore considered below in general terms, being divided according to the different kinds of vehicles:

Private cars.
Commercial vehicles, including goods-carrying vehicles, public service, private hire, and local authorities' vehicles.

Agricultural and forestry vehicles.
Vehicles of special construction, e.g., mechanical navvies, mobile canteens.
Motor traders' vehicles.
Motor cycles.

Insurers offer alternative kinds of policies, according to the extent of the cover required by the proposer. There are four kinds:

a Full comprehensive which covers loss of or damage to the Insured's own vehicle(s), third party liability for death of or bodily injury to members of the public or damage to their property, and, particularly for private cars, several additional forms of protection such as medical expenses and personal accident benefits for the owner.

b Third party, fire, and theft, under which the third party indemnity is exactly the same as that provided by the corresponding section of the comprehensive policy, plus fire and theft insurance for the Insured's own vehicle(s).

c Third party only—as in (*b*), but excluding fire and theft.

d 'Act' liability only. This policy provides an indemnity in respect of the liability (for death or bodily injury only) which it is compulsory to insure[1] under the terms of the Road Traffic Acts. 'Act' only cover is not favoured by Insurers.

F ENGINEERING INSURANCE (LIABILITY)[2]

Many types of engineering insurance likewise combine liability with property insurance. They are as follows:

a Boiler insurance. A boiler policy covers damage to the boiler or other apparatus described in the schedule to the policy, or to other property of the Insured, and liability of the Insured for fatal or non-

1 It is also compulsory to include similar liability for passengers to comply with the requirements of s.148(3) of the Road Traffic Act, 1972, which embodies the provisions of the Motor Vehicles (Passenger Insurance) Act, 1971.
2 Sometimes duplication of cover arises with conventional liability policies and, in so far as engine and electrical plant is concerned, third party cover is to some extent anachronistic as there is a general trend for this liability insurance to find its proper home in the liability market.

fatal injury to third parties or for damage to their property, arising as a direct consequence of explosion or collapse of the boiler or other plant specified. This section includes the insurance of power boilers, heating and domestic boilers, and pressure vessels, such as steam receivers and steam-jacketed pans.

b Engine insurance. An engine policy covers damage to the engine or machine by breakdown, while third party liability and damage to property of the Insured by flying fragments can be insured, if desired. Steam, gas, oil and diesel engines, refrigerating plant, and air compressors are within this section.

c Electrical plant insurance. The cover is similar to that of the engine policy and it relates to dynamos, motors, turbogenerators, and static plant, such as transformers and rectifiers.

d Lifting machinery insurance. Third party liability and other protection according to circumstances is arranged for passenger and goods lifts, cranes, hoists, and lifting tackle generally.

G AVIATION INSURANCE (LIABILITY)

Here again 'own damage' is combined with liability under comprehensive policies, but aviation insurance is transacted in a highly competitive market and the business has to face many problems by reason of the fluid state of underwriting. The huge sums insured present their own problems.

There is a demand, these days, for 'products' liability insurance to protect the manufacturer or repairer against the results of defective workmanship. Faulty design or bad workmanship might result in a very heavy claim which no single firm could bear without financial embarrassment.

The airport liability policy is a special type of public liability contract and covers (1) liability for bodily injuries or damage to property arising out of any accident at the airport caused by the fault or negligence of the Insured or his employees or by any defect in the premises or plant, (2) the food and drink risk where relevant, (3) loss of or damage to vehicles not belonging to the Insured, and (4) loss of or damage to aircraft not belonging to the Insured while on the ground in the care, custody, or control of the Insured.

4 General Principles (1)

There are certain general principles more or less common to all classes of insurance business. They are therefore dealt with in this chapter and the succeeding one in their relation to the main sections of insurance, with any modifications in their application to individual sections of the business.

These general principles are insurable interest, good faith, indemnity (with the corollaries of subrogation and contribution), and proximate cause. Such principles or doctrines are inherent in English Common Law, and they are affected also by Statute Law, particularly as regards insurable interest. Moreover, it is always possible to modify by contract any Common Law principle (provided the modification is not illegal) and an illustration of this is provided by the contractual duty of good faith, outlined later in this chapter.

When dealing with these principles of insurance, it is important to notice the appropriate leading cases. The judgments of the Courts have clarified the practical application of such principles.

Insurable interest is necessary in every contract of insurance. In the absence of good faith, no contract of insurance is valid. Indemnity provides for the sum recoverable to be limited to the extent of the Insured's interest in the subject-matter. There is, therefore, some inter-relationship, and the order adopted in this and the succeeding chapters is (*a*) insurable interest, (*b*) good faith, (*c*) indemnity, with (*d*) subrogation and (*e*) contribution as corollaries, and (*f*) proximate cause.

Insurable Interest

The principle of insurable interest is best approached by reference to three Statutes, the Life Assurance Act, 1774, the Gaming Act, 1845, and the Marine Insurance Act, 1906. The last-mentioned Act deals with marine insurance, but the law as laid down in many sections applies equally in principle to other classes of insurance.

Definition

This principle is defined in the Marine Insurance Act, 1906, Sect. 5(2):

> 'In particular a person is interested in a marine adventure where he stands in any legal or equitable relation to the adventure or to any insurable property at risk therein, in consequence of which he may benefit by the safety or due arrival of insurable property, or may be prejudiced by its loss, or by damage thereto, or by the detention thereof, or may incur liability in respect thereof.'

Another definition of insurable interest can be found in the case of *Lucena* v. *Craufurd* (1806), 2 Bos & PNR 269:

> 'A man is interested in a thing to whom advantage may arise or prejudice happen from the circumstances which may attend it. Interest does not necessarily imply a right to the whole, or a part of a thing, nor necessarily and exclusively that which may be the subject of privation, but the having some relation to, or concern in the subject of the insurance, which relation or concern by the happening of the perils insured against may be so affected as to produce a damage, detriment, or prejudice to the person insuring; and where a man is so circumstanced with respect to matters exposed to certain risks or dangers as to have a moral certainty of advantage or benefit, but for those risks or dangers, he may be said to be interested in the safety of the thing. To be interested in the preservation of a thing, is to be so circumstanced with respect to it as to have benefit from its existence, prejudice from its destruction. The property of a thing and the interest devisable from it may be very different; of the first, the price is generally the measure, but by interest in a thing every benefit or advantage arising out of or depending on such thing may be considered as being comprehended.'

Life Assurance Act, 1774

In the eighteenth century, there was an extraordinary wave of gambling under the guise of insurance, and policies were effected on the lives of public men without any insurable interest. The following extract from the Life Assurance Act, 1774 (otherwise known as the Gambling Act), is therefore of interest, more particularly because this Statute put an end to the pernicious practice in question:

> 'Whereas it hath been found by experience, that the making

insurances on lives, or other events, wherein the assured shall have no interest, hath introduced a mischievous kind of gaming: For remedy whereof, be it enacted ... that from and after the passing of this Act, no insurance shall be made by any person or persons, bodies politic or corporate, on the life or lives of any person or persons, or on any other event or events whatsoever, wherein the person or persons for whose use, benefit, or on whose account such policy or policies shall be made, shall have no interest, or by way of gaming and wagering; and that every assurance made, contrary to the true intent and meaning hereof, shall be null and void, to all intents and purposes whatsoever.'

The Act also provides that no 'policy or policies on the life or lives of any person or persons ...' shall be made 'without inserting in such policy or policies the person's name or persons' names interested therein or for whose use, benefit, or on whose account such policy is so made or underwrote.' Moreover, 'no greater sum shall be recovered or received from the insurer or insurers than the amount or value of the interest of the insured in such life or lives. ...'

Gaming Act, 1845

The Life Assurance Act, 1774, did not extend to 'insurances bona fide made by any person or persons on ships, goods, or merchandise,' hence the Gaming Act, 1845, was passed which covers the position as regards goods and merchandise and by Sect. 18 provides:

'All contracts or agreements, whether by parole or in writing, by way of gaming or wagering, shall be null and void; and no suit shall be brought ... for recovering any sum of money ... alleged to be won upon any wager, or which shall have been deposited in the hands of any person to abide the event on which any wager shall have been made.'

An insurance on goods without insurable interest is, in effect, a wager and therefore unenforceable.

Marine Insurance Act, 1906

The position as regards ships and cargoes is covered by the Marine Insurance Act, 1906, from which a quotation has already been given. It is only necessary here to quote Sects. 4 and 8.

'4 1 Every contract of marine insurance by way of gaming or wagering is void.

2 A contract of marine insurance is deemed to be a gaming or wagering contract:

a Where the assured has not an insurable interest as defined by this Act, and the contract is entered into with no expectation of acquiring such an interest; or

b Where the policy is made "interest or no interest," or "without further proof of interest than the policy itself," or "without benefit of salvage to the insurer" or subject to any other like term:
Provided that, where there is no possibility of salvage, a policy may be effected without benefit of salvage to the insurer.

8 A partial interest of any nature is insurable.'

Insurable Interest: General Application

Insurable interest applies generally to insurances of the person, property, liability, or any contingency which is properly the subject of a policy of insurance. Insurable interest is the legal right to insure and an insurance policy does not cover property, but relates to the Insured's *interest* in the property. This applies *mutatis mutandis* to all types of insurance.

ILLUSTRATIONS OF APPLICATION OF INSURABLE INTEREST

Insurances of the Person

Life assurance. In life assurance it is necessary to differentiate between (*a*) where the policyholder assures his own life, and (*b*) where the policy covers the life of another.

The life of a policyholder cannot be accurately valued in terms of money and there is no monetary limit to the amount for which a man may assure his life. In practice, life assurance premiums are paid mainly out of income, and the extent to which a man assures largely depends upon his will to save and his power to save. (Single premium policies are often paid out of capital.)

Where the life of another is assured, it is essential for the person assuring to have a financial interest in the life of the other person as, for instance, a creditor in the life of his debtor to the value of the debt. A wife has an interest in the life of her husband who is legally bound to support her, and so she can assure his life. This is recognized by the Married Women's Property Act, 1882. Apart from the husband and wife relationship, however, a mere dependency is not sufficient to support assurance. Thus, a father has no insurable interest in his son's life, while a son has no insurable interest in his mother's life, even though she performs domestic services for him. As regards industrial assurance, life-of-another policies have been permitted in well-defined limits, as it was recognized that a death might result in expense to a surviving near-relative, e.g. parent, stepparent or grandparent. Moreover, the legislature has provided for low limits on the amounts which can be assured by a life-of-another policy where the 'other' is a child. Historically, the reason for the latter limits was the temptation to infanticide in order to obtain the policy moneys. Various alterations, however, are made by the Industrial Assurance and Friendly Societies (Amendment) Act, 1958 (see p. 41).

Insurable interest must exist at the commencement of the assurance but not necessarily at the time of loss.

Personal accident and sickness insurance. The application of insurable interest here is similar to life assurance and calls for no specific comment.

Insurances of Property and Pecuniary Insurances

The application of the general principles of insurable interest to property can be illustrated both from marine and fire insurance.

Marine insurance. It should be noticed that insurance 'lost or not lost' can be effected when there is no information at the time relative to the safety of the subject-matter. In *Sutherland* v. *Pratt* (1843), 11 M & W 296, the plaintiff acquired an interest in merchandise after the date when the goods suffered damage but before news of this reached him, and a policy effected by him 'lost or not lost' was held to be valid. The effect of the term 'lost or not lost' is to make the insurance retrospective to the commencement of the voyage.

As regards the time when insurable interest must exist in connection with marine insurance contracts, the position is covered by Sect. 6(1) and (2) of the Marine Insurance Act, 1906, which also deals with 'lost or not lost' insurances. The sub-sections are as follows:

'1 The assured must be interested in the subject-matter insured at the time of the loss though he need not be interested when the insurance is effected.

Provided that where the subject-matter is insured "lost or not lost," the assured may recover although he may not have acquired his interest until after the loss, unless at the time of effecting the contract of insurance the assured was aware of the loss, and the insurer was not.

2 Where the assured has no interest at the time of the loss, he cannot acquire interest by any act or election after he is aware of the loss.'

PPI policies. In marine insurance practice, PPI ('policy proof of interest') contracts as defined by Sect. 4(2)(*b*) of the Marine Insurance Act, 1906, are issued. Policies of this type are used daily to insure such nebulous interests as shipowners' disbursements or increased value by reason of rising market.

The Marine Insurance (Gambling Policies) Act, 1909, makes clear that any person effecting marine insurance without interest or anticipation of interest is deemed guilty of an offence by way of gambling on loss by maritime perils.

Fire insurance. The majority of fire policies cover the insurable interest of the policyholder in material property set out in the schedule of the policy. Insurable interest is not limited to absolute ownership of property, but may arise in other ways as, for example:

a Joint owner.

b Mortgagor or mortgagee, the interest of the mortgagee being limited to the amount of the advance.

c Executor or trustee.

d Bailee.

e Lessor or lessee.

For insurable interest to exist, the Insured must be in some legal relationship to the property insured so that he benefits by its safety and is prejudiced by loss of or damage to the property in question. Insurable interest must exist both at the commencement of the insurance and at the time of loss.

Pecuniary insurances. Insurable interest is not difficult to find in some pecuniary insurances such as fidelity guarantee and contingency risks where the loss is easily assessable in terms of money.

An insurable interest also arises from a 'chose in action' which has been defined as 'a thing of which a man has not the possession or actual enjoyment, but has a right to demand by action or other proceeding'. Thus, a debt is a chose in action, and the possibility of non-payment of a debt is sufficient insurable interest to support a credit insurance. However, a mere expectancy does not constitute an insurable interest. In the leading case of *Lucena* v. *Craufurd (supra)* it was said that a 'mere expectancy even such as that of an heir apparent who is practically certain to succeed (as in a case when the ancestor is on his death-bed, 90 years of age, lunatic and intestate) has been considered to confer no insurable interest'. No more can a beneficiary under a will insure his interest because the will can be revoked at any time before the death of the testator.

The position is different, however, when the expectancy is founded on a legal right. Hence, the owner of a business can insure against loss of profits resulting from interruption of the business following fire.

Insurances of Liability

Under policies of this type, an indemnity is provided to the Insured in respect of his legal liability to pay damages, usually arising out of negligence or nuisance and, occasionally, under contract. In order to constitute insurable interest, the Insured must be under such a liability that he is prejudiced when it becomes operative (and therefore benefits in the absence of such liability).

Liabilities arising out of acts of negligence which are also criminal are insurable on the grounds that such acts are accidental. Thus, a motor insurance policy covering the Insured's liability for accidental injury caused by his negligence, even though gross and attended by criminal consequences such as manslaughter, will not be void as against public policy. Deliberate criminal acts are not insurable, and in *Hardy* v. *Motor Insurers' Bureau* (1964), 2 All ER 742, it was held that a motorist guilty of a deliberate crime resulting in payment of damages to an injured third party is not entitled to recover on the policy. However, if he does not pay the damages, the injured third party can recover against the Insurers.

ASSIGNMENT OR TRANSFER OF INTEREST

It is necessary to distinguish between assignment (*a*) of the *subject-matter of insurance*, e.g., a house insured under a fire or householder's policy may be transferred to a new owner, (*b*) of the *policy* so that the benefit of the contract is passed over to another Insured, and

(c) of the *policy moneys*, i.e., where the Insured directs the Insurers to pay the amount of a claim to a third party, and, provided the Insurers are protected by an adequate discharge, they are bound to comply.

Marine and life policies can be freely assigned (unless subject to restrictive clausing) but assignments of fire and accident policies are not valid without the consent of the Insurers—except changes of interest by will or operation of law. Assignments must be made before the Insured parts with his interest. Once he has lost this the policy concerned is void and cannot be assigned.

Insurances of the Person

Life assurance. Where the assignee wishes to have the right to sue in his own name, (a) he must have the equitable right to receive the money, (b) he must have a properly stamped assignment in writing, and (c) notice must be given to the Company in accordance with the Policies of Assurance Act, 1867. Companies must register all notices of assignment and the fee they may charge is limited to 25p. Incidentally, life policies are the only policies which can be assigned whether the assignee has an insurable interest or not. Life policies are frequently charged, assigned or otherwise dealt with, for they are valuable securities. It is for this reason that proof of title is always particularly important when dealing with life claims.

Insurances of Property and Pecuniary Insurances

Marine insurance. Assignment is dealt with by Sect. 50 of the Marine Insurance Act, 1906, which provides that 'A marine policy is assignable unless it contains terms expressly prohibiting assignment. It may be assigned either before or after loss. ... A marine policy may be assigned by indorsement thereon or in other customary manner.' In practice, a marine cargo policy is frequently endorsed in blank and becomes in effect a quasi-negotiable instrument. This, it will be appreciated, adds considerably to the convenience of mercantile transactions, as the policy can be negotiated through a bank along with other documents of title.

In hull policies, Underwriters' agreement to change of ownership of the vessel must be obtained, as ownership and management are important underwriting considerations.

Fire insurance. It has never been the practice in fire insurance to recognize assignment without the consent of the Insurers, and changes of interest in fire policies (unless by will or operation of law) are not valid unless and until the consent of the Insurers has been given. It was stated in *Lynch* v. *Dalzell* (1729), 4 Bro PC 431, that 'these policies (in this instance, fire policies) are not in the nature of them assignable, nor intended to be assigned from one person to another without the consent of the Office.' When there is a transfer of interest, the Insurers make all their usual inquiries and assignment may be recognized only subject to conditions: it forms a new contract.

The following extract from Porter's *Laws of Insurance* (8th edition, p. 299) summarizes the position:

'It seems universally to have been held that fire policies are personal contracts, and that the consent of the Insurers is necessary to the assignment thereof; while marine policies have always been assignable with their subject-matter, and life policies have been treated as reversionary interests, and allowed to be assigned, charged, or otherwise dealt with.'

Insurances of Liability

Here the practice follows fire insurance in principle.

Utmost Good Faith

In most types of contract the buyer needs protection from the seller. This has not always been recognized and until the passing of the Misrepresentation Act, 1967, most commercial contracts were governed by the Common Law doctrine of *caveat emptor* (let the buyer beware). This permitted each party to a contract to remain silent even in regard to facts which one believed would be operative upon the mind of the other. Thus, in a contract for the sale of goods the seller was under no duty to disclose defects; it was the duty of the purchaser to examine the goods and discover any defects for himself. This rule did not justify misrepresentation, but the remedies available for misrepresentation did not always compensate the buyer. The 1967 Act set out to remedy the shortcomings of the existing law and to give the buyer still greater protection as against the seller. In particular, it permits in certain circumstances rescission of a contract induced by misrepresentation, even if innocent, and the award of damages. It also limits the use of exemption clauses which seek to exclude liability of the seller for misrepresentation, as such clauses would defeat the object of the Act.

The Act is not likely to have any great effect on insurance contracts which have always been subject to the much more stringent rules of utmost good faith[1] (*uberrima fides*). This doctrine is essential on account of the fact that the full circumstances of the subject-matter of insurance are as a rule known to one party only, namely, the proposer, and the Insurers, in deciding whether or not to accept a risk, must rely primarily upon the information supplied to them by the proposer. As will be seen, this principle is rigidly applied by the Courts and it imposes the duty with equal stringency upon both Insured and Insurers.

The *inherent* or Common Law duty of utmost good faith must be distinguished from the *contractual* duty. The Common Law duty is the basis, but the parties to an insurance contract can either restrict or extend the duty as it exists at Common Law (see p. 104). This is of special importance in some classes of insurance, e.g., liability, in view of the additional conditions imposed by the declaration included in proposal forms.

The Inherent Duty of Utmost Good Faith

This doctrine requires both parties to a contract of insurance to make full disclosure of all material facts. A material fact for this purpose was defined in the case of *Rivaz* v. *Gerussi* (1880), 6 QBD 222, as a fact which would affect the judgment of a rational Underwriter in considering whether he would enter into a contract at all or enter into it at one rate or another.

The duty of disclosure imposed by utmost good faith is strictly interpreted by the Courts and is not limited to material facts which the proposer knows, but extends to those which he ought to know. At the same time, a statement of intention or of opinion must be clearly distinguished because, provided it is made in all honesty, there is no misrepresentation if it should subsequently prove to be untrue.

The law is clearly stated in the case of *Carter* v. *Boehm* (1766), 3 Burr 1909, where Lord Mansfield said:

---

1 'The general principles of law applicable to contracts of insurance do not differ in essence from those applicable to other kinds of contracts, and the rule with regard to the disclosure of material facts and the penalty for non-disclosure is rather a rule of construction for a particular type of contract.'—Anson's *Law of Contract*, 23rd ed., p. 237

'Insurance is a contract upon speculation. The special facts upon which the contingent chance is to be computed lie most commonly in the knowledge of the Insured only; the Underwriter trusts to his representations, and proceeds upon confidence that he does not keep back any circumstance in his knowledge to mislead the Underwriter into a belief that the circumstance does not exist, and to induce him to estimate the risk as if it did not exist. The keeping back of such a circumstance is a fraud, and therefore the policy is void. Although the suppression should happen through mistake, without any fraudulent intention, yet still the Underwriter is deceived, and the policy is void; because the risk run is really different from the risk understood and intended to be run at the time of the agreement ... Good faith forbids either party, by concealing what he privately knows, to draw the other into a bargain from his ignorance of that fact and his believing the contrary.'

The Marine Insurance Act, 1906, provides a clear guide and the following sections may be taken as applying *mutatis mutandis* to all classes of insurance:

'17 A contract of marine insurance is a contract based upon the utmost good faith, and, if the utmost good faith be not observed by either party, the contract may be avoided by the other party.

18 1 Subject to the provisions of this section, the assured must disclose to the insurer, before the contract is concluded, every material circumstance which is known to the assured, and the assured is deemed to know every circumstance which, in the ordinary course of business, ought to be known by him. If the assured fails to make such disclosure, the insurer may avoid the contract.

2 Every circumstance is material which would influence the judgment of a prudent insurer in fixing the premium, or determining whether he will take the risk.

3 In the absence of inquiry the following circumstances need not be disclosed, namely:

a Any circumstance which diminishes the risk;

b Any circumstance which is known or presumed to be known to the insurer. The insurer is presumed to know matters of common notoriety or knowledge, and matters which an insurer in the ordinary course of his business, as such, ought to know;

c Any circumstance as to which information is waived by the insurer;

d Any circumstance which it is superfluous to disclose by reason of any express or implied warranty.

4 Whether any particular circumstance, which is not disclosed, be material or not is, in each case, a question of fact.

5 The term 'circumstance' includes any communication made to, or information received by, the assured.

19 Subject to the provisions of the preceding section as to circumstances which need not be disclosed, where an insurance is effected for the assured by an agent, the agent must disclose to the insurer:

a Every material circumstance which is known to himself, and an agent to insure is deemed to know every circumstance which in the ordinary course of business ought to be known by, or to have been communicated to, him; and

b Every material circumstance which the assured is bound to disclose, unless it come to his knowledge too late to communicate it to the agent.'

The onerous duty of disclosure continues until the negotiations for the contract of insurance have been completed. After that, the duty arises again if an alteration is to be made to the contract, but it only applies so far as regards the alteration. The position at renewal depends upon whether or not renewal constitutes a fresh contract.

The Statements of Insurance Practice

The duty to disclose material facts has been modified by two 'Statements of Insurance Practice' that were published in the summer of 1977. The first, non-life statement was issued by the British Insurance Association and Lloyd's; this was followed by the second, long-term statement issued by the Life Offices' Association and the Association of Scottish Life Offices.

The reason for the publication of these codes of practice stems from the Unfair Contract Terms Act which came into force on 1 February 1977 and provides that all exclusion clauses in consumer and standard form contracts should be subjected by the courts to a reasonality test at the suit of the aggrieved customer. Insurance contracts are expressly excluded from the scope of the Act but in return for this concession the Department of Trade require the insurers to take positive steps to alleviate any lurking public suspicion that insurance exclusion clauses are at any time used unfairly and insurers responded with the issue of these statements.

The *non-life statement*, applicable to policyholders resident in the UK, and insured in their private capacity only, is as follows:

1 Proposal Forms

a The declaration at the foot of the proposal form should be restricted to completion according to the proposer's knowledge and belief.

b If not included in the declaration, prominently displayed on the proposal form should be a statement:
  i drawing the attention of the proposer to the consequences of the failure to disclose all material facts, explained as those facts an insurer would regard as likely to influence the acceptance and assessment of the proposal;
  ii warning that if the proposer is in any doubt about facts considered material, he should disclose them.

c Those matters which insurers have found generally to be material will be the subject of clear questions in proposal forms.

d So far as is practicable, insurers will avoid asking questions which would require expert knowledge beyond that which the proposer could reasonably be expected to possess or obtain or which would require a value judgment on the part of the proposer.

e Unless the prospectus or the proposal form contains full details of the standard cover offered, and whether or not it contains an outline of that cover, the proposal form shall include a statement that a copy of the policy form is available on request.

f Unless the completed form or a copy of it has been sent to a policyholder, a copy will be made available when an insurer raises an issue under the proposal form.

2 Claims

a Under the conditions regarding notification of a claim, the policyholder shall not be asked to do more than report a claim and subsequent developments as soon as reasonably possible except in the case of legal processes and claims which a third party requires the policyholder to notify within a fixed time where immediate advice may be required.

b Except where fraud, deception or negligence is involved, an insurer will not unreasonably repudiate liability to indemnify a policyholder.
   i on the grounds of non-disclosure or misrepresentation of a material fact where knowledge of the fact would not materially have influenced the insurer's judgment in the acceptance or assessment of the insurance;
   ii on the grounds of a breach of warranty or condition where the circumstances of the loss are unconnected with the breach.

The previous paragraph 2(*b*) does not apply to marine and aviation policies.

3 Renewals

Renewal notices should contain a warning about the duty of disclosure including the necessity to advise changes affecting the policy which have occurred since the policy inception or last renewal date, whichever was the later.

4 Commencement

Any changes to insurance documents will be made as and when they need to be reprinted, but the statement will apply in the meantime.

5 EEC

This statement will need reconsideration when the EEC Contract Law Directive is taken into English/Scots law.

The *long-term statement* is similarly worded with only minor differences of terminology mainly because materiality is more concentrated being almost completely limited to the life assured's physical characteristics. Both statements require the provision of a copy proposal to the policyholder in the event of dispute, but the life statement, recognizing that there is a trading in life policies and that the original proposer may not be the disputant, provides that information not relevant to the issue will be deleted if it is necessary to preserve confidentiality. There is also an undertaking to make copies of standard policy forms available on request if the prospectus or proposal does not give full details, as opposed to an outline, of the normal benefits offered.

The statements have no legal effect but their practical significance is great. Insurers accept that the declaration at the foot of the proposal should be restricted to completion according to the proposer's knowledge and belief. He is no longer under any obligation to speak accurately of facts which he does not know or which he cannot discover after reasonable enquiry. Proposal forms in respect of personal-lines insurance are being amended so that the declaration is shorter and more questions are being included since both statements agree that matters which insurers have commonly found to be material must now be the subject of clear question. At the same time the attention of the proposer is drawn to the consequences of the failure to disclose all material facts and is advised that when in doubt as to whether a fact is material or not it should be disclosed.

The non-life statement also includes a practice long adopted by the insurers whereby renewal notices carry a warning about the duty of full disclosure as it arises again at that time, and of the need to advise changes that might have occurred since inception of the last renewal date.

A further modification is made in the notification of claims, the statements providing that in lieu of strict time limits the claimant shall be required to report claims as soon as reasonably possible except in the case of legal proceedings on the non-life side where time limits may be involved. Insurers, for their part, undertake not to repudiate liability on the grounds of non-disclosure or misrepresentation of material fact where the knowledge would not have influenced the insurer's judgment in the acceptance or assessment of the risk. Nor will they unreasonably avoid liability when there is a breach of a policy condition and the circumstances of the loss are not related to the breach. But fraud, deception or negligence as to materiality may still entitle insurers to repudiate.

The long-term statement contains two special provisions to be included in life policies and documentation. The circumstances in which interest accrues after maturity must be made clear to the policyholder and he must also be informed whether he has any rights to a surrender value and if so what those rights are.

Rehabilitation of Offenders

The duty to disclose material facts has also been modified by the Rehabilitation of Offenders Act, 1974, which is designed to wipe the slate clean after a person has been convicted, has served his sentence and has not been reconvicted for a substantial period. Thereafter the offender will be able to act and speak as if he had neither committed the crime nor been convicted of it. Similarly, other people may not take cognisance of it and a person so protected by the Act may bring an action for defamation against anybody who discloses his criminal record.

Where a person has the protection of the Act his conviction is said to be spent. The length of the rehabilitation (i.e. the period which must elapse before the conviction can be considered spent) varies with the type of crime and length of sentence as follows:

Sentence	*Period of rehabilitation*
Probation	1 year
Non-custodial sentence	5 years
Imprisonment not exceeding 6 months	7 years
Imprisonment exceeding 6 months but not more than 30 months	10 years
Imprisonment exceeding 30 months and life imprisonment	None

The effect of this legislation on insurance is that a proposer is under no obligation to disclose a spent conviction no matter what the wording of the proposal form may be. Neither can the insurers seek information in an indirect way to determine whether there are any spent convictions. Moreover, if a spent conviction comes to light in the course of investigating a claim, it may not be used as a reason for repudiating liability. While an intermediary is normally obliged under the duty of utmost good faith to disclose material facts, Section 4 of the Act prohibits him from disclosing a spent conviction of which he has knowledge. It is clear that the result of this protective legislation may be that insurers could find themselves insuring people with a criminal record and this could be of practical significance in any class of insurance and particularly where motor and fidelity insurances are concerned.

Breaches of Utmost Good Faith

There are various circumstances in which the parties may be guilty of a breach of utmost good faith. They may be classified into four sections according to their effect upon the validity of the contract.

1 *Non-disclosure.* As the term implies, this refers to omission to disclose, but in law it is limited to those omissions which are made unintentionally or inadvertently or because the proposer did not recognize that the fact in question was material.

Before there can be non-disclosure, however, factors must exist from which the proposer could reasonably have been expected to recognize a material fact. This is illustrated by the following:

'The duty is a duty to disclose . . . If a reasonable man would have recognized that the knowledge in question was material to disclose, it is no excuse that you did not recognize it. . . . Let me take an example. I will suppose that a man has, as is the case with almost all of us, occasionally a headache. It may be that a particular one of those headaches would have told a brain specialist of hidden mischief. But to the man it was an ordinary headache indistinguishable from the rest. Now, no reasonable man would deem it material to tell an insurance company of all the casual headaches he had had in his life, and, if he knew no more as to this particular headache, there would be no breach of duty in not disclosing it. He possessed no knowledge that it was incumbent on him to disclose, because he knew of nothing which a reasonable man would deem material or of a character to influence the Insurers in their action.'[1]

2 *Concealment.* A breach of utmost good faith in this category relates to the intentional suppression of a fact which is material. The following is an extract from the judgment in *Brownlie* v. *Campbell* (1880), 5 App Cas 925, 953:

'In policies of insurance, whether marine insurance or life insurance, there is an understanding that the contract is *uberrimae fidei*, that, if you know any circumstance at all that may influence the Underwriter's opinion as to the risk he is incurring, and consequently as to whether he will take it, or what premium he will charge if he does take it, you will state what you know. There is an obligation there to disclose what you know, and the concealment of a material circumstance known to you, whether you thought it material or not, avoids the policy.'

3 *Innocent misrepresentation.* This relates to a statement which is inaccurate but which is made without any fraudulent intention. On

---

1 Moulton, L. J., in *Joel* v. *Law Union and Crown Insurance Co.*, [1908] 2 KB 863.

the contrary, it is believed to be true by the person who makes the statement.

4 *Fraudulent misrepresentation.* A breach of good faith under this heading relates to a statement made knowingly or without belief in its truth or recklessly without caring whether it be true or false. On the other hand, a false statement which is made merely through want of care in investigation of the facts is not fraudulent.

Effect of Breaches of the Duty

Where there is a breach of the duty of utmost good faith, the contract may be either void or voidable. Where there is fraudulent misrepresentation, the contract is void for the simple reason that the law will not assist a party to a fraud.[1] In the other instances, the contract is as a rule voidable, but where a misrepresentation concerns a matter of expectation or belief, it is deemed to be true and has no effect upon the validity of the contract if it is made in utmost good faith.

The Contractual Duty of Utmost Good Faith

In many contracts of insurance, the ordinary Common Law duty of utmost good faith is modified by the terms of the contract. This will be dealt with fully when studying the application of the duty of utmost good faith to the main sections of insurance.

ILLUSTRATIONS OF APPLICATION OF UTMOST GOOD FAITH

Insurances of the Person

Life assurance. Life assurance is in the nature of a permanent contract and a proposal form must in all cases be completed by the proposer. The wording of the declaration varies, but the following are typical:

> *Ordinary Life*: 'I, the proposed Assured, do hereby declare that all the answers to the foregoing questions are true, complete and correct to the best of my knowledge and belief, and I do hereby agree that this proposal shall be the basis of the contract of assurance between me and the .... Company Limited.'

1 If the Insurers choose to overlook fraud, the contract is valid, hence in this sense even fraud may render the contract only voidable.

Industrial Life: 'I declare that the policy to be issued on this proposal is to be taken out by me and that the premiums thereon are to be paid by me. I also declare that the foregoing particulars are true to the best of my knowledge and belief, that they shall be the basis of the said policy and that no material information has been withheld; and I agree to be bound by the conditions upon the policy, and that the assurance hereby proposed shall not be binding on the Company until the policy has been delivered.'

This is a contractual duty of utmost good faith and the same legal considerations arise *mutatis mutandis* as are explained below in connection with accident insurance.

The case of *Anstey* v. *The British Natural Premium Life* (1908), 24 TLR 871, is of interest because it illustrates the application of the doctrine of utmost good faith to Insurers, who must observe the terms of their printed prospectus. The following extract is given from *Macgillivray on Insurance Law*, 6th edition, at p. 718:

'Where a policy is expressed to be "indisputable," either from the commencement or after it has been in force for a specified time, it cannot be challenged on the ground of misrepresentation, unless it was procured by fraud.'

The answers of the Assured were warranted accurate, but the policy contained the condition that it 'will be indisputable from any cause (except fraud) after it shall have been continuously in force for two years.' One of the answers was not accurate, but there was no fraud, and more than two years had elapsed since the policy was effected. The Company argued that as there had been a misrepresentation and breach of warranty at the time the contract was effected, it never came into force at all, and therefore the indisputable condition did not apply. The Court of Appeal held that such a construction would reduce the condition to sheer nonsense, and that its obvious meaning was that after the lapse of two years neither misrepresentation nor breach of warranty could be advanced as a defence unless there was fraud.

Policies on life of another. Where a life assurance is effected on the life of another, there are two declarations which are usually worded as follows:

'I (the Life to be assured) do hereby declare that all the foregoing answers to the foregoing questions ... are true and correct to the best of my knowledge and belief ...

And I, the proposed Assured (the person in whose name the policy of assurance is to stand), do hereby declare that the foregoing answers to the foregoing questions ... are true and correct to the best of my knowledge and belief, and I do hereby agree that this proposal shall be the basis of the contract of assurance between me and the ... Company Limited.'

Insurances of Property

Marine insurance. The quotations given above from the Marine Insurance Act, 1906, in order to explain the Common Law principle of utmost good faith, indicate the application of this principle to marine insurance.

Fire insurance. The position is clearly expressed in the standard fire policy, condition 2 of which reads as follows:

'This Policy shall be avoided with respect to any item thereof in regard to which there be any alteration after the commencement of this insurance:

1 by removal; or
2 whereby the risk of destruction or damage is increased; or
3 whereby the Insured's interest ceases except by will or operation of law;
unless such alteration be admitted by memorandum signed by or on behalf of the Insurers.'

This condition extends the Common Law duty of utmost good faith.

Insurances of Liability

It is an almost invariable rule to require the proposer to complete a proposal form. This form incorporates a declaration which has been modified in accordance with the Statement of Practice (see p. 98). The following is a specimen wording:

'I/We warrant that the above statements made by me/us are true and complete to the best of my/our knowledge and belief and I/we agree that this proposal shall be the basis of the contract between me/us and the Company. I/We agree to accept a Policy in the Company's usual form for this class of insurance.'

The object of the compulsory third party motor insurance provisions of the Road Traffic Act, 1972, is to protect third parties, including passengers, who are injured by negligent motorists. The Statute in question therefore places certain limitations upon motor Insurers as regards repudiation of liability to third parties where there has been breach of utmost good faith. In effect, Insurers meet any claims by third parties for which their policyholders are legally liable, although there has been a breach of the duty of utmost good faith, unless the Insurers can obtain a declaration in accordance with Sect. 149 of the Road Traffic Act, 1972, that, apart from any provision contained in the policy, they are entitled to avoid payment on the ground that the insurance was obtained by the non-disclosure of a material fact or by a representation of fact which was false in some material particular. This, however, does not affect the *contractual* position between the Insured and the Insurers, so that if the Insurers make a payment to a third party solely by reason of these Statutory provisions, they have a right of recovery against their Insured for any sums so paid. (See also Motor Insurers' Bureau, p. 225).

5 General Principles (2)

As stated in Chapter 4 all these basic or fundamental principles are of equal importance. The present division of the subject into two chapters is designed merely for the convenience of the student.

Indemnity

Almost all policies of insurance, with the exception of insurances of the person, are contracts of indemnity and this is best explained by a quotation from the judgment in *Castellain* v. *Preston* (1883), 11 QBD 380, CA, as follows:

'The very foundation, in my opinion, of every rule which has been applied to insurance law is this, namely that the contract of insurance contained in a marine or fire policy (and that equally applies to accident policies) is a contract of indemnity and of indemnity only, and that this contract means that the Assured, in a case of loss against which the policy has been made, shall be fully indemnified, but shall never be more than fully indemnified. That is the fundamental principle of insurance and if ever a proposition is brought forward which is at variance with it, that is to say, which either will prevent the Assured from obtaining a full indemnity, or which will give the Assured more than a full indemnity, that proposition must certainly be wrong.'

The object of indemnity is to place the Insured after a loss in the same position as he occupied immediately before the event. There is no objection, however, to the proposer effecting an insurance for less than a full indemnity, unless the Insurers impose a special condition otherwise. An example is referred to in Chapter 9 (p. 185).

On the other hand, if it were possible for the Insured to effect an insurance by the terms of which he was permitted to make a profit in the event of loss, the temptation would always be present to desire the insured event and thus to obtain the policy proceeds. This would obviously be contrary to the public interest.

ILLUSTRATIONS OF APPLICATION OF INDEMNITY

Insurances of the Person

Life assurance. As already indicated, the principle of indemnity does not apply to life assurance, because different considerations arise under this type of protection. 'The contract of the Insurer may be to pay, on the happening of the event insured against, a certain or ascertainable sum of money irrespective of whether or not the Assured has suffered loss or of the amount of such loss if he has suffered any.' A definition of life assurance is given in *Dalby* v. *India and London Life Assurance Co.* (1854), 15 CB 385, as follows:

'The contract commonly called life assurance, when properly considered, is a mere contract to pay a certain sum of money on the death of a person, in consideration of the due payment of a certain annuity (i.e., premium) for his life, the amount of the annuity being calculated in the first instance according to the probable duration of the life, and when once fixed it is constant and invariable. The stipulated amount of annuity is to be uniformly paid on one side, and the sum to be paid in the event of death is always (except where bonuses have been given by prosperous offices) the same on the other.'

As previously stated, the amount for which a person is assured is governed by the amount of premium that he decides to pay.

Personal accident insurance. Personal accident policies, like life policies, are not contracts of indemnity. Nevertheless, Insurers usually require notice of any additional insurances effected, and endeavour to relate the extent of the benefits granted to the financial position of the Insured. In aviation insurance, however, the only limit in practice appears to be the Insurers' reinsurance arrangements, and as booking clerks issue coupons indiscriminately it is not practicable to make inquiries.[1]

Insurances of Property and Pecuniary Insurances

Marine insurance. The indemnity provided by a policy of marine insurance is 'in manner and to the extent agreed,' that is to say, not

1 If a person effects a personal accident insurance on the life of another person, the amount recoverable is the loss sustained by the person who effected the policy. In theory, therefore, such a personal accident insurance becomes a contract of indemnity, but it is often impossible exactly to assess the injury suffered, and a policy with fixed benefits may be issued.

a perfect indemnity. Claims must, of necessity, be settled on a cash basis and it would not be practicable to adjust losses on actual or market values, if only for the reason that the subject-matter varies in value during the period of insurance because of market fluctuation. Sect. 16 of the Marine Insurance Act, 1906, provides an insurable value, on which claims will be assessed in the absence of an agreed value in the policy. Insurable values as contemplated by the Act, however, are insufficient for modern commerce, and the practice, therefore, is to used *valued* policies for ships and goods. The value stated in such policies remains constant throughout the risk. This value, it should be noted, is arrived at, in the case of ships, by agreement between shipowner and Insurers and is usually well above market value; for cargo, it includes cost, charges, and estimated profit, as decided by the Assured. It is, of course, possible to issue unvalued policies, and this is the usual practice in connection with freight insurance, where a valued policy would be no advantage.

Fire insurance. Almost all contracts of fire insurance are contracts of indemnity on the lines set out in the general discussion of the principle. Exceptions are:

i Agreed value policies (otherwise termed valued policies) which are sometimes issued in respect of jewellery, works of art, or other property which is not subject to rapid changes in value. The sum insured must be computed in accordance with the figures of a professional valuer, and each item must be separately specified and valued. In the event of *total* loss of an item or items, the sum insured is payable without any adjustment for altered values. Partial losses are settled on the ordinary terms.

An *agreed value* policy must be clearly distinguished from a contract made subject to an *inventory and valuation clause.* Where an inventory and valuation of general contents has been prepared and a copy lodged with the Insurers, an inventory and valuation clause is incorporated in the policy under which the valuation is accepted by the Company as the basis of settlement in the event of loss, production of invoices or other evidence of cost not being required in respect of the items set out in the inventory. It is specifically provided, however, that the values will be subject to reasonable allowance for appreciation or depreciation at the date of the loss so that the policy is not a valued policy at all, but a contract on the ordinary basis. The liability of the Insurers, in all, will naturally not exceed the total sum insured by the policy.

ii Reinstatement policies. For some types of property, notably machinery, reinstatement while giving the Insured a bare indemnity is not always satisfactory to him. To be compensated for the market value after wear and tear have been taken into account may leave a heavy liability to be shouldered by the Insured. When old machinery can only be replaced by new, the difference between the cost of the new and the value received for the old may again be an onerous burden on a business. Therefore, reinstatement or replacement policies may be issued or an ordinary fire policy extended by endorsement to cover the difference between the value of the property at the time of loss and the actual cost incurred in reinstating the property. This represents a deviation from the doctrine of indemnity in practice, but such cover is issued subject to considerable discretion.

Pecuniary insurances. The measure of indemnity is a cash sum which can usually be ascertained from the books of account in the case of a commercial fidelity guarantee, while for many other guarantees a signed certificate by the proper authority is conclusive evidence of the amount of the loss.

Insurances of Liability

The amount payable by the Insurers is a cash sum to represent the cost of settlement of a third party claim, and the measure of indemnity, therefore, is this amount together with any costs and expenses incurred by the Insured with the written consent of the Insurers, and costs and expenses recovered from the Insured by any claimant. If, however, the limit of indemnity provided by the policy is insufficient to cover the cost of the claim, the policyholder will have to bear the difference. The importance of adequate insurance protection against public liabilities was highlighted by the case of *Hamp* v. *Sisters of St. Joseph's Hospital Mount Carmel Convent School* (1972). A schoolgirl suffered an almost total loss of sight as the result of a chemical explosion in the school laboratory. Damages amounting to £76,878 were awarded, but the defendant school was only covered to the extent of £25,000, so that it was faced with the task of raising over £50,000 from other sources.

In many contracts there is a policy condition which permits the Insurers at any stage to make a cash payment of the maximum sum (plus any costs incurred to date) for which they are liable, after which they cease to have the conduct and control of the claim and are not responsible for any costs and expenses incurred after the date of the payment.

Subrogation

At Common Law, subrogation arises only after payment has been made, and it is, in such circumstances, the Insurers' right 'to receive the benefit of all the rights of the Assured against third parties which, if satisfied, will extinguish or diminish the ultimate loss sustained.' It should be noted that:

'... the doctrine of subrogation is to be applied merely for the purpose of preventing the Assured from obtaining more than a full indemnity, the question is whether that doctrine as applied to insurance law can in any way be limited ... In order to apply the doctrine of subrogation, it seems to me that the full and absolute meaning of the word must be used, that is to say the Insurer must be placed in the position of the Assured ... As between the Underwriter and the Assured the Underwriter is entitled to every right of the Assured, whether such right consists in contract fulfilled or unfulfilled, or in remedy for tort capable of being insisted on, or already insisted on, or in any other right, whether by way of condition or otherwise, legal or equitable, which can be or has been exercised or has accrued, and whether such rights could or could not be enforced by the Insurer in the name of the Assured, by the exercise or acquiring of which right or condition the loss against which the Assured is insured, can be, or has been, diminished ... I use the words "every right of the Assured." I think that the rule does require that limit.' Brett, L. J. (*Castellain v. Preston* (1883), 11 QBD 380, CA).

The Subrogation Condition

An appropriate policy condition enables the Insurers to exercise the right of subrogation before payment has been made.[1] At the same time, it must be remembered that the right exists (after indemnity has been paid) apart from any policy condition.

The ability to exercise the right forthwith is often of material assistance—particularly under liability indemnities—because the Insurers as a rule undertake the entire conduct of claims and can commence proceedings against a third party in the Insured's name. The policy condition is usually worded as follows:

'The Company ... shall be entitled if it so desires to take over and

1 Under third party policies, the Insurers have the right to conduct all claims in the name of the Insured, and they can join (i.e., add) a third party in any proceedings which may be commenced.

conduct in the name of the Insured the defence or settlement of any claim or to prosecute in the name of the Insured for its own benefit any claim for indemnity or damages or otherwise and shall have full discretion in the conduct of any proceedings or in the settlement of any claim and the Insured shall give all such information and assistance as the Company may require.'

ILLUSTRATIONS OF APPLICATION OF SUBROGATION

Insurances of the Person

As already explained, as these are not contracts of indemnity, the principle of subrogation does not apply to them.

Insurances of Property and Pecuniary Insurances

Marine insurance. The principle of subrogation is clearly set out in the Marine Insurance Act, 1906, Sect. 79:

'79 1 Where the insurer pays for a total loss, either of the whole, or in the case of goods of any apportionable part, of the subject-matter insured, he thereupon becomes entitled to take over the interest of the assured in whatever may remain of the subject-matter so paid for, and he is thereby subrogated to all rights and remedies of the assured in and in respect of that subject-matter as from the time of the casualty causing the loss.

2 Subject to the foregoing provisions, where the insurer pays for a partial loss, he acquires no title to the subject-matter insured, or such part of it as may remain, but he is thereupon subrogated to all rights and remedies of the assured in and in respect of the subject-matter insured as from the time of the casualty causing the loss, in so far as the assured has been indemnified, according to this Act, by such payment for the loss.'

Subrogation applies only after payment of loss. Examples are recoveries from carriers and other third parties. The Insurer is entitled to recover only up to the amount which he has paid in respect of rights and remedies.

Fire insurance. Subrogation may come into operation when a fire has been caused by negligence of a third party. Thus, in *Roskill* v.

Cooke (1932), it was alleged that a fire had originated in a wood block in the party wall. It was held, however, that the plaintiff had failed to discharge the onus of proof of the cause of the fire. In *Jefferson* v. *Derbyshire Farmers Ltd.*, [1921] 2 KB 281, a motor garage was leased by the owner to a firm of motor engineers and the latter agreed with the defendants to allow them the use of the garage for their motor lorries. An employee of the defendants struck a match and lighted a cigarette while drawing motor spirit from a drum, and then threw the match on the floor. This caused a serious fire which destroyed the garage and contents. The owner and lessees successfully brought this action against the defendants on the grounds of the negligence of their servant.

Motor insurance. Subrogation also arises in motor insurance as, for example, where an insured motor vehicle is damaged owing to the negligence of a third party against whom the Insurers will therefore claim in an endeavour to recover the cost of repairs paid by them under their policy. Subrogation rights are sometimes not exercised because of the existence of a claims-settling agreement between Insurers (see p. 183).

Glass insurance. Another illustration is afforded by the position under a glass policy where the glass insured has been broken by the negligence of an independent window cleaner, passer-by, or motorist.

Pecuniary insurances. Subrogation does not often arise in connection with insurances against pecuniary loss. An illustration met with in practice concerned an employee who obtained money by forging the signature of his employer on cheques, and after payment of the amount due, the Insurers obtained recoupment from the bank, who had omitted to detect the forgery.

Insurances of Liability

If a claim is made against the Insured as principal and he has obtained an undertaking from the contractor to indemnify him, the Insurers in dealing with the claim will be entitled to the benefit from the right of recovery against the contractor. If a claim is made against a retailer on account of food poisoning (and the claimant does not join the wholesaler as a defendant), then the Insurers who deal with the matter under the retailer's public liability indemnity can recover from the wholesaler who supplied the food, if liability can be established against the wholesaler.

Contribution

Contribution ensures the equitable distribution of losses as between Insurers. Contribution arises in the case of contracts of indemnity where the same interest, the same peril, and the same subject-matter are insured with more than one Insurer. It prevents the Insured from recovering more than the full amount of his loss and thus supports the principle of indemnity.

'In the case of double insurances of the same interest with different insurance companies the Assured will not be entitled to recover more than the full amount of the loss which he has suffered.' (*Scottish Amicable Heritable Securities Association Ltd.* v. *Northern Assurance Co.* (1883), 11 R (Ct of Sess.) 287.)

Where there is double or multiple insurance, the Insured according to Common Law can claim the whole loss from one of the Insurers concerned, or he may claim against all. In the former case, the Insurer who pays more than his share is enabled to enforce contribution from the others, but the right does not arise until after payment has been made.

'In marine insurance a rule which has long been recognized is that when the Assured has recovered to the full extent of his loss under one policy, the Insurer under that policy can recover from other Underwriters who have insured the same interest against the same risks a rateable sum by way of contribution. The foundation of the rule is that a contract of marine insurance is one of indemnity, and that the Insured, whatever the amount of his insurance or the number of Underwriters with whom he has contracted, can never recover more than is required to indemnify him. The different policies being all with the same person and against the same risk are therefore regarded as truly one insurance, and if one of the Underwriters is compelled to meet the whole claim, he is entitled to claim contribution from the other Underwriters, just as a surety or cautioner who pays the whole debt is entitled to rateable relief against his co-sureties or co-cautioners. There is no reason in principle ... why the same rule should not be applied to other classes of insurance which are also contracts of indemnity.' (*Sickness and Accident Assurance Association* v. *General Accident Assurance Corporation* (1892), 19 R (Ct of Sess.) 977.)

The Contribution Condition

The Common Law position is modified by a policy condition, the effect of which is to require the Insured to claim against all the Insurers concerned and to recover a *pro rata* proportion from each. This is clearly expressed in a passage from the judgment in *North British and Mercantile Insurance Company* v. *London, Liverpool and Globe Insurance Co.* (1877), 5 ChD 569:

> 'Where there are several policies, and where there, in point of fact, is a double insurance, then in order to do away with the old practice of the Insured recovering the whole from one of the several insurance offices, and then the one from whom it was recovered being put to obtain contribution from the others, this clause (the contribution condition) was put in to say that the Insured should, in the first instance, proceed against the several insurance companies for the aliquot parts for which they are liable in consequence of that condition.'

ILLUSTRATIONS OF APPLICATION OF CONTRIBUTION

Insurances of the Person

As already explained, these are not contracts of indemnity and therefore the principle of contribution has no application.

Insurances of Property

Marine insurance. The appropriate sections of the Marine Insurance Act, 1906, are Sects. 32 and 80, which are as follows:

> '32 1 Where two or more policies are effected by or on behalf of the assured on the same adventure and interest or any part thereof, and the sums insured exceed the indemnity allowed by this Act, the assured is said to be over-insured by double insurance.
>
>   2 Where the assured is over-insured by double insurance—
>
>   *a* The assured, unless the policy otherwise provides, may claim payment from the insurers in such order as he may think fit, provided that he is not entitled to receive any sum in excess of the indemnity allowed by this Act;
>
>   *b* Where the policy under which the assured claims is a valued policy, the assured must give credit as against the

valuation for any sum received by him under any other policy without regard to the actual value of the subject-matter insured;

c Where the policy under which the assured claims is an unvalued policy he must give credit, as against the full insurable value, for any sum received by him under any other policy;

d Where the assured receives any sum in excess of the indemnity allowed by this Act, he is deemed to hold such sum in trust for the insurers, according to their right of contribution among themselves.

80 1 Where the assured is over-insured by double insurance, each insurer is bound, as between himself and the other insurers, to contribute rateably to the loss in proportion to the amount for which he is liable under his contract.

2 If any insurer pays more than his proportion of the loss, he is entitled to maintain an action for contribution against the other insurers, and is entitled to the like remedies as a surety who has paid more than his proportion of the debt.'

Sect. 32 deals with the principle of contribution generally, while Sect. 80 shows its application as between Insurers.

In the case of marine insurance, double insurance is sometimes effected knowingly as may happen if a finance corporation is not prepared to accept a policy underwritten by certain Insurers as an approved policy.

In marine insurance practice, there is no contribution clause inserted in contracts as in fire insurance, but the principle exists, between Insurers, and the Insured cannot obtain more than statutory indemnity. If he does, it is held in trust for the Insurers who are entitled to it according to the principle of contribution.

Fire insurance. The policy condition usually inserted in fire policies reads as follows:

If at the time of any destruction of or damage to any property hereby insured there be any other insurance effected by or on behalf of the Insured covering any of the property destroyed or damaged, the liability of the Insurers hereunder shall be limited to their rateable proportion of such destruction or damage.

The application of contribution varies according to whether the policies are concurrent or non-concurrent. If they are concurrent, that is, of the same range and cover precisely the same property, contribution applies in proportion to the sums insured. In the case of non-concurrent policies, that is, policies of different range, one insuring property not covered by the other, there is a difference of opinion as to the proper basis of contribution. Another complication arises where policies are subject to average, and the method will vary according to the kind of average clause concerned (see also p. 184). It is not necessary for the purpose of this general text-book to go into detail.

Insurances of Liability

Occasionally there may be more than one liability policy in force, in which case the general practice is that the policies contribute equally, rather than proportionately, to the loss, although the limits of indemnity may be different. But this rule is qualified to the extent that no policy can become liable for an amount exceeding its limit of indemnity.

For example, there may be two policies with limits of indemnity of £25,000 and £75,000 respectively. Any loss up to £50,000 is shared equally, as each is liable up to £25,000, but if a claim exceeds £50,000, the policy with the higher limit of indemnity is liable for the whole of the excess, subject again to its own limit of indemnity.

Proximate Cause

The rule is that the immediate and not the remote cause is to be regarded—*causa proxima non remota spectatur*. This was well expressed by Bacon when he said:

'... it were infinite for the law to consider the cause of causes, and their impulsions one of another, therefore, it contenteth itself with the immediate cause, and judgeth of acts by that without looking to any further degree.'

In the case of *Becker Gray and Co.* v. *London Assurance Corporation*, [1918] AC 101, Lord Sumner said that 'cause and effect are the same for underwriters as for other people. Proximate cause is not a device to avoid the trouble of discovering the real cause or the "common-sense cause," and, though it has been and always should be rigorously applied in insurance cases, it helps the one side no oftener than it helps the other. I believe it to be nothing more nor less than the real meaning of the parties to a contract of insurance ... the *causa proxima* rule is not merely a rule of statute law, but is the meaning of the contract writ large.' In another well-known case, *Pawsey and Co. v. Scottish Union and National Insurance Co.* (1907), it was stated that 'proximate cause means the active, efficient cause that sets in motion a train of events which brings about a result, without the intervention of any force started and working actively from a new and independent source.'

The practical working of the above, however, often involves difficult problems for solution. It must be remembered that a loss may not be occasioned merely by one event; there may be concurrent causes or a chain of causes with the sequence either unbroken or interrupted. A further complication is the operation of perils which are excepted by the terms of the policy.

The position may be briefly summarized as below:

1 If there is a *single cause* which is an insured peril, this is obviously the proximate cause of the loss and there is a valid claim under the policy.

2 If there are *concurrent causes* with no excepted perils involved, the loss is recoverable provided one of the causes is an insured peril. If there are exceptions involved and the consequent losses can be separated, there is liability for those caused by the insured peril, but if the circumstances are such that the perils are inseparable, then the Insurers are not liable at all under the contract.

3 If there is a *direct chain of events* with no exceptions concerned, the insured peril is the direct and natural cause of the loss. On the other hand, if an excepted peril precedes the operation of the insured peril so that the loss caused by the latter is the direct and natural consequence of the excepted peril, there is no liability.

4 In those cases where there is a *broken chain of events* with no excepted peril involved, it is possible to separate the losses and the Insurers are, of course, liable only for that caused by an insured peril. Where there is an excepted peril concerned, the subsequent loss caused by an insured peril will be from a new and indirect cause because of the interruption in the chain of events, so that the Insurers will be responsible for loss caused by the latter. The same principle will apply where loss occurs by an insured peril and there is subsequently loss by an excepted peril with, however, a break in the chain of events.

ILLUSTRATIONS OF APPLICATION OF PROXIMATE CAUSE

Insurances of the Person

Life assurance. Proximate cause is not of much practical importance in connection with life assurance, but it did arise where war risks exclusions clauses were concerned. Some life policies are extended to cover so-called disability benefits, such as weekly conpensation for incapacity by accident or disease, or double benefits may be payable in the event of death by accident, when the same considerations arise as those dealt with below under personal accident insurance.

Personal accident insurance. In *Lawrence* v. *Accidental Insurance Co.* (1881), 7 QBD 216, a person suffered from fits and was accidentally shot while on the ground in a fit. It was held that this was death by accident. In *Etherington* v. *Lancashire and Yorkshire Accident Insurance Co.*, [1909] 1 KB 591, a policyholder sustained an accident while hunting. He was unable to walk after the accident and, as a result of lying on wet ground before being picked up, he contracted pneumonia. There was an unbroken chain of causation between the accident and the death, and the proximate cause of the death, therefore, was the accident and not the pneumonia.

Insurances of Property and Pecuniary Insurances

Marine Insurance. According to the Marine Insurance Act, 1906, the position is:

'55 1 Subject to the provisions of this Act, and unless the policy otherwise provides, the insurer is liable for any loss proximately caused by a peril insured against, but, subject as aforesaid, he is not liable for any loss which is not proximately caused by a peril insured against.

2 In particular:

a The insurer is not liable for any loss attributable to the wilful misconduct of the assured, but, unless the policy otherwise provides, he is liable for any loss proximately caused by a peril insured against, even though the loss would not have happened but for the misconduct or negligence of the master or crew;

b Unless the policy otherwise provides, the insurer on ship or goods is not liable for any loss proximately caused by delay, although the delay be caused by a peril insured against;

c Unless the policy otherwise provides, the insurer is not liable for ordinary wear and tear, ordinary leakage and breakage, inherent vice or nature of the subject-matter insured, or for any loss proximately caused by rats or vermin, or for any injury to machinery not proximately caused by maritime perils.'

Proximate cause as related to marine insurance is conveniently summarized in *A Handbook to Marine Insurance* (Dover), 6th edition, p. 412, as follows:

'The proximate cause of a loss is that cause proximate to the loss, not necessarily in time, but in efficiency. Remote causes may be disregarded in determining the cause of a loss, but the doctrine must be interpreted with good sense, so as to uphold and not defeat the intentions of the parties to the contract. There must be a direct and uninterrupted sequence between proximate cause and ultimate loss; if any new intervening cause arises between primary cause and ultimate loss, such new intervening cause will rule out consideration of preceding causes, subject to its possessing the qualities of reality, predominance, efficiency.'

Fear of the happening of a peril does not constitute that peril as the proximate cause of a loss. Losses proximately caused by delay are excluded by the Act. Thus, loss of market or deterioration of goods by delay or loss of charter is not recoverable, although the delay is caused by a peril insured against. Where, however, goods are destroyed by fire during delay caused by an insured peril, there is a recovery under the policy.

An interesting and well-known marine case on the subject of proximate cause is that of *Montoya* v. *London Assurance Corp.* (1851), 6 Exch. 451; 20 LJ Exch. 254, when (to quote Arnould) 'A vessel loaded with hides and tobacco shipped a quantity of sea water which rotted the hides but did not come directly into contact with the tobacco or the packages in which it was contained; the tobacco, however, was spoiled by the reek of the putrid hides. It was held, that in this case the perils of the sea were the proximate cause of the loss on the tobacco as well as on the hides.' It will be realized that the chain of causation leading from a peril of the sea, namely, the incursion of sea water, was unbroken.

It is not necessary for the purposes of the present work to deal in detail with the application of the doctrine of proximate cause to total losses and partial losses.

Fire insurance. Proximate cause sometimes occasions difficulties in fire insurance, largely because of the operation of excepted perils.

If the property insured is burned, but the fire was preceded and brought into operation by an excepted peril, the legal position depends upon whether the excepted peril was the proximate or only the remote cause of the loss. Thus, in *Tootal Broadhurst Lee Co. v. London & Lancashire Fire Insurance Co.* (1908), where an earthquake, which was an excepted peril, caused fire which spread and involved many buildings some distance away from the scene of the original fire, it was held that the earthquake (i.e., the excepted peril) was the proximate cause. It was not the remote cause as the fire had spread by natural causes (e.g., by wind or by one thing catching fire from another) and there was no intervening cause to break the chain. It may happen that a fire and an excepted peril are concurrent causes, when the position depends upon whether or not the losses can be separated (see p. 119).

Motor insurance. During World War Two, various accidents occurred where it was necessary to decide whether the proximate cause was the result of the operation of an insured peril or war risks, for example, 'own damage' to a motor car caused by passing over a bomb crater in the highway during the black-out.[1]

Glass insurance. Another illustration is provided by the case of a glass policy under which the fire risk was excluded. A fire broke out in the vicinity and certain persons in the crowd broke the shop windows in order to steal. It was held that the fire was the remote cause of the damage, the proximate cause being the violence of the mob.

Pecuniary insurances. Under this heading, there are rarely difficulties with proximate cause. The intention of the parties to the contract (and, for that matter, of the defaulting employee) under a fidelity agreement is seldom in doubt. However, if a policy covered fraud and dishonesty, but excluded misappropriation of goods, an employee might steal goods and subsequently convert them into money. No claim would then arise under the guarantee because the proximate

1 Each case depended upon the facts, and the time which elapsed between the making of the crater and the happening of the accident was material.

cause of the loss would have been the stealing of the goods, and the conversion into money the remote cause. The possibility of complications can arise in the case of two defaulting employees in the same employment, only one of them being guaranteed. If they act in collusion and share the proceeds, the combined amount of the loss cannot be properly regarded as payable under the policy, which covers one employee only, even allowing that the amount guaranteed is sufficient, on the argument that the dishonest acts of the insured employee made the *whole* of the loss possible. As regards the amount taken by the employee who is not covered, the fact that the insured employee, by collusion, made this possible is merely a remote cause. As regards the uninsured employee the dishonest act of *taking* his share of the money involved is the proximate cause.

Insurances of Liability

A motorist might damage immobile property where the real cause of the accident was the explosion of some fireworks which were being carried in the car in connection with the motorist's trade, contrary to the policy conditions. Another example of the operation of the doctrine of proximate cause under this heading would be the granting of a public liability indemnity to protect a man in one capacity, whereas his liability in a particular case arose while he was undertaking some added duties not within the scope of the indemnity.

6 Types of Insurance Contracts

The basic principles of insurance already discussed can be seen in proper perspective only against the background of the general law. Moreover, the general principles of the law of contract apply to insurance contracts. A contract of insurance is a legal bargain between parties on terms to which they both agree, and its characteristics differ only in detail from those of a contract for the sale of a sack of coal or for tutorial services.

With the exception of certain fidelity guarantees, contracts of insurance are simple contracts executed under hand (as distinct from deeds or specialty contracts which are executed under seal).

Simple Contracts

Three of the primary elements of all simple contracts are offer, acceptance, and consideration. These are now discussed, with special reference to their application to insurance contracts.

Offer

The offer usually comes from the proposer, that is, the person who desires to effect an insurance, and the offer is known as the proposal. In order to be effective, it must be communicated to the other party, the Insurers. The proposal may be made verbally as, for instance, over the counter of an Insurance Company, on the telephone, or to one of the Insurers' outside representatives, or it may be made in writing by means of a letter, or by the completion of a proposal form. Practice varies to some extent in each main branch of insurance, as follows.

Insurances of the person. It is an invariable rule to require the proposer to complete a form of proposal in which there are detailed questions designed, *inter alia*, to disclose the name, address, occupation, and age of the proposer, his general health and pursuits, and questions relating to assurance history. In addition, a statement of family history, names of references and of the proposer's medical attendant are required for life assurance risks. There is also a declaration as described on p. 104. (Under group life schemes, proposal forms are not required from the individual concerned, but a collective form must be completed by the firm.)

Insurances of property. In marine insurance it is customary for brief details of the risk proposed for insurance to be shown on an original slip[1] which is submitted by the broker to the Underwriter. The latter inserts the amount that he accepts and initials the slip. No proposal form is used. In fire insurance, offers are made in any of the ways mentioned above. As a rule, proposal forms are not used, but exceptions to this rule are proposals in respect of farming stock insurances, and insurances for small amounts on household goods or stock in trade. For other classes of property insurance, such as motor, theft, and 'all risks', it is customary to use a proposal form which includes the usual type of declaration. Marine practice is largely followed in aviation insurance, but where Insurers accept business direct through their own agents, for example, from private owners, proposal forms are obtained.

Insurances of liability. Proposal forms are also used extensively for liability insurance and contain a declaration on the lines mentioned for life assurance and some property risks.

Acceptance

Acceptance is not effective until it is communicated to the party who made the offer. The Insurers intimate their acceptance of the proposal and indicate that they are willing to assume the risk on payment of the premium. Sometimes they assume the risk forthwith either by their letter of acceptance[2] or by the issue of a formal cover note. When the offer has been accepted, the proposer becomes the Insured. (Acceptance can be—and often is—verbal.)

Insurances of the person. When the Office have had the proposed

---

1 It is called an *original* slip because it is the first document used in placing the insurance, and it takes the place of a proposal form in non-marine insurance.
2 Acceptance of an offer through the post is communicated when the acceptance has been posted.

life medically examined (except under non-medical schemes) and have obtained satisfactory reports from the referees and the medical attendant (if such are required), they notify their acceptance of the proposal, intimating that the assurance does not commence until the first premium has been paid. The proposer is usually given 21 or 28 days in which to pay the premium, but if this time is exceeded, it may be necessary to submit to a further medical examination, and in any event, a declaration as to continued good health will be required.

The practice in life assurance illustrates the way in which the position as to offer and acceptance may shift. If, instead of an unconditional acceptance, the proposal is accepted subject to a condition (usually, as in life assurance, payment of the first premium), this acceptance becomes a counter-offer. This counter-offer is accepted by the proposer when he fulfils the condition. The matter is not usually of very great importance, although it is occasionally necessary clearly to establish where the offer and the acceptance lie.

Insurances of property. Where marine risks are concerned, acceptance is effective immediately the Underwriter initials the original slip, but the commencement of risk may be before or after the date of acceptance. In fire insurance, there may be a simple acceptance communicated verbally, a premium debit note may be sent, on which it is indicated that the risk is held insured pending the issue of a duly stamped policy, an official cover note may be issued, or cover may be granted by means of a letter. In motor insurance, however, it is necessary to issue a cover note in special form, incorporating a temporary certificate of insurance, in order to comply with the provisions of the Road Traffic Act, 1972. The insurance is not effective, for the purposes of the said Act, until the certificate has been 'delivered' by the Insurers to the person by whom the policy is effected.

Insurances of liability. So far as insurances of liability are concerned, the general procedure follows that of property insurance relating to fire risks.

Consideration

Consideration consists of some right, interest, profit, or benefit accruing to the one party or some forbearance, detriment, loss, or responsibility given, suffered or undertaken by the other. In the case of insurance contracts, the consideration moving from the Insured to the Insurer is the premium, and the consideration moving from the Insurer to the Insured is the promise to indemnify.

The policy usually recites that the Insured has paid or agreed to pay the premium, but, once acceptance has been communicated, the Insurers are liable to indemnify the Insured whether or not the premium has been paid at the time of a loss. Where it is intimated that the insurance does not commence until the premium is paid, as happens with life assurance, no risk attaches until this is done, as already noted.

In *Thompson v. Adams* (1889), 23 QBD 361, which concerned a fire insurance arranged at Lloyd's, a loss occurred after the slip had been initialled, but before the policy had been submitted by the broker to the Underwriters for signature. It was unsuccessfully contended on behalf of the Underwriters that the slip did not create a binding obligation, but was merely a preliminary contract subject to a policy being presented within a reasonable time, so that, if the policy was not presented, the insurance would have to be treated as abandoned. It is clear from this case that, after a loss, the Underwriters cannot escape from the contract contained in the slip. But in marine insurance the contract must be embodied in a marine policy before the case can come into the Courts (Marine Insurance Act, 1906, Section 22). In *General Accident Insurance Corporation v. Cronk* (1901), 17 TLR 233, the defendant undertook to pay the premium if the risk was accepted, and it was held that this created a liability to pay the premium on acceptance and that there was no question of the Insured having to approve of the policy tendered to him before he could be asked for the premium.

The premium may be adjustable at each renewal date in order to reflect adequately the extent of the risk. On the other hand, a discount may be allowed on account of no claim having arisen during the preceding period of insurance, or because of an undertaking to renew for a number of years. Special scales and methods of computation are used for short period insurances, i.e., for periods of less than one year.

A deposit may be paid in respect of temporary cover. Incidentally, temporary cover which is granted pending payment of the premium is always subject to a time limit, because Insurers naturally wish to see negotiations completed within a reasonable period.

In certain circumstances, total or partial refunds of premium are allowable. The right to a refund of premium is, generally speaking, dependent upon whether there is total or partial failure of consideration. A full refund may be allowable if the insurance is *ultra vires*, because it is of a kind which the Company is not authorized to grant, or there may not have been genuine agreement (*consensus ad idem*). Even where there is failure of consideration, the Insured is not entitled to a refund if he has been guilty of fraud, or to his knowledge has entered into an illegal contract and the risk has attached. Partial refunds of premium are allowable in various circumstances as, for example, under a cancellation condition or where the premium is adjustable, say, on wages, and the wages, during the period of insurance, have fallen short of the estimated figure.

Other Features of Simple Contracts

The other features of simple contracts apply equally to insurance contracts, and seldom involve any difficulties. These features are: (1) the requirement that there should be *agreement* between the parties, i.e., consent arising out of common intention, (2) *legality* of the contract, and (3) *capacity* of the parties to contract. As regards capacity, minors, i.e., persons under 18 years of age, are subject to certain disabilities, but Insurers freely enter into contracts with minors, and such contracts are generally enforceable because they are for the minors' benefit.

When Writing is Essential

The majority of simple contracts are effective whether or not evidenced in writing and may even be inferred from conduct.

In the case of insurance, however, contracts of marine insurance before they are admissible before a Court must be in writing as required by the Marine Insurance Act, 1906, Sect. 22. In the same way, contracts of fidelity and solvency insurance must be in writing in order to comply with the unrepealed part of the Statute of Frauds, 1677, Sect. 4.

Insurance contracts are, as a matter of practice, always evidenced in writing in order that their terms may be perfectly clear to both parties, and all life policies must be stamped in accordance with the requirement of the Stamp Act, 1891, as amended.[1]

Specialty Contracts

Certain Court and Government guarantees are dealt with in the fidelity guarantee department and they are in the form of a deed. A

1 Unless stamp duty is compounded, see p. 133.

deed, instead of being executed under hand, must be executed under seal and its validity depends on this formality, hence specialty contracts are sometimes termed 'formal contracts.' The principles governing offer and acceptance, discussed under the heading of simple contracts, likewise apply to specialty contracts. Evidence of acceptance, however, may have to be given in some special way, as, for instance, under certain Government bonds where the authorities require the issue of a cover note in a particular form. Incidentally, it is not possible to cancel bonds issued by the fidelity guarantee department in the same way as a fire insurance may be cancelled. A bond is in many instances a permanent contract, and if the Insurers desire to be relieved of the risk, it is in some instances necessary to apply by summons in Chambers—a procedure very rarely adopted.

If a receiver[1] dies, the receivership terminates, subject, however, to liability to account up to the date of the death.

Under a specialty contract, no consideration is required, but Insurers naturally charge a premium, or fee, for the risk undertaken.

A bond must be sealed, and delivered—'I deliver this as my act and deed.' It is always also signed at the present day. When a bond is given by an Insurance Company, it is executed by the affixing of the seal in accordance with the provisions of the Company's Articles of Association.[2] Legality, agreement (*consensus ad idem*), and capacity of the parties are essential elements, in the same way as they are with simple contracts.

Variation of Terms

It is often necessary to vary the terms of an insurance contract and this can be done by means of endorsement, in order to save the trouble and expense of entering into an entirely new contract.

The wording of the ordinary marine policy is to a large extent no longer in conformity with present-day practice, but it is still used because practically every phrase has been the subject of judicial interpretation. The difficulty is overcome by the use of standard marine clauses which are, of course, attached at the time of the issue of the policy and suitably modify the contract. In accident and fire

1 A receiver is a person appointed by the Court, e.g., to act for a mental patient, and security has to be given by means of a bond.
2 The Articles of Association usually provide that the seal shall be affixed in the presence of a Director and Officer of the Company, who sign their names as having witnessed the sealing.

contracts also, it is frequently the practice to issue new policies with 'endorsements'[1] attached. Endorsements on bonds, for instance, increasing or decreasing the amount of the penalty, must as a rule be executed in the same way as the original bond.

Rules of Construction

Contracts of insurance are interpreted according to well-known rules of construction formulated in the course of Court practice.

The drafting of policies requires great care because, while the principal rule of construction is that the intention of the parties must prevail, that intention must be gathered from the policy itself. Moreover, if there is any ambiguity, then the policy is construed against the Insurers and in favour of the Insured, because the Insurers were the drawers of the document.

Policies are, as a rule, printed in standard form and the particulars relating to each individual insurance are inserted in writing (which includes typewriting). It may happen that there is a contradiction between printed and written portions of a policy and in such circumstances the written part prevails, as it is deemed to indicate more clearly the real intention of the parties. The same principle applies to the interpretation of endorsements which are attached to policies in order to vary their terms.

The phraseology of a policy must be construed in the plain, ordinary, and popular sense (unless the context indicates some special meaning), and, while the rules of grammar must be observed in interpretation, the primary rule holds good that the intention of the parties must predominate. Technical terms are freely used in the business of insurance and such technical terms must always be given their strictly technical meaning, unless there is clearly an indication to the contrary.

Any express term in a policy overrides an implied term, except where there is an inconsistency by so doing. At the same time, the contextual interpretation must be observed and also the *ejusdem generis* rule. This rule means that where specifications of particular things belonging to the same genus precede a word of general significance, the latter word is confined in its meaning to things

1 An endorsement varies the terms of an original contract, hence 'endorsements' attached to new policies at the time of issue are not endorsements proper. They are used merely as a convenience in policy drafting.

belonging to the same genus and does not include things belonging to a different genus.[1]

Policies in scheduled form (see p. 139) are often more easily construed than others. This is because in such policies it is provided that the policy and schedule shall be read together and that any word or expression to which a specific meaning has been attached in any part of the policy or of the schedule shall bear such specific meaning wherever it may appear.

It is usual in scheduled policies to print any such terms (e.g., 'Company') with an initial capital letter, and this facilitates clear expression of the intention of the contract. In any event, the whole of a policy must be regarded and not a particular clause only. Moreover, the majority of policies are prepared on uniform lines so far as regards their general terms and conditions, and, in the event of a dispute, the Court will have regard to the effect of any particular construction upon other cases. The Court, therefore, will not interpret a policy in any way contrary to general principles for the purposes of one particular instance only.

Validity of Contracts

Validity of contracts can be considered under four headings, and the general principles apply equally to contracts of insurance. It will be recognized that policies of insurance must contain all the essential elements discussed above when dealing with simple and specialty contracts respectively. If there is any defect, the contract will come within one of the headings studied below. It is here appropriate to stress the fact that, of the many insurance contracts entered into every year, the vast majority are valid. Of the few which are invalid, the majority fall within the category of voidable contracts (see below).

a Illegal contracts. Illegal contracts, that is to say, contracts which are contrary to law, cannot be sustained and are wholly without legal effect. This hardly ever arises in practice in connection with insurance

1 This is illustrated by the case of *King* v. *Travellers Insurance Association Ltd.* (1931), 48 TLR 53. There was a condition in the policy that 'jewellery, watches, field-glasses, cameras and other fragile or *specially valuable* articles must be separately declared and valued' and it was held that furs or fur coats were *not* 'specially valuable articles' within the meaning of the condition.

contracts, but it would be illegal in time of war to insure goods belonging to an enemy alien resident in an enemy country.

b Void contracts. A contract may be void, and a good illustration under the heading of insurance is a contract obtained by fraud.[1] It should be recognized, however, that while all fraudulent contracts are void, all void contracts are not necessarily fraudulent. Occasionally, a dishonest person will effect an insurance in respect of property which does not exist and will then endeavour to recover under the policy for an alleged loss. Obviously, the contract is void.

c Voidable contracts. Under this heading are included those policies where it is open to the Insurers to repudiate liability because of some defect in the terms of the contract as, for instance, misrepresentation on the part of the Insured. As explained in Chapter 4 (p. 96), the duty of utmost good faith requires the disclosure of all material facts, and this duty may be still more onerous where it is a contractual duty, as required by a signed proposal form and declaration. Strictly speaking, if there is in such circumstances *any* inaccuracy in the answers given on the proposal form, the contract is voidable, but Insurers do not necessarily take advantage of their legal right to repudiate liability. Indeed, many contracts of insurance, if strictly interpreted, could be repudiated under this heading, as proposers sometimes fail to give full details of the risk proposed for insurance—for example, the correct description of the construction of buildings proposed for fire insurance. Any minor inaccuracies are often overlooked by Insurers, provided the policy is corrected for the future.

d Unenforceable contracts. The best illustration for the present purpose of an unenforceable contract in the case of insurance is an unstamped life policy. It is not invalid, but unenforceable because it does not comply with the provisions of the Stamp Act. A policy can, however, be stamped after execution on payment of the duty, plus a penalty, when it can be used as evidence in civil proceedings in the usual way.

1 If, however, an Insurer overlooks fraud in any particular case, the contract is valid (see also p. 104).

Stamp Duty

Policies of insurance and assurance were made subject to revenue stamp duty as provided by the Stamp Act, 1891, and subsequent legislation. The Finance Act, 1970, made extensive changes to the stamp duties affecting a wide variety of documents and transactions. The provisions are contained in ss. 32 and 33 and Schedules 7 and 8, Parts IV and V of the Act. Among other changes, these provisions took into account the introduction of new currency under the Decimal Currency Act, 1967, and the introduction of decimalization in 1971. The table below shows the rates currently in force in so far as they affect policies of insurance.

Under the Finance Act, 1956, s.38, stamp duty may be compounded, and many Insurers take advantage of these provisions. Instead of each policy being stamped, a note is inserted therein, 'The appropriate Stamp Duty has been or will be paid to the Commissioners of Inland Revenue in accordance with the provisions of . . .' (the appropriate statutory reference is here shown).

Types of Insurance Contracts

Description of Instrument or Head of Charge	Duty Payable	FA 1970 Sched. 7, paras.
1 Policy of insurance other than life insurance	NIL	1(2)(b)
2 Policy of life insurance where amount insured exceeds £50 but does not exceed £1,000:		17(1)
For every £100 or part of £100 of the amount insured	5p	
Where the amount exceeds £1,000: For every £1,000 or part of £1,000 of the amount insured	50p	
3 Policy of life insurance for period not exceeding 2 years	5p	17(2)
4 Policy of re-insurance A policy of life insurance made solely in connection with re-insurance of a risk to which a policy duly stamped under head 'Policy of Life Insurance' relates is now chargeable thereunder only if under seal (or in Scotland only if it has a clause of registration).	Duty limited to 50p	17(3)

7 Proposal and Policy Forms

Proposal forms are used for many types of insurance, while policy forms are, of course, essential for all classes of insurance business.

It is always useful to obtain a selection of proposal forms and policy forms used for different classes of business so that comparisons and contrasts can be made. Quite apart from the different shapes and sizes of these forms, as used by different Insurers, they vary within wide limits, although the intention is the same. The object of proposal forms is to give the Insurers full particulars of the risks against which insurance protection is desired, while policy forms provide evidence of the contracts into which the parties have entered.

Proposal Forms

Where proposal forms are used, as a rule they constitute the means of communicating the *offer* to the Insurers, as explained in the previous chapter. At the same time, proposal forms often play a very important part in advertising the advantages of the type of insurance concerned; some Insurers pay particular attention to this feature in the drafting and general lay-out of their forms. It is also customary to indicate on the form a brief statement of the cover which is provided by the appropriate policy, or the terms and conditions of the insurance may be set out in full. There is something to be said for the latter method, because it tends to avoid misunderstandings.

GENERAL FEATURES

As already noted, no proposal forms are used in the practice of marine insurance. Instead of a proposal form, an original slip is prepared by the broker, based upon the information given to him by the proposer. (A specimen original slip is given on page 135.)

A. Broker & Co

TARKWA S.S. &/or STRS. APPD. or H/C

UK via L'POOL/LAGOS

500 BALES COTTON PIECE
GOODS VD. £5,000

ALL RISKS (INST. CARGO CLS.)
INCL. WAR, S.R. & C.C.
(INST. CLAUSES)
0·3125% + 0·0375% War

£2,500	}	*Initials of*
1,500	}	*Underwriters, date*
1,000	}	*and reference*

(This method is similarly adopted for most of the non-marine business placed at Lloyd's.)

It will have been noted in the previous chapter that proposal forms are used for certain types of fire insurance only, while proposal forms are invariably required in connection with life, other forms of property insurance, and liability insurances. There are certain features of proposal forms, whether used in personal, property or liability insurances, which are common to all such forms, and for convenience of exposition these are dealt with below. At the same time, the wording of these common inquiries varies within limits, according to the class of business concerned.

Features relevant to particular forms are studied later in this chapter. *For the convenience of the student, the questions common to all proposal forms are marked with an asterisk on the specimen forms included in this chapter, so that he may readily note the other inquiries which are peculiar to each class of business.* Package deals are now being offered and some of the questions are then incorporated as statements in the declaration. If the proposer is unable to warrant the applicability of the wording of such statements, a package policy is not possible.

QUESTIONS IN COMMON

1 *Proposer's name.* This is, of course, required for the purposes of identification. The name must be given in full and if other parties are interested in the insurance as, for instance, freeholder and mortgagee, all the names must be stated. In life assurance, the proposer for assurance is not necessarily the same as the person whose life is to be assured, and life proposal forms make provision for both names to be inserted. In the case of women, the proposer is asked to state whether Miss or Mrs, or, preferably, whether the proposer is single, married, or widowed.

2 *Proposer's address.* This is, once again, required for identification and also may be necessary to assess the risk. Where the property insured is not situated at the proposer's place of residence as, for example, a motor car which may be kept elsewhere, it is also necessary to have the address where the property is kept, as the situation is often a factor in rating.

3 *Proposer's profession or occupation.* This may be of material value to the Underwriter in rating the risk, particularly where life and personal accident insurances are concerned.

The particulars under (1), (2), and (3) enable the Insurers to insert the name, address, and description in the policy in accordance with long-standing legal and insurance practice.

4 *Previous and present insurances.* The proposer is required to state whether he has held or at present holds any insurance with another Insurer in respect of the risks proposed for insurance. The average man who is convinced of the benefits of life assurance effects additional policies as his income increases, and the same should be true of personal accident and sickness insurance. Sometimes, it is found convenient for a firm to spread its fire insurances over several Insurers without arranging the insurances on a schedule basis. On the other hand, if previous insurances have been held, the experience may have been unsatisfactory and for this reason the proposer is required also to state whether any Insurer has declined to accept or renew an insurance, so that the Insurers to whom the proposal is made may have an opportunity of consulting the previous Insurers for full details of their experience. The fact that Insurers consult each other in this way is well known to the public, and it is to this extent a protection to Insurers against unsatisfactory business being

offered to them. In proposal forms for motor and liability insurances, this question is often worded in more detail, as follows:
Has any Company or Underwriter at any time

a declined a .... proposal from the proposer?

b required an increased premium or imposed special conditions?

c cancelled or refused to renew an existing ....
policy held by the proposer? If so, give the name of the Company or Underwriter.

5 *Claims experience.* The claims experience is of special importance to Insurers. If there have been many claims in the past, it may reveal that the proposer is a careless person, or that the physical hazard is abnormal. The Insurers will then give special attention to the proposal before deciding upon acceptance or declinature and they may impose, in the event of acceptance, specially restrictive conditions.

The wording of this question in a fire proposal form is simply 'Has the proposer sustained loss by fire? If so, state particulars,' whereas in connection with motor insurance, for instance, the proposer is required to give details of all claims during the last three or five years, divided into settled and outstanding claims with particulars of the estimated further liability under outstanding claims. He may also be required to divide the claims among 'own damage,' third party, and other losses.

6 *Sum insured.* The sum or sums for which property is to be insured against fire, the sum assured under a life assurance policy, and the sum insured or limit of indemnity, as the case may be, under a liability insurance, must be indicated on the respective proposal forms so that the premium may be fixed and the monetary extent of the obligations which it is proposed that the Insurers should undertake may be clearly known. Irrespective of individual methods of rating, the sum insured or limit of indemnity is obviously a factor in the assessment of the premium.

7 *Date and signature.* All proposal forms must be dated and signed.

8 *Agent's recommendation.* Some Insurers require an agent's recommendation on their proposal forms as, for instance, 'To the best of my knowledge and belief the proposer whom I have known personally for .... years is of good reputation and I recommend acceptance,' followed by the date and signature of the agent. (Many

insurances are negotiated direct and there is then, of course, no question of an agent's recommendation.)

SPECIMEN FORMS

Insurances of the Person

A life proposal form is given on pp. 146–7 for use where the proposer is the person whose life is proposed to be assured.

The special questions are many. In the first instance, it is possible to effect life assurance under one of many tables drawn up by Assurers to show premiums payable for specified benefits. The proposer is therefore asked to state the type of assurance desired, whether or not with participation in profits, whether family protection benefits are required, the term of the assurance, and how frequently premiums are to be payable. Other questions relate to such matters as place and date of birth, whether married or single, health, habits, foreign residence, aviation, and family history. The information on family history is useful to the actuary and to the medical examiner, more particularly as some diseases have hereditary tendencies.

Insurances of Property

Theft insurance resembles fire insurance in that the object of the policy is to provide an indemnity in respect of loss of or damage to the Insured's own property. It is not practicable within the space of this chapter to give a specimen proposal form for each class of property insurance, but a private car motor proposal form has been included in view of the popularity of this type of insurance. For the same reason a household proposal form has been included.

Insurances of Liability

A combined employers' liability/public liability proposal form is included on p. 152. The object of the special questions is self-evident, as they largely relate to factors affecting the physical hazard. The questions concerning employees give some indication of the magnitude of the risk. Cover may be effected under either or both of the sections.

Policy Forms

Policy forms, like proposal forms, vary within wide limits as between the different classes of insurance, but they have certain features in common. This is true even of the marine insurance policy, although on the surface it is very different from the forms of policies used for other classes of business.

The policy is not the contract itself, but the evidence of the contract. In most cases, the contract has been entered into and concluded some days or weeks before the policy is issued to the Insured. In recent years, there has been an increasing tendency to standardize policy forms. In this connection, the student should note that the scheduled policy is now in use by many Insurers. The essential feature of such a policy is that all the typewritten matter is grouped together in one place, namely, in the schedule. The following exposition is based upon the scheduled type of policy.

MAIN SECTIONS

Generally speaking, policies are divisible into certain well-defined sections and these are as follows:

1 *Recital clause or preamble.* The opening section of the policy is termed the recital clause because it recites the parties to the contract, and if the insurance is based upon a proposal form and declaration, this is also mentioned.

2 *Operative clause.* The operative clause sets out the circumstances in which the Insurers agree to make a payment or its equivalent to the Insured. The wording of this clause naturally varies considerably according to the class of insurance concerned, and in the case of comprehensive policies the clause is of considerable length as, for instance, private-type motor car insurances. For convenience, the operative clause may be divided into certain sections.

The exceptions refer to the risks which are specifically excluded from the terms of the contract. As a general rule, it would be impracticable to issue a policy without exceptions, and it should be noted that, where the operative clause of a policy is divided into sections, there may be exceptions to each section and also general exceptions, the latter being applicable to the policy as a whole.

3 *Attestation clause.* This clause governs the signature of the policy

and its wording depends upon the practice of the Insurers concerned for the execution of documents.

4 *Conditions.* All policies are subject to conditions.[1] There are certain conditions which are implied, namely, that (i) good faith be exercised in all material circumstances, (ii) the Insured has an insurable interest in the subject-matter, (iii) the subject-matter is in existence when the contract is effected, and (iv) the subject-matter is so identified that the Insurers know the risk to be undertaken. When speaking of 'conditions' in the present sense, however, the express policy conditions are in mind, namely, those which are set out in the policy itself. Policies generally contain express conditions, with the exception of marine and life contracts and certain fidelity bonds.

5 *Schedule.* In the schedule will be found certain particulars common to most classes of policies and others peculiar to the type of insurance under consideration. The particulars common to most policies include details of the policy number, first and annual premiums, renewal date, names and addresses of the parties, and the period of insurance, with the date of signature of the policy and a space for the signature or initials of the policy examiner.

Policy forms do not now always follow the pattern given, especially when they are printed by the computer. Some Insurers, too, are introducing simplified wordings.

With this general introduction, notes are appended on the policies issued in connection with the three main classes of insurance.

GENERAL FEATURES

Insurances of the Person

Life assurance policies embrace many different types of contracts as, for instance, whole life assurances, endowment assurances, family income policies, children's endowment assurances, and annuities.

Generally speaking, the operative clause of a life policy is a brief statement as, for instance:

'Now this Policy witnesseth that, provided the Company receives the Premium as stated in the Schedule at the times and in the

1 Special considerations apply to marine insurance, and it is not practicable to go into detail in a book of this type.

manner therein specified, the Company will, on proof being given to the satisfaction of the Directors of (1) the occurrence of the Event described in the Schedule, (2) the title of the person or persons claiming, and (3) the age of the Life Assured, pay the Sum Assured hereunder, together with (if this Policy is issued With Profits) any further sum which may be appropriated by way of Bonus in addition thereto, to the Proposer or to the executors, administrators, or assigns of the Proposer, on the delivery up of this Policy and the receipt for the last premium due.'

All the facts peculiar to each policy are stated in the schedule.

Insurances of Property and Pecuniary Insurances

In marine insurance a standard policy form is used. This has been almost unaltered for 300 years, but it is brought up to date by the addition of standard clauses issued by the Institute of London Underwriters on behalf of the whole market.

The Opening, or Assignment clause (subject to restrictive clauses in hull policies) allows for the use of the policy by any person having a proved beneficial interest in the policy:

'Be it known that . . . . as well in . . . . in name, as for and in the name and names of all and every other person or persons to whom the same doth, may, or shall pertain, in part or in all, doth make Assurance and cause . . . . and they and every of them to be insured.'

The form used by the Companies is slightly different from the Lloyd's SG[1] form, the main difference being in the Binding Clause. In the SG Policy it reads:

'And so we, the Assurers, are contented, and do hereby promise and bind ourselves, each one for his own Part, our Heirs, Executors, and Goods, to the Assured, their Executors, Administrators, and Assigns, for the true Performance of the Promises, confessing ourselves paid Consideration due unto us for this Assurance by the Assured.'

Every Lloyd's Underwriter has a separate and unlimited liability,

1 The letters SG signify Ship and Goods, as the policy form wording refers to both ship and goods, dating from the old days when the common adventure was in one ownership.

The Companies and Lloyd's now use separate forms of policies for hull and cargo.

whereas the liability of a Company is limited according to its constitution. (Liability under an individual contract is naturally limited by the sum insured.)

Lloyd's and Companies' combined policies are signed on behalf of all Underwriters concerned at the respective Policy Signing Offices.

In fire insurance there are several policy forms used, namely, the ordinary form for private dwellings, the standard form used for other risks, the extra perils form, and the form(s) used for profits insurances.

Insurances of Liability

In liability insurance the layout of the form follows that for fire Insurance, but the operative clause will obviously differ and the following is an example of an operative clause in a public liability form:

'Now this Policy witnesseth that in consideration of the Insured having paid or agreed to pay to the Company the first premium the Company hereby agrees subject to the terms, exceptions and conditions contained herein, or endorsed or otherwise expressed hereon, that during the period of insurance or during any further period in respect of which the Insured shall have paid and the Company shall have accepted the premium required for the renewal of this Policy the Company will, subject to the limits of indemnity of the Policy, indemnify the Insured against:

All sums which the Insured shall become legally liable to pay as damages in respect of:

a accidental death of or bodily injury to or illness or disease contracted by any person,

b accidental loss of or damage to property

arising anywhere in connection with the business and occurring during the period of insurance.

All litigation expenses incurred with the consent of the Company will be paid in addition to the liability of the Company for compensation.[1]

In the event of the death of the Insured the Company will in respect of the liability incurred by the Insured indemnify the

1 If the Insured in the course of the business undertakes work for a Principal, the Principal may be provided with an indemnity. A personal indemnity may also be given for directors or employees of the Insured.

Insured's legal personal representatives in the terms of and subject to the limitations of this Policy provided that such legal personal representatives shall as though they were the Insured observe, fulfil and be subject to the terms, exceptions and conditions of the Policy so far as they can apply.'

EXPRESS CONDITIONS

Insurances of the person. Life policies are subject to special conditions but do not contain express conditions on the lines of those found in some property and liability insurances. There are, however, certain provisions, sometimes termed either 'regulations' or 'privileges,' and they refer, *inter alia*, to the following matters:

Foreign residence—occupation—indisputability. Unless otherwise provided in the schedule, the policy is free from all restrictions as to occupation, residence, and travel.

Renewal premiums. Thirty days of grace are normally allowed, and provision is made for the case of death after a renewal premium has become due, but has not been paid.

Reinstatement and non-forfeiture. Provision is usually made for:

1 reinstatement if one full year's premium has been paid and the policy is not renewed after the thirty days of grace;

2 surrender value or paid-up policy—if two or more years' premiums have been paid, the policy may be surrendered to the Assurers for a cash payment or a paid-up policy may be issued for a reduced sum assured;

3 non-forfeiture of policy—the surrender value of the policy can be available out of which to meet unpaid premiums to keep the policy in force.

Insurances of property and liability. With the exception of marine and aviation insurances, the express conditions for property and liability policies are more or less identical and are conveniently discussed below.

1 *Notification to Insurers.* It is essential that the way in which losses are to be notified and in which other communications are to be sent

to the Insurers should be clearly stated. It is usually provided that if notice is not given in the manner specified, then there will be no liability under the policy for any loss or damage sustained.

2 *Loss procedure.* It is necessary to set out the procedure to be followed when a loss occurs. The wording of this condition naturally depends to some extent upon the class of insurance concerned. Notice must be given as soon as possible; in a case of loss of or damage to the Insured's own property, evidence of value is required; while under a liability indemnity provision is made for the Insurers to deal with the claim. The Insurers are enabled under the condition forthwith to prosecute in the name of the Insured for their own benefit any claim for indemnity or damages, so that *subrogation* rights apply immediately, whereas at Common Law the Insurers would not be subrogated to alternative rights and remedies until after a claim had been settled.

3 *Cancellation.* Policies provide for the contract to be cancelled by the Insurers, and in such event a *pro rata* return of premium for the unexpired portion of the current period will be allowed. The condition may also give the Insured the right to cancel the contract, when a refund will be allowed after applying the Company's short period rates of premium. (Fire policies do not as a rule contain a cancellation condition.)

4 *Adjustable premiums.* If the premium is adjustable, the method of adjustment is governed by a special policy condition so that the Insurers obtain the necessary figures on which to make the adjustment and can insist upon the payment of any requisite additional premium.

5 *Contribution.* If there is more than one policy in force on the same subject-matter and the contract is one of indemnity, the Insured must not recover more than the total amount of his loss, and this condition ensures that all the Insurers concerned shall contribute. It modifies the Common Law position, because at Common Law an Insured can claim the whole of his loss, if so desired, against one Insurer who then is involved in the trouble of seeking contribution from the Co-insurers. The condition requires the Insured to claim against all his Insurers from each of whom he can recover a *pro rata* contribution only.

6 *Insured to take precautions.* It is a primary principle of insurance that the Insured should take as much care of his property as if he

were not covered by insurance. This condition draws the attention of the Insured to this obligation and the wording, of course, varies according to the type of insurance concerned.

7 *Arbitration clause.* Almost all policies contain an arbitration clause which governs the method of settlement of disputes as to amount. The public are inclined to misunderstand the technical business of insurance, and the publicity of court actions with abridged Press reports often aggravates this misunderstanding. Arbitration is therefore a preferable means of settlement of disputes because (*a*) the case is heard in private, (*b*) it is often less costly than litigation, and (*c*) there is certainly not the delay involved in legal actions.

Until 1958 all disputes were referred to arbitration, but since that time it has been agreed by members of the British Insurance Association and Lloyd's that, as regards UK business, disputes as to amount only are to be covered by the arbitration condition, leaving questions as to liability to be settled by the court. Disputes as to liability can still be settled by arbitration if the Insured prefers this. Before this alteration to the arbitration condition, very few claims were dealt with in this way, and now there are fewer still.

Specimen Life Proposal Form

Type and term of assurance	*Sum to be assured	With or without profits	Family protection benefit (if any) £ per annum for years	How frequently premiums are to be payable

Statement to be made by the proposed Life Assured...
Please give all relevant information. Ticks and dashes are not sufficient.

*1 Name in full (block letters)

   Married or single

   Age **next** birthday

*   Address (block letters)

   Date of birth
   Place of birth

*   Occupation
(please be specific)

   Maiden name if
   a married woman

2   Do you expect to take part in motor cycle racing, flying (except as a passenger on a recognised air service) or any hazardous activity ?
If so, please give details

   Do you expect to reside abroad ?
If so, please give details

*3 Is your life already assured with this Company ?
Has a proposal to this Company or any other Company been declined, postponed, withdrawn or accepted on special terms ?
If so, please state in each case which Company and the approximate date of the proposal

4   What are the name and address of your medical attendant or (if you have not required medical attention personally) of your family doctor ?

   How long has the doctor named known you ?
Have you consulted him during the last five years ?
If so, state when and for what reason

   Have you consulted any other doctor during the last five years ?
If so, state when and for what reason and give the name and address of the doctor

continued over

Items 5, 6, 7 and 8 need not be completed if you are to have a medical examination

	Please state 'Yes' or 'No'	Answer each question separately and if 'yes' please give full details **including dates**

5 Have you ever had or do you suffer from :

a) Rheumatic fever or rheumatoid arthritis ?

b) Faints, fits, giddiness or nervous trouble ?

c) Tuberculosis, pleurisy, asthma or other chest trouble ?

d) Digestive trouble with or without ulceration ?

e) Heart or arterial trouble or raised blood pressure ?

f) Diabetes, actual or suspected ?

g) Kidney or bladder trouble or venereal disease ?

h) Any other serious illness, operation, accident or condition ?

6 Height in shoes .... ft. .... in. .... Weight in indoor clothes .... st. .... lb. (as tested recently on a reliable machine)

7 Do you smoke ? If so, what is your daily consumption—Cigarettes........ Pipe tobacco........oz. Cigars........

8 If any of the following have died please give age at death and cause of death

Father .... Brothers

Mother .... Sisters

9 I declare that the foregoing statements are true and complete. I understand that this proposal and declaration, my statements (if any) to the Assurance Company's medical examiner and any other declaration made by me relating to this proposal will be the basis of any contract resulting from this proposal. I consent to the Assurance Company's seeking information from any doctor who has attended me and from any company to which I have made a life assurance proposal and I authorise the giving of such information. **I confirm that I have checked, and found correct, any statements in this proposal that are not in my own handwriting.**

Signature of the proposed Life Assured .... Date ....

Specimen Private Car Proposal Form

All questions must be answered fully. Delete Yes or No as applicable.

A DETAILS OF PROPOSER AND DRIVERS

1 Proposer

Full name: (Mr/Mrs/Miss)
(Block letters, please)

Full address
(Block letters, please)

Postcode .... Tel. No. ....

2 Drivers

a) State the following details of all persons including yourself who, to your knowledge, will drive the car.

Full name	Age	Occupation (if more than one, give details of each)	Period of recent car driving experience in the British Isles	Type of driving licence held and date of passing driving test
Proposer as above				
Other drivers				

b) Have you and the above drivers resided in the British Isles for the past 3 consecutive years?   Yes/No

If 'No' give details

*3 Driving History

Have you or any of the above drivers

a) had any accident or loss during the past 4 years whether covered by insurance or not?   Yes/No

If 'Yes' give details	Name	Date	Cost and circumstances

b) had any convictions in the past 4 years, or is any prosecution pending, for any offence in connection with a motor vehicle?   Yes/No

If 'Yes' give details

4 Health

Do you or any of the above drivers suffer from defective vision or hearing (not corrected by spectacles or hearing aid), or from any physical or mental disability, infirmity or disease ?

Yes/No

If 'Yes' give details

*5 Insurance History

a) Have you been or are you now insured in respect of any motor vehicle ?

Yes/No

If 'Yes' state name and address of insurer and policy or certificate number

b) Have you or any of the above drivers been refused insurance at normal rates and terms during the past 4 years ?

Yes/No

If 'Yes' give details

B DETAILS OF CAR(S)

1 Details (Note. Your estimate of present value must include accessories and spare parts)

Make and model	Engine capacity	Year of make	Registered letters and number	Type of body	Seating capacity	Date of purchase	price paid by you	Estimate of presentvalue

Note. In the case of a sports car or high performance car state period of driving experience in such cars.

2 Modifications

Has the car been modified to give an increased performance from the makers' published specification or is it intended to do so ?

Yes/No

If 'Yes' give details

3 Garaging

a) Is the car usually kept at a different address from that of the proposer ?

Yes/No

If 'Yes' state address where usually kept

b) Is the car usually kept in a garage overnight ?

Yes/No

If 'No' state where it is kept

4 Ownership

a) Are you the owner of the car and is it registered in your name ?   Yes/No

If 'No' give the name and address of
i) owner

ii) person in whose name the car is registered

b) Is any finance company interested in the car ?   Yes/No

If 'Yes' give the name and address of the company

C CLASS OF USE

a) Will the car be used solely for social domestic and pleasure purposes ?   Yes/No

If 'No' will the other use be
i) solely by you in person in connection with your business ?   Yes/No

ii) on your business, or that of your employer or partner, by your employees or other persons ?   Yes/No

iii) for commercial travelling in your business ?   Yes/No

iv) in connection with the Motor Trade or for hire or reward ?   Yes/No

b) Will the car be used for any other purposes by you or any other person ?   Yes/No

If 'Yes' give details

c) Will the car be used for racing, competitions, trials or rallies (other than road safety rallies and treasure hunts) ?   Yes/No

If 'Yes' give details

D COVER

Please indicate the type of cover required: Comprehensive ☐   Third Party Fire and Theft ☐   Third Party ☐

E OPTIONAL DISCOUNTS Please indicate the discounts required:

Driving restricted to: One named driver ☐   Yourself and your spouse ☐

If a Comprehensive policy is required do you wish to bear the first amount of each claim for loss of or damage to your car (other than by fire, theft or shattered windscreen) ?

If so, indicate the amount   £15 ☐   £25 ☐   £50 ☐

Note. Any such contribution is additional to the compulsory amounts of £25 and £50 for young and inexperienced drivers.

continued over

F PERIOD OF INSURANCE

I require insurance for a period of one year commencing on

Note. If you are entitled to a 'no claim discount' please attach the renewal notice from previous insurer confirming entitlement.

Before signing this proposal please read the following declaration carefully. As it is an offence under the Road Traffic Act to make any false statement or withhold any material information to obtain a Certificate of Motor Insurance great care must be taken to ensure that the form is completed correctly.

Declaration

I/We declare that the particulars in this proposal are true to the best of my/our knowledge and belief and that nothing materially affecting the risk has been concealed by me/us.

I/We undertake that the car or cars to be insured

a) will not be driven by any person who to my/our knowledge has been refused motor vehicle insurance or continuance thereof

b) is or are in a roadworthy condition.

I/We agree that this proposal shall be incorporated in and taken as the basis of the proposed contract between me/us and the Company.

Signature   Date

Note. The Company is **not on risk** until a temporary cover note or Certificate of Motor Insurance has been delivered to the Proposer.

Specimen Employers' Liability/Public Liability Proposal Form

*Name of Proposer in full
(Block letters, please)

Tel. No.

*Address (Block letters, please)

Postcode

*Address of Business Premises, if different from above

Postcode

*Business (Describe fully and, if a contractor or engineer, state exact nature of work. State whether manufacturer, processor, importer, wholesaler, warehouseman or retailer)

Please tick boxes as appropriate

Cover required   Section I   Liability to Employees ☐   Section II   Liability to the Public ☐

Complete the Sections for which cover is required

Section I   Liability to Employees

Note. 'Employees' includes labour only masters and persons supplied by them, labour only sub-contractors and persons employed by them, self-employed persons and persons hired from any public authority, firm or individual. Payments to all such persons must be included in column **B**.

1 Description of all Employees	A Estimated number	B Estimated annual wages and salaries
Clerks, commercial travellers and managerial Employees (not engaged in manual work)		£
Working directors (fees should not be included) Manual		£
Non-manual		£
Employees using wood-working machinery other than lathes, fret-saws and the like		£
All other Employees (give full description of work)		£
		£
		£
		£

continued over

2 Is the annual wage-roll expected to increase by more than $33\frac{1}{3}\%$ over the next 3 years? Yes ☐ No ☐ If 'Yes', state estimated wage-roll 3 years hence £

3 Details of machinery driven by mechanical power
a) Wood-working

b) Other

4 a) Does Proposer comply with the regulations made under the Factories Act or other regulations applicable to the business? Yes ☐ No ☐

b) Has Proposer ever been prosecuted under the Factories Act? Yes ☐ No ☐ If 'Yes', give details

5 Will Proposer manufacture, dress, handle or use asbestos, silica, material containing silica or any other substance which may be harmful to health? Yes ☐ No ☐
If 'Yes', give details

6 Has Proposer a foundry? Yes ☐ No ☐

*7 Have any incidents occurred during the last 5 years resulting in death, injury or disease to Proposer's Employees? Yes ☐ No ☐
If 'Yes', give details

Date of occurrence	Brief details of each incident (whether a claim was made or not)	Cost (if any) of claim paid £	estimated outstanding £
		£	£
		£	£
		£	£

Section II Liability to the Public

*1 Limit of indemnity (please tick amount required) £100,000 ☐ £250,000 ☐ £500,000 ☐

2 Details of all premises Description, e.g. office, factory etc. To what part do public have access?
Address

3 Is Proposer responsible for any berth or for the berthing or mooring of any water-borne craft?　　Yes ☐　　No ☐

If 'Yes', give details

---

4 Will chemical effluent or fumes or anything of a noxious nature be discharged?　　Yes ☐　　No ☐

If 'Yes', give details

---

5 a) State whether any electric, oxy-acetylene or similar welding or cutting equipment, blow lamps or blow torches are used　　Yes ☐　　No ☐

If 'Yes', give details, including annual wages paid to employees using such equipment

b) Will such equipment be used away from Proposer's premises?　　Yes ☐　　No ☐

---

6 Estimated annual wages paid to all employees working　a) at the premises £　　　b) away from the premises £

---

7 Will any work be sub-contracted to established firms holding their own insurances?　　Yes ☐　　No ☐

If 'Yes', give details and relevant estimated annual contract prices

---

8 a) Give details (if applicable) of treatment and services provided by Proposer other than products supplied

	Estimated current annual turnover £
	£
	£
	£

b) Is annual turnover expected to increase by more than 33⅓% over the next 3 years?　　Yes ☐　　No ☐　If 'Yes', state estimated turnover 3 years hence £

---

9 a) Give details of products supplied by Proposer. (Include purpose of use and if a product or any part of it is imported, state source)

	Estimated current annual turnover £
	£
	£
	£

continued over

3 b) Is annual turnover expected to increase by more than $33\frac{1}{3}$% over the next 3 years? Yes ☐ No ☐ If 'Yes', state estimated turnover 3 years hence £

c) Are printed conditions of sale used in every case? Yes ☐ No ☐

If 'Yes' please attach a specimen of each printed wording in use, including warranties given. Specimens of brochures, other sales literature and any instructions for use should also be provided.

d) What system of check is in operation for the purpose of discovering possible defects in products?

e) Do any products contain poisons, acids or other ingredients which could be harmful to health? Yes ☐ No ☐

If 'Yes', give details

f) Are any products supplied used in
   If 'Yes', give details, including annual turnover
   i) aircraft or aerial devices? Yes ☐ No ☐
   ii) computer equipment? Yes ☐ No ☐
   iii) motor vehicles? Yes ☐ No ☐

g) Is cover required for liability in respect of advice, design or specification in connection with products supplied? Yes ☐ No ☐

Note. Liability in respect of advice, design or specification given for a fee cannot be included.

If 'Yes', state whether design work is undertaken or advice is given in connection with products supplied and, if so, give details, including qualifications of persons involved

h) Are any products supplied to the U.S.A. or Canada? Yes ☐ No ☐

10 a) Has proposer any representation outside the United Kingdom? Yes ☐ No ☐

If 'Yes', state annual turnover £

b) Are any visits made or is work undertaken outside the United Kingdom? Yes ☐ No ☐

If 'Yes', are they always under the direct control of a handler? Yes ☐ No ☐

11 Are any guard dogs used? Yes ☐ No ☐

12 Does Proposer own, possess, hire in or use any unlicensed mechanically propelled vehicles which do not require a Certificate of Motor Insurance? Yes ☐ No ☐

If 'Yes', give description
   a) Unlicensed vehicles at Proposer's premises
   b) Unlicensed vehicles away from Proposer's premises

•13 Have any incidents occurred during the last 5 years resulting in death, injury or disease to members of the public or damage to their property? Yes ☐ No ☐

If 'Yes', give details

Date of occurrence	Brief details of each incident (whether a claim was made or not)	Cost (if any) of claim paid £	estimated outstanding £
		£	£
		£	£
		£	£

General questions to be completed in all cases

1 Give details of all lifts, hoists, cranes, steam boilers, steam containers and other pressure vessels

a) Description	Maximum load or pressure	Purpose of use

b) Are they inspected regularly to comply with statutory regulations? Yes ☐ No ☐ If 'Yes', by whom?

2 Will any radioactive substances or other sources of ionising radiations be handled or used? Yes ☐ No ☐ If 'Yes', give details

3 Will any explosives or other dangerous substances be stored, handled or used? Yes ☐ No ☐ If 'Yes', give details

•4 Has Proposer previously insured in respect of a) Liability to Employees? Yes ☐ No ☐ b) Liability to the Public? Yes ☐ No ☐

If 'Yes', give details, including name(s) of insurers

•5 Has any insurer ever a) declined a proposal, refused renewal or terminated an insurance? Yes ☐ No ☐ b) required an increased premium or imposed special conditions? Yes ☐ No ☐

If 'Yes', give details

Declaration

I/We declare that the above statements made by me/us or on my/our behalf are true to the best of my/our knowledge and belief and I/we agree that this proposal shall be the basis of the contract between me/us and the Company. I/We agree to accept a Policy in the Company's usual form for this class of insurance.

Signature   Date

(Signing this form does not bind Proposer to complete the insurance)

Specimen Household Proposal Form

*Name of Proposer (in full) .... (Mr./Mrs./Miss)

*Address ....

*Occupation .... Occupation of Husband/Wife ....

Cover required from ....

Address of Private Dwelling to which Insurance is to apply (if different from above) ....

1. Is the Dwelling a flat or maisonette? .... If so, has it a separate locked entrance under your sole control? ....   YES/NO**

2. Are the Buildings built of brick, stone or concrete and roofed with slates, metal, tiles or concrete?   YES/NO**

   If "NO" please state construction.

3. Are the Buildings of the Private Dwelling
   - (a) specially liable to damage by storm, tempest, flood, subsidence or landslip?   :   :   :   YES/NO**
   - (b) used other than for residential purposes? :   :   :   :   :   YES/NO**
   - (c) regularly left unoccupied other than for shopping, recreation or holidays?   :   :   YES/NO**

4. Does the total value of articles of Gold, Silver or other precious metal, Jewellery or Fur exceed one-third of the value of Contents to be insured (excluding property insured under the All Risks Section)?   :   :   YES/NO**

*5. In respect of any of the risks proposed for insurance
   - (a) have you or any member of your family ever sustained a loss or made a claim?   :   :   YES/NO**
   - (b) has the acceptance or renewal of any insurance been declined or made subject to special terms or increased premium?   YES/NO**

** Delete the answer which does not apply. If the answer to questions 3, 4 or 5 is "YES" please give further details here:

HOUSEHOLD SECTION

	State sums to be insured
THE BUILDINGS of the Private Dwelling (including allowance for fees)	£
Do you wish the Society to cover the first £15 of each loss on Buildings caused by Storm Tempest Flood Escape of Water Malicious Damage and Impact? (See Summary of Cover) : : YES/NO	£
THE CONTENTS: Household Goods and Personal Effects	£
Specified items	£
	£
	£

ALL RISKS SECTION
(available only if Contents insured)

Please state below the sums to be insured. Except for items 1, 2, 3, 4 and 5 each article to be insured must be separately described and valued. Receipts or valuations will be required for articles exceeding £100 in value.

The Sum Insured by Item 1 must represent the maximum value of such property with the Policyholder and his family when away from home.

1. **Clothing and Personal Effects** (away from home)
   Minimum Sum Insured £100   £ ....

2. **Miscellaneous articles of Jewellery Watches and Furs** not exceeding £50 each article   £ ....

3. **Miscellaneous Photographic Equipment and Binoculars** not exceeding £50 each article   £ ....

4. **Sporting Equipment** relating to
   ....   £ ....

5. **Camping Equipment**   £ ....

Do you wish to cover Personal Money?   YES/NO

6. ....   £ ....

7. ....   £ ....

8. ....   £ ....

9. ....   £ ....

10. ....   £ ....

11. ....   £ ....

12. ....   £ ....

Do you wish to cover Credit Cards?   YES/NO
If so, state Card Numbers ....
By whom issued ....

DECLARATION

I hereby
  (i) **declare that my answers are true to the best of my knowledge and belief and that I have not withheld or concealed any material information**
  (ii) agree that this Proposal and Declaration shall be the basis of the Contract between me and the Company
  (iii) declare that I am willing to accept a Policy subject to the terms exceptions and conditions prescribed by the Company therein.

Date............   Signature...............

The liability of the Company does not commence until acceptance of the Proposal by the Company.

8 Reinsurance

Where the amount on any one risk or risks which form one hazard is such that it is beyond the limits which it is prudent for one Insurer to carry, it is necessary to effect reinsurance.[1]

Large risks are encountered in all sections of insurance business and for this reason reinsurance is required in all departments with the object of providing a greater spread of risk so that a heavy claim, while made upon the one Insurer who issued the policy, is in fact borne by a number of Insurers. The general principles of reinsurance are common to all sections of insurance, subject, of course, to modifications in their adaptation to individual classes of business.

It is essential that the utmost good faith be observed at all times between the direct Insurer and the Reinsurer. Insurable interest is also vital in all contracts of reinsurance, and it has been held that the issue of a policy with the acceptance of liability thereunder by the direct Insurer is sufficient to constitute such insurable interest. At the same time, the original Insured acquires no rights under a reinsurance contract which operates solely between the direct Insurer and the Reinsurer. If the direct Insurer should become insolvent, recoveries under reinsurances form part of the general assets available for distribution among all creditors. If a Reinsurer fails to meet his obligations, the direct Insurer is still liable in full to the Insured. All contracts of reinsurance are contracts of indemnity only, whether or not the policy issued by the direct Insurer (e.g., personal accident insurance) is one of strict indemnity. This is because the Reinsurer undertakes to indemnify the direct Insurer in respect of a proportion (and occasionally the whole[2]) of the amount of liability incurred to the policyholder.

---

1 Reinsurance can be arranged either with another direct Insurer or with a specialist reinsurance Office, that is, one which accepts no direct business.

2 A risk is sometimes wholly reinsured where a Company issues a policy in respect of a class of business which it does not ordinarily transact.

Definitions

The following are definitions of terms generally used in reinsurance:

a Direct Insurer—the Insurer who accepts the risk from the proposer and who, so far as the policyholder is concerned, is alone responsible for the obligation undertaken.

b Reinsurer—the Insurer who grants a guarantee (or accepts a reinsurance)[1] from the direct Insurer.

c Ceding Insurer—the Insurer who obtains a guarantee (or places a reinsurance).

d Cession—the amount given off by way of reinsurance and therefore the amount accepted by the Reinsurer.

e Reinsurance policy—the contract of reinsurance, except in fire practice where it is termed a guarantee, or guarantee policy.

f Retention, or holding—the proportion of the risk which the direct Insurer holds on his own account.

g Line—the amount of the retention of the direct Insurer; a Reinsurer may accept one or more lines (or a fraction of a line).

h Retrocession—a reinsurance of a reinsurance, i.e., where the Reinsurer desires to reduce the limit of his liability in respect of business accepted.

i Reinsurance commission—the amount paid by the Reinsurer to the ceding Company as a contribution to the acquisition and administration costs. It is calculated on a percentage of the premium received by the Reinsurer.

j Profit commission—a percentage of the earned profits which the Reinsurer agrees to return because the profit earned on business passing under a reinsurance treaty is deemed to be due to skill and care in the conduct of the business by the direct Insurer.

1 In fire insurance, the terminology is slightly different from that in accident insurance. The ceding fire Insurer *obtains a guarantee*, while the ceding accident Insurer *places a reinsurance*. Similarly, the fire Reinsurer *grants a guarantee* and the accident Reinsurer *accepts a reinsurance*.

Different Kinds of Reinsurance Contracts

There are three main methods by which reinsurance may be effected, and the extent to which these methods are used respectively must, of course, depend upon the practice of Insurers and the scope of their resources. These three methods are: (*a*) facultative, (*b*) treaties, and (*c*) pools.

a Facultative

This is the oldest method of reinsurance and it necessitates the consideration of each risk separately. Its drawback is the amount of work involved and the time taken to place a risk because, after the direct Insurer has decided upon his own retention, it is necessary to submit the details of the risk, with the amount available for reinsurance, to one or more other Offices. There is uncertainty that each Office to which the offer is made will accept the business, while the amount of the acceptance is entirely within the discretion of each Reinsurer.

The procedure is to submit a slip to each Reinsurer giving details of the risk, with the rate(s), and the amount of the ceding Company's retention. The Reinsurer then initials the slip with the amount of his acceptance, and this process must be repeated until the whole of the risk has been placed. Cover is not usually granted to the proposer until the reinsurances have been fixed. The next step[1] is to issue a request note which contains formal particulars of the risk, and the Reinsurer then issues a take note. The take note is often stamped in order to avoid the necessity of the further issue of a formal guarantee policy. Renewals have to be dealt with individually by the issue of renewal statements on the part of the Reinsurers, followed by advice by the direct Insurers of renewals, lapses, and cancellations, and later settlement in account. There is usually a time-lag of three months, more particularly where the direct business is through a credit agent who has a quarterly account. If any Reinsurer does not wish to continue on a risk after next renewal date, due notice must be given, and the direct Insurers then endeavour to find another Reinsurer to accommodate them.[2]

Where facultative fire reinsurance is arranged between members of the Fire Offices' Committee, it is stated on the request note, take note, and guarantee policy, that the transaction is subject to the rules

1 If a slip is not used, the first step is the issue of a request note.
2 This does not apply to life reassurance.

adopted by the Fire Offices' Committee for the regulation of guarantee transactions, otherwise terms of the Reinsurer's acceptance must be separately agreed for each reinsurance. The rules give the direct Insurers certain rights as to the nature of the indemnity and settlement of claims which would otherwise have to be provided for specifically.

Although facultative reinsurance has of recent years taken second place because of the popularity of treaties, it is still important as a means of reinsuring special risks outside the scope of the usual treaty or in order to absorb a surplus after treaty facilities have been exhausted.

b Treaties

Under this method of reinsurance, an agreement is entered into between the direct Insurer and the Reinsurer (either one Company or several), whereby the ceding Company agrees to cede and the Reinsurer agrees to accept all insurances offered within the limits of the treaty. This means that automatic protection is secured and that it is obligatory for the Reinsurer to accept all risks within the scope of the treaty. The direct Insurer, therefore, can grant cover immediately for any proposal accepted within the limits of the treaty.

1 *Quota share treaty.* Under this type of treaty, a fixed proportion of a given class of insurance as a whole is ceded. If, for example, reinsurance is arranged on a 50 per cent basis, the Reinsurer accepts half of each risk, obtains half the premiums (less commission), and bears half the claims, while the ceding Company retains the balance of 50 per cent. Commission is, of course, a matter of mutual arrangement. This type of reinsurance has the advantage of simplicity, but its disadvantage is the necessity of paying away premiums on small risks instead of retaining the whole for the direct Insurer's own account. There is no risk of selection against the Reinsurer, all business coming to the treaty.[1]

2 *Surplus treaty.* The direct Insurer merely places on the treaty any part of the risk, i.e., the surplus, which it is not desired to retain. It follows that if a certain risk is wholly retained, there is no surplus to place on the treaty. If a treaty is arranged so that three, four, or more lines are secured in this way (a line being the amount of the direct Insurer's retention) the latter can thus accept automatically

[1] Normally such treaties would be subject to a maximum liability in respect of any one risk.

a risk which is four or more times the size of his own holding, but for any larger risk the balance must be reinsured facultatively.

3 *Excess of loss treaty.*[1] An Insurer decides the maximum amount he is prepared to bear on any one loss and seeks reinsurance under a treaty whereby the Reinsurers will be responsible for the amount of any losses and above the amount retained by the direct Insurer. There may be an upper limit to the treaty so that if the Insurer, for instance, is content to bear the first £3,000 of any loss, the treaty Reinsurers will bear any loss over £3,000, but not exceeding, say, £100,000. For cover beyond that limit, a further excess of loss treaty may be negotiated, or the direct Insurer may be content to bear the possibility of a claim exceeding £100,000.

4 *Stop loss treaty.* This is a modern variation of excess of loss whereby the loss ratio of the ceding Insurer is stopped at an agreed percentage, and if the loss ratio in any year exceeds that percentage the Reinsurers bear the difference. Stop loss reinsurance can be arranged in addition to a surplus treaty.

Of the foregoing methods of reinsurance, (1) and (2) are proportionate in that the premiums are shared and the losses are paid by the Insurers and the Reinsurers in proportions agreed before the loss. Methods (3) and (4) are known as non-proportionate in that the premiums are not necessarily divided between the Insurer and the Reinsurer in the same proportion as they pay claims. They are more commonly used for motor and general third party risks.

In (1) and (2) above, details of risks placed on the treaty and of subsequent alterations may be advised to the Reinsurers periodically by bordereaux, but this has never been universal. The need to reduce administrative costs has resulted in this practice becoming less common, but the Reinsurers are supplied (usually quarterly) with a statement of premiums and losses and have the right to inspect the appropriate reinsurance records of the Insurers. The Reinsurers do not require to be advised of risks accepted under (3) and (4), but are advised of all claims likely to involve them in a payment under the treaty.

c Pooling Schemes

These schemes are adopted mainly for catastrophe risks, that is, where the happening of an insured event may involve unusually

1 Facultative reinsurance may also be arranged in this way.

heavy loss, damage, or liability (e.g., where a large number of persons may be injured), so that the total claims upon the Insurers will be considerable. All claims (and all losses) may be pooled, or the surplus above a fixed retention, or an agreed excess of loss, may be dealt with in this way. Each member, in effect, receives back a share of his own cessions and a like share of the cessions of others, so that each is liable for only a comparatively small share of a wide spread of business. Material damage and liability pools have been organized by the British Insurance (Atomic Energy) Committee to deal with the huge amounts involved in atomic energy risks.

Some examples of the way in which these various methods are used for different classes of insurance follow.

Insurances of the Person

a Life Assurance

Cover may be secured for life reassurance either facultatively or by automatic treaty. Until recently the general practice in this country was to place reassurances facultatively, but much more use is made nowadays of automatic treaties.

Most reassurances are effected by ceding a share of the original policy, and this is described as reassurance on original terms. The Reassurance Agreement, 1900 (to which many Offices have adhered), sets out the general principles that normally apply, but it also provides for the possibility of reassuring at the rate of premium, rate of bonus, and policy conditions of the Office accepting the reassurance. This latter system is rarely used at the present time.

A more recent development is the risk premium system of reassurance under which the mortality risk alone is reassured. The whole of the actuarial reserves are thus retained by the ceding office.[1] The amount at risk for each year of the reassurance is calculated by subtracting the reserve from the initial amount at risk under that part of the policy which is reassured. The reassurance premium is obtained by applying the rate of risk premium for the age at the

1 By the level premium system in life assurance, where the risk covered increases yearly, more is received in early years than is required to meet the cost of the risk. The excess is accumulated and, in theory, is held 'in reserve'; this is the actuarial reserve.

commencement of the policy year to the amount at risk for that year.

A direct writing Office has the choice of reassuring facultatively or by automatic treaty, and either method can be used in conjunction with the risk premium system or reassurance on original terms. The needs and circumstances of the Office will determine which combination is adopted.

The chief reason for reassurance is that Offices desire to protect their funds from losses arising out of claims for large amounts, and hence it is usual to fix the retention at a reasonable figure, depending upon the size of the Office and the distribution of the sums assured.

An automatic treaty saves much time and work, especially for Offices which have a large number of reassurances to place. It is the custom for the Reassurer, in accepting business under a treaty, to allow special reassurance commissions which include an allowance for overhead expenses. A young Office or an Office which is growing rapidly can secure some contribution towards the heavy procuration expenses and thus reduce its expense ratio which otherwise would be high in comparison with other Offices.

When reassurances are accepted from overseas, it is usual to grant cover in original currency, and if such business is transacted on the risk premium basis the problem of investment of reserves does not arise and there is no concern regarding liability to foreign taxes on interest earnings. On the other hand, some reassurance treaties are arranged on original terms and provide for the deposit of actuarial reserves either in cash at a guaranteed rate of interest or in securities.

The professional Reassurer may be in a position to offer special facilities for the underwriting of sub-standard risks, and sub-standard treaties provide that the Reassurer accepts an agreed proportion of each policy. Special risks may be allocated to a pool where the risk may be shared by several Companies.

b Personal Accident Insurance

In this class of business it is customary to enter into a surplus treaty so that provision is made for the cession only of that part of an original insurance which remains after the ceding Office's retention has been decided.

Most Companies have an excess of loss protection against unknown accumulations, so that they can limit the amount of their liability in respect of an accident involving a number of people, for example, an air crash.

Insurances of Property and Pecuniary Insurances

a Marine Insurance

One of the commonest forms in which cargo business is transacted is by means of Open Covers. The Open Cover provides that the Underwriter will accept from his client all his insurances coming within the scope of the cover, up to an agreed amount per vessel. If an Underwriter has a number of Open Covers, there are occasions when several of his clients may be shipping full lines by the same vessel.[1] Again, branches and agencies may accept lines on vessels on which the Underwriter is already fully interested and it then becomes necessary for the Underwriter to reinsure the excess of the limit that he has decided upon for the particular vessel.

For both hull and cargo, reinsurance may be effected in a number of ways, but the methods commonly adopted are those described below under (i) facultative reinsurance, and (ii) (*a*) excess of line covers or treaties, but excess of loss covers are increasingly popular:

(i) *Facultative.* This method is used when the Underwriter is aware of his commitments before the vessel sails, or where he wishes to reinsure risks which are unusually heavy, but which for one reason or another he has been obliged to accept.

(ii) *a Excess of Line.* For protection against an accumulation on a particular vessel, a safer method of reinsurance is by means of an excess of line (referred to as such in the marine market, although it is really a form of surplus reinsurance). Cover is arranged with a number of other Underwriters who each agree to accept a proportion of the reinsuring Underwriter's excesses, up to a fixed limit. A schedule showing the reinsuring Underwriter's retentions for various classes of vessels is prepared and the Reinsurers agree to be bound by all settlements made by the original Underwriter. Bordereaux are sent to the various Reinsurers periodically and policies are usually issued by the Reinsurers in respect of such bordereaux.

(ii) *b Excess of Loss.* This is another form of reinsurance which is sometimes used. This method assumes that the original Underwriter

---

1 Merchants and shippers take out Open Covers with Underwriters, and each Cover has a maximum in any one bottom (or vessel). Obviously, the steamers' names are not known until the shipments go forward, so it may happen that several merchants may make 100 per cent shipments under their Open Covers and all the shipments may go forward in the same vessel.

will carry any loss on any one vessel or location up to an agreed amount and that the Reinsurers will bear the excess over that amount, up to a given limit. This method does away with the need to advise Reinsurers of shipments in which they are interested, which means a large saving of work in the original Underwriter's office. One premium only is paid annually, but the fixing of the premium presents many difficulties.

b Fire Insurance

The main method of reinsurance favoured by fire insurers is that of surplus treaties. There is not very much useage made of the facultative method nowadays. Surplus treaties are arranged in lines so that with a ten-line treaty the direct Insurer is able to place on the treaty ten times his own retention. If, after this, there is still a balance left, it is, of course, necessary to reinsure that balance facultatively. A treaty sometimes requires the direct Insurer to place reinsurances on the treaty to the utmost capacity before going outside for accommodation. Fire Insurers sometimes have two treaties, namely, a first surplus treaty under which amounts in excess of the direct Insurer's retention are accommodated to an agreed number of lines and a second surplus treaty under which a proportion of any further surplus is taken. Yet again, the treaty may be so arranged that particulars of the risks ceded are advised to the Reinsurers periodically, or the treaty may be a 'blind' one, no details of individual cessions being given to the Reinsurers, but merely accounts of premiums and losses submitted once a quarter. Where large fire insurances are arranged on a collective or scheduled basis as explained on page 75, each co-insurer may effect reinsurance for his own share of the risk.

c Theft Insurance

Reinsurances for this class of business are dealt with by surplus treaties, as described above.

d Pecuniary Insurances

Fidelity guarantee reinsurances may be arranged on quota share, surplus or excess of loss bases and sometimes on a facultative basis.

Insurances of Liability

For public liability and motor insurances the excess of loss treaty is the popular type of reinsurance, but for Companies with small accounts a quota share treaty is often used, particularly for motor insurance business, and this is sometimes combined with an excess of loss reinsurance.

Present-day Problems

Reinsurance business is beset with many difficulties and this applies particularly to the purely reinsurance Office.

The acquisition costs of the business have risen considerably. Commission, for example, in the early days of facultative reinsurance ranged from 20 to 25 per cent,[1] but when treaties became general with the greater spread of business, rates of commission advanced to 30 or 40 per cent. If in theory the ceding commission only covers the direct Insurer's original cost, then it is only fair that the ceding Insurer should be recompensed by way of a participation in the profits made by Reinsurers. The amount of such a profit commission varies from 10 to 25 or 33⅓ per cent of the net profit made by the Reinsurer after some allowance (often five per cent of gross premiums received) for the Reinsurer's own expenses.

The very natural desire of Companies to obtain a *quid pro quo* for the business they give makes the demand for reciprocity more and more insistent and it becomes harder and harder to meet. In view of the difficulty of obtaining a reciprocal amount of business for that which they give away, the Companies tend to give more and more attention to profit commission. They may not take advantage of full treaty facilities on poor quality business, so as to 'underwrite' the treaties and guard their profit commission.

All these matters are in essence the internal problem of the Companies and would not affect the insuring public, unless and until they assumed such magnitude as to restrict the reinsurance market, with the result that the Companies would have to restrict the amount they were prepared to grant and so reduce the facilities now available.

1 This does not apply to life reassurance.

The Reinsurance Broker

A reinsurance broker is one who (solely or in addition to direct business) concerns himself with the arranging of reinsurance treaties. He sometimes also places facultative reinsurances.

As reinsurance is transacted beyond national borders, a very specialized knowledge of the various insurance markets and of the standard terms and conditions prevailing is required.

A reinsurance broker may be required to draft the treaty but this is not usual for the large Companies. With reinsurances placed at Lloyd's where the services of a broker are essential, he does this and also does all the detail work.

9 Claims

Claims occur under all types of insurance policies; indeed, payment of claims constitutes the main service of insurance to the community. In the life department, a payment is made under almost every policy[1] because the sum assured is, as a rule, payable on death (which is bound to occur sooner or later), or on an earlier date as, for instance, under an endowment assurance which matures after a fixed term of years. Under other types of insurances, claims may or may not arise, as they depend upon the happening of fortuitous events. Insurers have built a reputation for the prompt and generous treatment of claims, and this is without doubt one of the most effective means of advertisement for any Insurer.

The negotiation and settlement of claims arising in connection with the various classes of insurance involve a measure of similarity of procedure. Nevertheless, the requisite claims technique is one of the most complicated features of insurance business, necessitating a wide knowledge of insurance, a fund of common sense with the good judgment of values which goes with it, a working knowledge of the law, and ability to hold a balance between the interests of the Insured and the Insurers.

In this work on the elements of insurance, it is first of all necessary to deal with those features of claims which are more or less common to all insurances. Later, the points which arise in the handling of claims in the main classes of insurance are considered.

Features in Common

Preliminary Particulars

It is obvious that the Insurers cannot be liable to meet a claim unless they receive notice of that claim. It is important, therefore, to stipulate what will constitute notice to the Insurers of any claim, for

---

1 The exceptions are term assurances and policies which are surrendered or lapsed.

the purposes of the policy under which it arises. If the Insured does not give notice in the prescribed way, then, strictly speaking, the Insurers are not liable for the claim, although it would be only in an extreme case that they would seek to avoid liability on this ground. Early notification is necessary so that the Insurers may make whatever preliminary investigations they may deem expedient. Delay may seriously prejudice their position and this is particularly true of certain types of liability insurance claims.

For the majority of claims, Insurers require completion of their own form as this gives the essential particulars in convenient order.

Immediately the form is received by the Insurers, they confirm that the policy is in force, that the premium has been paid and so satisfy themselves that there is a prima facie claim under the policy. It is customary to extract from their records details of the policy concerned on an appropriate form, in order to avoid constant reference to records throughout the subsequent negotiation and settlement.

The Next Stage

At this stage, the treatment of a claim will largely depend upon its magnitude. If the claim is for a small amount, it is more than probable that the Insurers will send a cheque in full settlement without further inquiry. Nothing creates a better impression upon the policyholder than prompt settlement of claims. Indeed, it helps to counteract the popular misconception that Insurers endeavour to avoid the payment of claims or, at any rate, try to reduce the amount claimed as far as possible. Many claims, however, are for large sums and further details may be required, while negotiations will inevitably take place over a period of time. Here again, it should be noted that the time factor is often to the Insured's advantage, for, where material damage is concerned, he may discover that the extent of his loss is more serious than it was thought to be when the preliminary notification was given to the Insurers.

Serious claims are often dealt with by adjusters and others with specialized knowledge, either on the Insurers' own staff or members of independent firms. This feature will be studied in detail when claims are considered in relation to the main classes of insurance.

Important Factors

Promptitude has been mentioned already, but tact is equally important. If the claims negotiator is not tactful, he often turns a friend into an enemy and seriously prejudices the Insurers' interests. It may be necessary to refuse payment because a claim is outside the terms of the contract. If so, there are always two ways of saying 'no,' and it is essential to give an explanation of the reason why a claim cannot be paid. Most policyholders are reasonable, and if the reason why the claim is not permissible is explained to them, they will usually accept the position with good grace. On the other hand, if they appear to be dissatisfied, it is always important to do everything possible to clear up any misunderstanding, remembering that the layman is not an insurance expert and may not so readily appreciate the position as a trained insurance man. In this connection, tact demands that a policyolder should have the position explained to him in non-technical terms, so that, provided he has ordinary common sense, he will be able to follow the Insurers' reasoning.

All kinds of questions arise which demand a display of tact. By way of illustration, a claim may be made in respect of a peril which is excluded from the contract, or in respect of loss or damage caused by a peril which could have been insured, but which the Insured elected not to cover when he effected the policy. In such circumstances, nothing more effectively convinces the Insured of the equity of the Insurers' attitude than to be able to produce documentary evidence of his decision to bear the particular risk himself, as may happen where a negative answer was given in a proposal form to a question relating to extra benefits. The practical application of the principle of indemnity often involves awkward situations, more particularly when the Insured has an exaggerated idea of the value of his goods, or when he mistakenly thinks that no allowance should be made for depreciation. The position is not difficult to explain and usually results in complete satisfaction.

Another personal quality which may be emphasized is the need for attention to detail. Care should be taken to collect every available piece of information, which must be sifted so that it is ready for use as and when necessary. The majority of claims are amicably settled, but a detail which, when noted, may have appeared to be unimportant may later assume considerable importance because of an unexpected turn of events which could not possibly have been foreseen.

Insurances of the Person

a Life Assurance

i *Death claims.* In order to establish a claim by death under a life policy, documentary evidence must be furnished. The age of the Life

Assured must be confirmed, unless age has already been admitted. Proof of death is also required by means of the death certificate. This will show the cause of death and may indicate a disease which was not disclosed, but which should have been made known to the Assurers at the time of the proposal. Evidence of title is also important, because life policies are frequently assigned. The Office may have notices of assignments in its records, and the date on which notice is received regulates the priority in the right to sue. The policy must be produced and the holder of the policy is usually the person entitled to the money.

The amount payable is calculated, that is, to the sum assured is added any bonus that may have accrued (if a with-profits policy) and any loans and/or outstanding interest deducted.

The Office has an obligation to see that the stamp duty on documents is adequate.

ii *Endowment claims.* Negotiations for the payment of the proceeds of an endowment assurance at maturity are usually started about a month before the due date. Notification of the amount due is sent and the requirements of the Office stated.

Occasionally, life-of-another endowment assurances are granted as, for example, an assurance to a wife on the life of her husband. Title questions can become involved in the event of the failure of the marriage. Positions in which one party has title but the rival claimant has the policy need handling with judgment.

iii *Proof of age.* In life assurance the age of the Life to be assured is important because premium and annuity rates are based upon age attained at inception of the contract. It is preferable that evidence of age should be furnished at the outset, but this is frequently not insisted upon. Such proof, however, is required before a claim is made under whole life policies, and in the event of death occurring during the currency of an endowment assurance. The evidence may be waived under maturing endowment assurances.

Where there has been an overstatement of age, the excess of premium paid may be refunded, with or without interest. In the event of understatement of age, insufficient premiums have been charged and the life Office may—

a charge the appropriate arrears of premium;

b reduce the sum assured; or

c alter the term of an endowment assurance.

iv *Loss of policy*. As mentioned in Chapter 4, life policies are frequently charged or assigned, and proof of title to policy moneys is of the utmost importance when dealing with claims. Production of the policy is required because, normally, possession of the policy indicates a right to a claim under it of all or part of the proceeds. The policy, however, is not the contract but merely evidence of it.

If the policy cannot be produced, the Office must proceed with caution for, prima facie, this raises a presumption that the policy has been charged. No hard and fast rules can be laid down as to the type and extent of the inquiries that should be made when the policy is missing; so much will depend on the particular circumstances.

If the life Office records did not show any notice of interest or any inquiry at any time on the part of a third party, the existing contract could be terminated on the loss of a policy and a new assurance effected in its place by completion of a new proposal form with a statutory declaration of the loss of the original policy. Such a declaration and probably an indemnity also would be required if a copy of the lost policy were issued instead.

Inability to produce the policy after a careful search may mean that it is either genuinely lost or dealt with in some manner, and it is because of the possibility of assignment that life Offices are reluctant to issue a duplicate policy.

b Personal Accident Insurance

The Insured, on notification of a claim, is requested to complete the appropriate form, and he is required to submit a report from his medical attendant. Furthermore, it is a condition of the policy that he shall place himself under the care of a registered medical practitioner.

When the Company have considered the claim form and the medical report form, they will notify the Insured of the benefits payable under the policy, if the claim is admissible. As a rule, the contract provides that no payment shall be made until the termination of disability. This is done in order to assist settlement. Most policies also stipulate that there shall be a limit of 52 or 104 weeks in respect of partial and total incapacity. Periodical inquiries will be made as to the progress of the Insured, and if the period of incapacity seems unduly long for the nature of the injuries concerned, it may be advisable to arrange for an independent examination by the Company's own medical officer. On the other hand, if the claim concerns the loss of limbs or eyesight, capital sums are payable and the insurance automatically terminates. The same applies to fatal injury claims, and the Insurers should be given the opportunity for their representative to be present at any coroner's inquest, fatal inquiry, or post-mortem examination.

Insurances of Property and Pecuniary Insurances

a Marine Insurance

Marine claims differ in many respects from those arising under other classes of business. In the first place, the conditions on which marine risks are covered are many and varied, and when a loss occurs it is just as important to discover the cause as the extent of the loss. Again, in the case of cargo claims, the Insurers, more often than not, deal with a different party from the one taking out the policy, this being because a marine insurance policy may have been assigned. The cause and extent of the loss are agreed with the policyholder by an independent surveyor, who does not concern himself with policy conditions, and the question of liability is decided by the Insurers from documents.

Marine claims fall into the following main groups:

i *Cargo claims.* Many marine cargo policies show the name of the Lloyd's or Companies' agent at destination. It follows that in the event of loss or damage application must be made to this agent for survey.

When an agent, Lloyd's or otherwise, is advised of damage, he will appoint a suitable surveyor to carry out the survey himself. The surveyor will ascertain the cause of the loss and will agree the extent with the consignees. The agent will then issue to the consignees, in return for a fee, a report incorporating the surveyor's findings and supplying information on such points as the date of arrival of the steamer, the date of discharge, date of delivery to consignees' warehouse, and the date of application for survey. This information and other details may be important when liability is under consideration.

If the policy provides for payment of claims at destination, the consignees present the documents to the agent for consideration. If the policy does not so provide, the documents are sent to the Office issuing the policy. These documents comprise the policy, copy of bill of lading, the invoice, and the surveyor's report. The first three of these are known as the documents of title, and, if the policy and bill of lading are properly endorsed, are sufficient evidence on which to pay the holder any claim recoverable under the policy, even though that person may not be the original Assured, provided he has an insurable interest at the time of loss, e.g., a buyer under a c.i.f. (cost, insurance, freight) contract.

The above is based on Company procedure. There is a variation for Lloyd's, because all insurances at Lloyd's must be placed through a Lloyd's broker, and the Assured must therefore authorize the broker to collect the claim instead of dealing with the Insurers direct. Fundamentally, the procedure is similar.

The first step taken by the Underwriter or agent is to examine the policy to ascertain whether the loss is recoverable thereunder. If so, the extent of liability is then ascertained.

In marine insurance, claims are based on the insured value, i.e., the agreed value, and in the case of a total loss the amount insured by the policy is paid. In the case of partial loss, it is necessary to ascertain the percentage of depreciation, which is applied to the insured value. When goods arrive damaged at destination, the percentage of depreciation is ascertained by comparing the gross sound arrived value with the gross damaged arrived value. These values are based on market values on arrival, and if there are fluctuations in the market, the sound and damaged values will rise and fall in sympathy. Therefore, the percentage of depreciation will always remain constant. The surveyor will endeavour to agree the depreciation with the consignees. If agreement cannot be reached, it may be necessary to sell the goods in order to ascertain the depreciation. If this is necessary, the gross proceeds are compared with the gross amount which the goods would have realized if sold in sound condition on the same day and the percentage of depreciation calculated. The Underwriter then pays the same percentage of the insured value plus sale charges and survey fees.

Example

Gross sound arrived value of goods		£900.00
Realized gross at sale		£450.00
	Loss	£450.00 (or 50%)
Insured value—£1,000.	50% =	£500.00
	Sale charges	10.00
	Survey fees	5.25
	Claim	£515.25

By using gross values the true depreciation is obtained. In this connection, it will be seen that if the sound value of the goods rose to £1,200, one would expect to realize £600 from goods damaged to the same extent. By using gross values the percentage of depreciation remains constant, irrespective of the state of the market. If items such as duty and sale charges were taken into account, the depreciation would vary during market fluctuations, owing to the fact that the same amount would be deducted from both sound and damaged values.

ii *Hull claims.* In hull claims, the cost of repairs is paid in full, subject to the limit of the insured value, and not as a proportion of the insured value as in the case of cargo.

When a vessel sustains damage, the brokers advise the leading Underwriters, who appoint a surveyor to represent them. The surveyor appointed by Underwriters inspects the damage in company with the ship's surveyor, and a specification of the necessary repairs is drawn up. A price for the work is obtained from a suitable repairer and, if approved, the contract is arranged.

When the work is completed, all the documents and vouchers are put into the hands of a professional average adjuster, who examines them and states the amount recoverable under the policy. In many cases, the shipowner takes advantage of the fact that the vessel is under repair to have other work done on his own account, and this usually involves an apportionment of certain expenses.

iii *Collision claims.* Damage caused by a vessel to another, i.e., as a third party liability, has been held not to fall within the scope of an ordinary marine policy, as it was not loss of or damage to the subject-matter insured, but in practice the clauses which are used for the insurance of hulls do agree by a *separate* contract to cover loss of or damage to another vessel when caused by the insured vessel, to the extent of three-fourths, it being customary for the remaining fourth to be insured by a mutual Club (known as a Protection and Indemnity Club) in which the shipowners' vessel is entered. This cover is only in respect of damage caused to another ship or vessel, its cargo or loss of use of the other vessel, and does not extend to cover other property, e.g., piers and stages, and loss of life.

iv *Freight claims.* Freight, i.e., reward for carrying goods, or hire money for chartering of a vessel or part thereof, provides an insurable interest. It is a pecuniary interest and the claims are adjusted on the principle of indemnity. Freight paid by a merchant 'lost or not lost' in respect of his goods which are shipped, i.e., prepaid freight, does not require a special insurance as the amount of freight prepaid is merged into the values of the goods, and the insured value is therefore sufficient to cover both the value of the goods and the freight paid thereon.

Other features

i *General average.* General average is peculiar alike to cargo, ship, or freight (see p. 183). It is dominated to a great extent by the York-Antwerp Rules[1] and has the result of spreading the loss and expense incurred for the general safety over the various interests concerned. General average consists of sacrifice and expenditure, and the resultant amount assessed to be due from the respective parties is called general average contribution. General average is usually recoverable under a policy covering the ship, cargo or freight. In the case of an accident producing a general average, it is customary for a firm of average adjusters to be appointed. If there is particular average damage to the ship, the adjusters will draw up one statement which will cover this and the general average contribution that is due from the various parties. When general average is incurred, security is taken by the shipowners from the cargo before it is delivered, either by requesting payment of a cash deposit or submission of an Underwriters' guarantee.

ii *Salvage.* While the popular meaning of this word is the recovery of what is left after loss, it also signifies the amount of remuneration to a salvor who is employed to rescue a ship and/or cargo *under contract*, for example, under Lloyd's Standard Form of Salvage Agreement. Alternatively, salvage may be awarded to a salvor who has been instrumental in helping to salve a ship and/or its cargo independently of any contract; in other words, salvage may be the voluntary act of a third party.

Salvage charges are not general average nor sue and labour charges. In practice, however, they may be apportioned on the lines of general average and are recoverable from Insurers if incurred in connection with a peril insured against.

1 The York-Antwerp Rules regulate the adjustment and apportionment of general average. They were drafted as the result of international agreement and were last amended in 1974.

iii *Sue and labour charges.* Every policy contains a clause which provides that:

'In case of any loss or misfortune it shall be lawful to the Assured ... to sue, labour, and travel for, in and about the defence, safeguards, and recovery of the said goods ..., and ship, ... without prejudice to this insurance; to the charges whereof we, the Assurers, will contribute ...'

In other words, this is an encouragement to the Assured to take all steps to minimize or avert further loss, and the Insurers, in their turn, undertake to pay the charges, even in addition to a total loss claim.

b Fire Insurance

Many fire claims are for small amounts only, such as damage to carpets by live coals falling from grates and the burning of clothing while airing. It is usual to obtain completion of a claim form, and so long as the policy is in force and covers the property concerned, a cheque is usually sent by return of post.

Other fire claims, however, require detailed investigation. Such investigation may be undertaken by the Insurers' own officials if the amounts involved are not considerable, but as a rule large claims are passed to a firm of independent adjusters who investigate on the Insurers' behalf and in due course submit their report recommending payment of an agreed amount.

Practical features. Under the conditions of the standard fire policy, the Insurers may elect to reinstate or replace the insured property. The majority of fire claims are settled by means of cash payments, but where, for example, there is refusal to reduce an exaggerated claim, or a request to reinstate under Statute,[1] the Insurers will adopt this course. If they elect to reinstate, they are bound to do so and cannot later make a cash payment instead.

In the case of a claim for building damage, the Insured usually obtains an estimate from his builders. The adjusters check the specification, quantities, and prices, and when agreement has been reached, the Insured signs a form of acceptance, whereupon the Insurers settle the claim by a cash payment. The cost of architects'

1 In order to prevent arson, the Fires Prevention (Metropolis) Act, 1774, requires Insurers to expend insurance money in reinstatement up to the limit of the sum insured, if requested to do so by any party having an interest in the property or upon suspicion that a claim is fraudulent.

and surveyors' fees for plans, specifications, quantities, and tenders is usually borne by the Insured, unless there is a special item in the policy to cover such cost.

Where the claim relates to goods, it is necessary to take into account depreciation or appreciation in order to observe the basic principle of indemnity. Reasonable business proof of loss is required, but the production of invoices or other evidence of cost is not necessary where the insurance is based on a professional inventory and valuation.

If the fire has been occasioned by the negligence of a third party, the Insurers by the exercise of subrogation rights may be able to recover from that third party any amount paid under the policy.

Loss apportionments: several Insurers. Frequently, several Offices will be interested in a loss, and this necessitates apportionments between such Offices.

If all policies cover the same property and are worded in a similar manner they are said to be concurrent, even if the amounts are not the same. When the property covered is not identical (e.g., an item in one Insurer's policy may cover stock only and the other policy, or policies, may contain an item covering both stock and fixtures and fittings), the policies are said to be non-concurrent.

Where concurrent policies (i.e., where the terms of the contracts are identical) are concerned, they contribute to a loss *pro rata* according to sums insured. The position is more complicated if non-concurrent policies (i.e., where the terms of the contracts vary) are involved. Moreover, average (see p. 184) introduces a further factor so that there are concurrent average policies and non-concurrent average policies. The extent of under-insurance is then an important consideration in assessing the Insurers' liability.

There are various well-known methods of apportionment, but it is unnecessary in this book to go into further detail.

Salvage. In many cases, there is salvage, but the Insured has no right of abandonment of salvage. The value of salvage must be taken into account in assessing the loss, although, if they choose, the Insurers may pay in full and take over the salvage.

c Theft Insurance

Theft, 'all risks,' and similar claims which are in respect of the Insured's own property or for which he is responsible are dealt with on the same general lines as fire claims. The Insured is required to complete the appropriate claim form, to notify the police, and to furnish to the Insurers full details of the property lost, stolen, or destroyed, with particulars of the value of the property at the date of purchase or acquisition, and the present value. As these policies are contracts of indemnity it is, of course, necessary to make allowance for depreciation or appreciation, within the terms of the contract.

If the insurance is based upon an inventory and valuation made by a professional valuer, this forms the basis of settlement, subject to allowance for depreciation or appreciation. Occasionally, agreed value (also known as 'valued') policies are issued and, in the event of total loss, the agreed values are payable without any question of depreciation. Jewellery and fur claims are sometimes settled by giving an order for an agreed sum upon any specified jeweller or furrier.

The Insurers are usually given the option under the terms of the policy to reinstate, replace, or repair the property, or to make a cash settlement.

d Motor Insurance

The majority of own damage claims under motor policies are dealt with by means of authorizing the necessary repairs to be effected and paying the account. If claims are substantial, they may be placed in the hands of the Company's own engineer or of a consulting automobile engineer. With a view to controlling the cost of repairs to damaged cars, the British Insurance Association have introduced a pilot Garage Pricing Scheme (see p. 210).

e Fidelity Guarantee

Claims under this heading are divisible into the four main sections of the business—commercial guarantees, local government guarantees, Court bonds, and Government bonds.

Commercial fidelity guarantees are based upon the employer's statement, in which are given full details of the system of check and method of supervision, and the first step in dealing with a claim is to ascertain in what way the system of check or method of supervision has broken down, and, incidentally, to make certain that no changes have been made under this heading since the guarantee was effected. If the defaulter can be traced, he should be interviewed as soon as practicable in order to recover, if possible, any of the money which was taken and has not yet been spent, while he may have life policies or other valuable securities, the benefit of which can be obtained in reduction of the amount of the loss. The loss itself is as a rule easily ascertainable by reference to the Insured's books.

Claims under many Court and Government bonds do not permit of the usual investigation because the guarantors, by the terms of the contract, agree to accept the certificate from the authority concerned, signed by its appropriate official, as evidence of the amount of the loss, without any further question. This also applies, in many instances, to claims made under guarantees to local government authorities.

Insurances of Liability

Three important questions arise in connection with all claims under liability indemnities: (*a*) are the Insurers liable to indemnify the Insured under the terms of the policy? (*b*) is the Insured legally liable to the third party? and (*c*) if so, to what extent? The answers to questions (*b*) and (*c*) are often doubtful, particularly where bodily injuries are caused, so that discussion or even litigation may be needed to clarify the position.

By the terms of the policy, the Insured is required to give notice of all accidents, whether or not a claim has been made. This enables the Insurers to investigate the circumstances forthwith so as to be ready to deal with any claim which may subsequently be intimated by the injured party.

The Insured is usually required to complete a notice of accident form, but where the accident appears to have been serious, the Insurers will invariably include in their investigations a visit to the scene of the accident. In the case of road accidents, an abstract of the police report may be obtained as this may give the names of additional witnesses. All witnesses should be interviewed and statements obtained from them.

If there is no defence on the grounds of liability, settlement on the best terms must be made, with a binding discharge obtained from the third party. If, however, the claim involves serious bodily injuries, an immediate settlement is not practicable; a medical examination should be carried out in the presence of the claimant's doctor. Where the injuries have proved fatal, the Insurers arrange for legal representation of the Insured at the inquest or fatal inquiry. It is more than probable that the third party (or his legal personal representative) will have instructed solicitors to act for him, with whom a compromise settlement may eventually be made or proceedings may be instituted.

Sometimes, the third party is insured and the claim can be brought within the scope of a claims-settling agreement with the other Insurers. This often happens where motor vehicle road accidents are concerned.

Marine third party claims have been dealt with above (see p. 177).

Appendix on Average

Average affects the negotiation and settlement of various types of property claims, as summarized below.

a Marine Insurance

The word 'average' is of French origin and it has a special meaning in marine insurance—entirely different from the significance of the word in other classes of insurance. The marine insurance meaning, briefly, is 'damage or partial loss,' hence the terms 'particular average' and 'general average.'

Particular average relates to partial loss or damage to ship or cargo proximately caused by a peril insured against and which is fortuitous. Examples are damage caused by fire to ship or cargo or heavy weather damage.

General average is a contract of affreightment liability and does not apply to marine insurance unless the property is insured; it means either sacrifices of property or expenditure as, for instance, when the common adventure is imperilled, and the object of the sacrifice is the preservation of the common adventure. Such losses are made good by the contribution of all the parties concerned, and may or may not be covered by insurance. Illustrations of general average losses are the burning of ship's stores and gear as fuel, the breaking down of bulkheads in an endeavour to extinguish fire on board, and, in the case of cargo, the jettisoning of cargo for the purpose of lightening a ship when in peril, or damage caused by water or chemicals used to extinguish fire. Where there is a general average adjustment and insurance is involved, the marine Insurers have a direct liability for sacrifice with subrogated rights and also pay the contribution in question, provided that the general average has arisen as the result of a peril insured against.

In marine policies the Memorandum excludes certain particular average losses if under a stated percentage unless the warranty is broken by a named casualty. But in practice most policies are issued irrespective of percentage, although quite a number persist as, for example, 'To pay Average if amounting to 3 per cent each package or on the whole.' In other words, if the claim is under 3 per cent, it is not paid; if it is over, then it is paid in full without deduction.

b Fire Insurance

Average has a different meaning in fire insurance. All fire policies, with the exception of domestic ones, are now subject to average,[1] so that, if the sum insured does not adequately represent the full value of the property at risk, the Insured will not be fully indemnified.

Pro rata condition of average. Certain fire insurances have always been subject to the *pro rata* condition of average as, for example, the insurance of building plant and materials on a building site, where the amount of property at risk will vary from time to time. In the case of insurance on buildings, in the general way a separate sum insured must be allocated to each building, but if a proposer insists on two separate buildings being covered in one sum, the insurance is made subject to the *pro rata* condition of average. The condition reads as follows:

> Whenever a sum insured is declared to be subject to average, if the property covered thereby shall at the breaking out of any fire or at the commencement of any destruction of or damage to such property by any other peril hereby insured against be collectively of greater value than such sum insured, then the Insured shall be considered as being his own Insurer for the difference and shall bear a rateable share of the loss accordingly.

It will be recognized that this condition is a protection to the Insurers against under-insurance; thus if the sum insured is £50,000

---

1 In the report of the Monopolies Commission on the supply in the United Kingdom of fire insurance on property in the United Kingdom, 1972, it was recommended that the application of average to all industrial and commercial fire insurances should be discontinued. Admittedly, average is a rough and ready methcd of adjusting premiums and achieving equity between Insured. Nevertheless, Insurers will no doubt seek to retain it until some better system is devised for dealing with under-insurance.

and the total value of the property at risk is £100,000, then if a loss of £25,000 is sustained, the sum payable is as follows:

$$\frac{£50,000}{£100,000} \times £25,000 = £12,500$$

In fire insurance, 'first loss' policies are sometimes issued. This is where the sum insured is deliberately fixed at less than the full value of the property insured. Such policies, other than those insuring sprinkler leakage, incorporate a form of average which usually relates the declared value of the property on which the premium is calculated to the value at risk at the time of the loss.

Special condition of average. The special condition of average, otherwise known as the 75 per cent or three-fourths clause, is applied to the insurance of growing crops and agricultural produce, other than livestock. Its object is similar to that of the *pro rata* condition of average, but instead of requiring the proposer to insure for the full value, the sum insured must represent at least 75 per cent of the value of the property at risk. This modification arises out of the fact that the quantity of property at risk on a farm varies considerably over the year and it would be unreasonable to impose the ordinary condition of average, whereby the Insured is prejudiced if the sum insured at the time of the loss represents something less than the full value of the property at risk. The clause reads as follows:

Whenever a sum insured is declared to be subject to the special condition of average, then if such sum shall at the breaking out of any fire or at the commencement of any destruction of or damage to the property by any other peril hereby insured against be less than three-fourths of the value of the property insured in that amount, the Insured shall be considered as being his own Insurer for the difference between the sum insured and the full value of the property insured at the time of such fire or at the commencement of such destruction or damage and shall bear a rateable share of the loss accordingly.

The application of the condition is similar in principle to that set out above. For example, if the sum insured is £6,000 and the full value of the property is £10,000 with a loss of £2,000, then the condition applies because the sum insured is less than three quarters of the total value of the property at risk, namely, £7,500. The sum payable is as follows:

$$\frac{£6,000}{£10,000} \times £2,000 = £1,200$$

Two conditions of average. The first of the two conditions is the *pro rata* one, and the second is really a contribution clause. The two conditions are set out together as follows:

1 Whenever a sum insured is declared to be subject to average, if the property covered thereby shall at the breaking out of any fire or at the commencement of any destruction of or damage to such property by any other peril hereby insured against be collectively of greater value than such sum insured, then the Insured shall be considered as being his own Insurer for the difference and shall bear a rateable share of the loss accordingly.

2 But if any of the property included in such average shall at the breaking out of any fire, or at the commencement of any destruction of or damage to such property by any other peril hereby insured against, be also covered by any other more specific insurance, i.e., by an insurance which at the time of such fire or at the commencement of such destruction or damage, applies to part only of the property actually at risk and protected by this insurance and to no other property whatsoever, then this policy shall not insure the same except only as regards any excess of value beyond the amount of such more specific insurance or insurances, which said excess is declared to be under the protection of this policy and subject to average as aforesaid.

The first condition is applied to:

a Insurances covering merchandise at public wharves, docks and warehouses, i.e., mercantile insurances;

b An insurance which is so arranged that there are specific items covering contents of specified buildings and a floating item covering the contents of all buildings to apply in any loss after the specific items have been exhausted. In such an instance it is usual to require that all insurances covering the property be worded concurrently. The floating item is also made subject to the second condition.

c Theft Insurance

Theft policies are sometimes made subject to average. A theft policy is issued subject to the full value being insured, or else the full value is declared, and if the insurance is for a lesser sum—a 'first loss' contract—the rate of premium is adjusted accordingly. In this way theft practice differs from fire practice where it is not customary to adjust rates according to the amount at risk. Average, however, is not invariably applied to 'first loss' policies.

It sometimes happens that when a claim arises and it is found that the full value warranty has been disregarded, the Insurers prefer not to repudiate liability, as they have the right to do, but rather to settle a claim by applying average, subject to the Insured agreeing to revise the sum insured for the future.

10 Insurance Administration

In any business enterprise, good organization is an essential feature of efficient management. This is specially true of insurance because of the complexity of the business and the importance of providing first-class service to the insuring public. Insurance is old-established, and satisfactory methods of general organization have been evolved from long experience. Organization, however, can never be static, because there are always new methods being devised in office practice generally.

It is no exaggeration to say that Insurance Offices, generally speaking, are in the forefront in the adoption of new ideas so that, for instance, automation now plays an important part in the work of practically every Insurance Office.

While there are different sections of insurance, the general principles of organization and routine are the same; they are merely adapted to the special needs of each section. Again, individual Offices vary in their methods.

Insurance is a highly skilled and specialized business and demands of those responsible for its administration qualifications of the highest degree. There is ample scope for initiative and the use of different talents in the conduct of the business. It has often been remarked that there are no insuperable barriers in the business, so that every junior has the possibility of eventually rising to the position of chief executive.

Insurance Organization

A traditional pattern of organization[1] is shown in the chart on page 190, but the classification is not rigid. Moreover, the chart is not a guide to seniority. The division between the executive and the staff cannot be clearly defined, as much depends upon the size of the

1 In recent years, however, as a result of investigations by management consultants, there is a growing tendency to move towards a functional type of organization, such as is illustrated by the chart on p. 196.

Company. Generally, however, all men with titled positions (e.g., general manager, fire manager, accident superintendent) rank as insurance officers, while the remainder of the staff are insurance officials, or clerks. There is a considerable variety of titles, dependent to some extent upon the size of the organization. By way of illustration, the offices of general manager and secretary may be combined, departmental heads may be termed managers or superintendents, or there may be both managers and superintendents.

HEAD OFFICE

Board of Directors

The directors of an Insurance Company are not always full-time directors. They may be persons of standing in the professional, commercial or social world, and they are appointed because of the knowledge of their particular sphere which they can bring to the deliberations of the board. The modern tendency, however, is to appoint senior executives from within the Company to a seat on the board. Sometimes, elevation to a seat on the board may occur at the time of retirement of a general manager, because this is a way in which to retain his counsel which, after a lifetime in the business, must be of obvious advantage to the board.

The day-to-day conduct of the business is in the hands of the executive (discussed later), but the board concerns itself with questions of policy, and those directors who are bankers, lawyers, or specialists in any other sections of the business world can bring their specialized knowledge to bear upon the Company's affairs in the interests of all concerned. It is nowadays unusual to have a restricted directorate as, for instance, a Company originally formed to cater for the legal profession, with a provision in its Articles of Association that directors must be either barristers or solicitors. The general constitution of the board and retirement of directors in rotation will be governed by the Articles of Association and by the Companies Acts.

There is a chairman of the board and as a rule also a vice-chairman. In addition, the board is usually split into various committees, or a special committee or sub-committee may be appointed for consideration of some particular problem and report to the board. The chairman presides at all board meetings and, while the board appoints a chairman annually, it is customary to elect the same

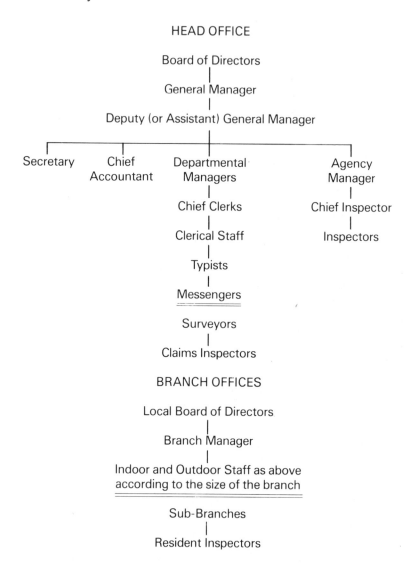

HEAD OFFICE

Board of Directors
|
General Manager
|
Deputy (or Assistant) General Manager

| Secretary | Chief Accountant | Departmental Managers | Agency Manager |

Departmental Managers
|
Chief Clerks
|
Clerical Staff
|
Typists
|
Messengers

Agency Manager
|
Chief Inspector
|
Inspectors

Surveyors
|
Claims Inspectors

BRANCH OFFICES

Local Board of Directors
|
Branch Manager
|
Indoor and Outdoor Staff as above
according to the size of the branch

Sub-Branches
|
Resident Inspectors

N.B. – This table is not complete. In a life office, for instance, there is the actuary who may, or may not, be also life manager. There may also be an investment manager and a registrar. Some motor Insurers have their own staff engineers.

The secretary and chief accountant have clerical and typing staffs, typists may work for the surveyors and inspectors, and the messengers serve the office as a whole.

person over a term of years. The directors usually retire[1] once every three years and, if eligible,[2] may seek re-election.

General Manager

The general manager is the chief executive officer of an Insurance Company unless there happens to be a managing director. This official as a rule does not deal with underwriting and departmental problems, which are in the hands of departmental managers, but the latter are always free to consult the general manager when in their opinion it is necessary to do so. He is concerned with policy, and visits to branches and connections at home and abroad will fall within his duties.

In smaller Companies or Companies transacting one class of business only, as, for instance, life assurance, the general manager may combine with his duties those of actuary, and may therefore be concerned not only with general policy but also with underwriting. In the larger Companies there is an increasing tendency to share the responsibilities of general management among two, three or more general managers, with a chief general manager at the top of the pyramid.

Deputy (or Assistant) General Manager

This is often the title of the second executive and it is usually the stepping-stone to general managership. Sometimes, the title is deputy general manager, which implies that he acts in the place of the general manager when the latter is absent and may therefore suggest a slightly senior position to that of assistant general manager. In large Companies, there may be more than one assistant general manager.

Secretary

The secretary of an Insurance Company, like the secretary of any other company, is primarily concerned with board matters, including the preparation of the agenda and the drafting of the minutes, and he must see that the Company conforms with all legal requirements. Staff matters, welfare, maintenance and repairs sometimes fall within

1 This periodical retirement of directors likewise applies to the chairman.
2 The Companies Act, 1948, provides that a director who has reached the age of 70 may not be re-elected unless the Company in general meeting passes an ordinary resolution of which special notice has to be given.

the purview of the secretary. He may also deal with investments, subject to the board of directors, but there may be an investment manager who is a financial specialist. The directors are as a rule influential business men, and they naturally take a special interest in the Company's investment policy. Insurance Companies often grant loans, and the secretary, working in collaboration with the Company's solicitors, arranges for the preparation of mortgage deeds and for the repayments. Some Companies have a separate registrar whose duties concern the keeping of the register of shareholders, the issue of notices, registration of transfers, and payment of dividends.

Assistant Secretary

As the term implies, this official assists the secretary, but if the Company is a small one there is as a rule a secretary only.

Chief Accountant

The chief accountant is responsible for the accounts and the preparation of the annual returns. He has assistants according to the size of the Company.

Departmental Managers

The head of each of the main departments has a title and is of executive rank, such as fire manager or accident manager. The actuary is a very important official of every life Assurance Company. Directly under the departmental managers there may be assistant managers or superintendents, while in some Companies there is a superintendent and not a manager of each department, as, for example, fire superintendent or accident superintendent (see also p. 189). Whether or not the departmental chief is known as a manager or superintendent, he is directly responsible to the general manager. In the marine department, the corresponding official is known as the marine underwriter. Then again, some Companies have titled officials in charge of claims as, for instance, a claims manager or claims superintendent. In marine insurance the official is called an adjuster of claims, which is not to be confused with average adjusters who are independent firms of professional adjusters.

Clerical staff. There is usually a chief clerk in each department, whose responsibility is normally the general supervision of the department, and under him senior clerks or section leaders who have the charge of special sections, according to the way in which the work of the office is divided.

Typists. Most Companies have a separate typing section and this is in the charge of a superintendent or head typist. Under her there are the shorthand typists, the audio typists, and copy typists, including policy writers. The chief officials usually each have a private secretary who is separate and distinct, that is, not attached to the typing pool.

Messengers. There is a housekeeper or head messenger[1] and, under him, messengers and office cleaners. The messengers usually deal with the dispatch of the post; one is normally assigned to the general manager and to each departmental manager. A messenger may also operate the telephone switchboard, or there may be a separate telephonist.

Surveyors

There is usually a chief surveyor and under him a number of surveyors according to the size of the Company. They may be divided into fire and accident surveyors, or some surveyors may undertake both fire and accident surveys, particularly in connection with theft and public liability proposals. The term 'surveyor' is, of course, used in a special sense because the primary function of a surveyor is to estimate the risk from an insurance point of view and to suggest improvements in the risk; insurance surveyors do not necessarily possess professional surveying qualifications, but there is an increasing tendency for them to become Surveyor Members of the Incorporated Association of Architects and Surveyors.

Claims Inspectors

These officials are part of the claims department. As a rule, they are mainly concerned with accident losses, as any large fire losses are dealt with by independent adjusters. Once legal proceedings are commenced, the case must go to a solicitor to enter appearance; the claims inspector, however, will have made most of the preliminary inquiries and he can thenceforth work in close conjunction with the Company solicitor.

1 The housekeeper and head messenger are sometimes two different persons.

Agency Manager

The agency manager is concerned with the home business-getting organization or field staff. Some Companies do not have a separate agency manager, these functions being performed by the chief executive official or by an assistant general manager. In any event, the importance of this section of the work cannot be over-emphasized, because new business is the life-blood of any Insurance Company.

An agency manager has control of the agency department. The work of the department varies with different Companies but it normally deals with the appointment of agents; recruitment, training and control of new business inspectors; allocation of areas of operation of branches, district offices and sub-district offices; appointment of local directors; statistics of new business; advice to senior management on transfer and promotion of outdoor staff; and in some Offices publicity comes within this department. As a rule, the agency department does not deal with overseas or with marine business.

Inspectors

Inspectors may be divided into chief, senior, and junior inspectors. They are primarily concerned with the general cultivation of agencies and with obtaining business, although they may settle minor losses, collect overdue accounts, undertake small surveys, and generally represent the Company in their districts.

BRANCH OFFICES

Local Board of Directors

Some Branch Offices have a local board of directors, composed as a rule of prominent men in local professional, commercial, or social life. They are accordingly chosen because of their local standing and their ability to influence business to the Company.

Branch Manager

The branch manager must possess wide knowledge, for any fair-sized branch deals at first hand with most of the problems encountered at Head Office. The success of a branch manager, moreover, is largely assessed in terms of new business premium income of a profitable nature, and much of his time may be spent in outdoor work. Inspectors of agents are, of course, attached to each branch and usually work directly under the branch manager, unless there is an agency super-intendent. The remaining personnel varies with the size of the branch. A full branch is one which has authority to underwrite (referring special cases only to Head Office) and issue policies and settle claims, whereas a sub-branch, which may be little more than a call office, is usually in the charge of a resident secretary or resident inspector who is responsible to the branch manager of the full branch.

City branches. These are general public branches in a Company's home town, and sometimes the city branch is housed in the same building as Head Office.

New Trends in Insurance Organization

Fundamental changes are taking place in the organization of Insur-ance Companies and, as indicated on p. 196, the traditional pattern of organization is giving place to a new concept of functional organization. Although new to insurance, this concept has been in evidence in industry generally for a number of years, and several factors have led to its introduction into the world of insurance. These include the recurrence of mergers—the modern term for amalgam-ations—which have given rise to larger groups, with the need for rationalization, the increasing use of management consultants by Insurance Companies, and the new emphasis which is being placed on profitability. It has been said, 'The typical insurance company (i.e., organized on the traditional pattern) is not organized like a business firm at all. It is organized like a giant professional office.'

The chart on p. 196 indicates how some Companies are tackling this problem by changing their Head Offices so that they are organized more by function rather than by different types of underwriting.

HEAD OFFICE

Chief Underwriter

The fire and accident departments are merged into one general department under the control of the chief Underwriter. This enables the insurances of a particular client to be handled by one Underwriter instead of by several separate Underwriters.

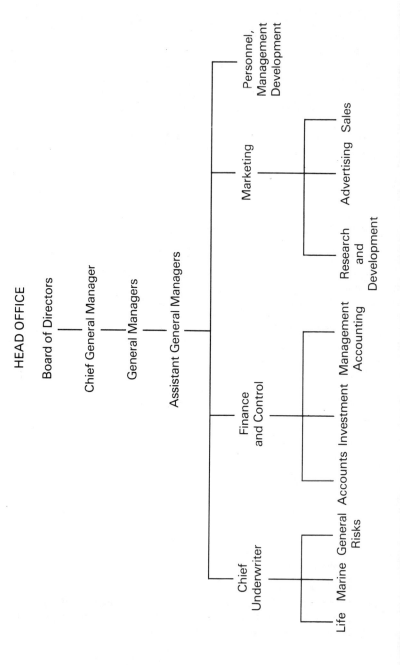

HEAD OFFICE

Board of Directors

Chief General Manager

General Managers

Assistant General Managers

Chief Underwriter
- Life
- Marine
- General Risks

Finance and Control
- Accounts
- Investment
- Management Accounting

Marketing
- Research and Development
- Advertising
- Sales

Personnel, Management Development

Marketing Manager

Marketing is treated as a separate function and the marketing manager carries out the duties of the agency manager under the traditional organization, but also uses more sophisticated techniques such as market research and product development.

Financial Manager

Other activities which have been traditionally part of the chief executive's responsibility include budgeting, profitability and investment, but in the new organization these responsibilities are entrusted to the overall control of a financial manager who may well have had similar responsibilities in other industrial concerns.

Personnel Manager

For many years staff recruitment, training and career development were handled by the secretarial department, although more recently some of the larger Offices have appointed staff managers and training officers responsible to the chief executive. However, the modern functional trend is to appoint a personnel manager who is a trained specialist in this field and who may well have qualifications such as a diploma of the Institute of Personnel Management. The personnel manager has his own organization which has a responsibility for manpower planning, recruitment, training and management development.

Agents

The majority of new business obtained by Insurance Companies comes to them through brokers and agents. At the same time they also accept business direct from the public, and a few Companies have no agents at all, securing all their business direct. In fact, there is an increasing emphasis today on direct selling, with some Companies marketing insurance through a shop in a store. Companies operating pilot schemes of this nature report favourably on their experience, since the counter service in the big stores jogs people's memories and has resulted in many enquiries and much high quality business, particularly in the field of motor insurance. Alongside of this, many of the smaller branches are being replaced by compact selling units comprising one or two salesmen supported by a small clerical staff. (Canadian and Australian life Offices operating in the UK also engage in direct selling, and their outside representatives are usually called Underwriters.)

The term 'agent' covers a wide variety of intermediaries and may relate to agents for the Insured, to agents for the Insurers, or to those who act in both capacities. There are various part-time agents, such as solicitors and accountants, who may do little more than introduce business, leaving the Company to arrange all details with the proposer. Then there is the insurance broker and the Lloyd's broker who are members of the British Insurance Brokers' Association and who are full-time specialists (of professional status), able and willing to give their connections expert advice, dealing with new business, renewals, and claims.

Agents are remunerated by commission, the rates varying for the different classes of business. Although an insurance broker is remunerated by the Insurers, he is agent for the Insured as well as for the Insurers.[1]

Credit Agents

A credit (or account) agent is formally appointed by the Insurers and his powers are usually set out in a letter of appointment. He issues renewal notices on behalf of the Insurers and gives receipts for premiums collected which are remitted to the Office, as a rule quarterly, less commission. He may grant cover, within limits, for certain classes of business without reference to the Office.

Cash Agents

A cash agent is not empowered to grant cover or to issue renewal receipts. As a rule, he merely introduces business, on which he is paid commission, all details including renewals being dealt with by the Insurers direct. Sometimes, however, renewal notices are sent to cash agents.

---

1 A contrary view was expressed in the Queen's Bench Division of the Commercial Court in *Anglo-African Merchants* v. *Bayley Ltd. and Anr.*, [1969] 2 All ER 421. This was followed in *North & South Trust Co.* v. *Berkeley* (1971), 1 All ER 980, when it was held to be inconsistent for the agents of the plaintiff to act as agents of the defendant without the plaintiff's leave. If this should become settled law an insurance broker would be in all matters relating to the placing of the insurance the agent of the insured only.

Home Service Agents

Home service agents are in a class by themselves. They are employees of industrial life offices on a full-time basis, collecting weekly or monthly and other premiums at the homes of the policyholders, and obtaining new business.

Agents Overseas

There is also the type of agent appointed in foreign countries with very wide powers, issuing policies and paying claims, and merely accounting periodically to Head Office in this country. Such agents are granted a power of attorney.

Centralization and Decentralization

In the course of time, many Branch Offices have been opened by Insurers in view of keen competition and the desire to give the best possible service. This development is sometimes criticized as wasteful, although much depends upon the type of business and nature of the Insurers' connections. There are no hard and fast rules, and although there has been this marked tendency towards decentralization, there have been forces operating in the opposite direction such as the amalgamation of Companies, whether or not they happen to retain their own identity to preserve goodwill, and the introduction of computers.

The merits and demerits of centralization and decentralization were usefully summarized in a lecture delivered before The Insurance Institute of London on the 17 December, 1945, by Mr W. L. Catchpole, entitled 'Insurance Organization: Centralization or Decentralization?'

Centralization
Merits: 1 Uniformity of policy, practice, and routine is attained.
2 The fullest and most economical use is made of mechanized methods.
3 Experts and specialists are concentrated at the most advantageous centre.
4 The branch is relieved of work which impedes business-getting.

Demerits: 1 Concentration of work in locations where overhead charges may be heavy.

2 Separation of the administration from healthy direct contact with the public.

3 Enterprise in gaining public favour tends to be replaced by an unhealthy rivalry for important Head Office administrative posts.

4 Possible deterioration in the status of the majority of the employees.

5 Concentration of power in the hands of a few.

Decentralization

Merits: 1 It falls into line with enlightened democratic sentiment.

2 It gives power to local officials who understand local conditions best.

3 It provides the public with a prompt and efficient local service.

4 It has a stimulating effect on branch staff morale.

5 It encourages group co-operation, thereby improving the standing of the industry and contributing to social progress.

6 It teaches the branch staff.

Demerits: 1 'Little despotisms' may arise at the branches.

2 Experts may be uneconomically dispersed.

3 Too much branch freedom may obstruct the smooth working of the organization.

4 Branches may be swamped with routine work.

5 Wasteful effort in trying to make every branch expert in everything.

Since this summary was drawn up in 1945 much has been done by Insurers to mitigate the demerits of both systems. For example, under a centralized system the concentration of work has been moved from London and the big cities to centres where overhead expenses are less heavy. Regionalization, described below, has helped to overcome the problem of an uneconomic dispersal of experts in decentralized systems. In addition, progressive personnel policies designed to provide the maximum of job satisfaction have eliminated many of the problems of 'unhealthy rivalry', 'deterioration of status' and 'little despotisms'.

Regional or Zonal Organization

Regional or zonal organization is a recent development of home branch control. The United Kingdom is divided, according to the spread of business, into six or more regions and each region comprises several counties. There is a regional or zonal office, which is virtually a 'head office' with a regional or zonal manager in charge, and the office is very largely autonomous in its own area. Each regional office has several branches under it. The regional office is naturally subject to general head office control which, as a rule, directs policy only. This is a special type of decentralization.

The system is designed to give more effective local service, since business is speeded up by the elimination, as far as possible, of the need for reference over long distances. Initiative is thrown outwards, while branches are made production centres without the need for each branch to have its team of technical experts. The technicians can be concentrated in the regional office.

Those who do not favour this system claim that the advantages of expedition are relatively illusory in view of telephone and postal communications, and that it is uneconomical to have six or more offices which are virtually 'head offices' with specialists at work on the same problems. Added weight is given to the views of opponents of regionalization by the increasing use of computers with random access facilities. On the other hand, regionalization goes a long way towards combining the merits of centralized and decentralized systems while at the same time avoiding many of the demerits of both systems.

Office Premises and Equipment

Lay-out and Furniture

A great deal of attention is paid to the lay-out of a modern office; indeed, there are consultants specializing in what is called office landscaping which ensures the optimum use of floor area with the general appearance of spaciousness. Privacy is provided for supervisors by portable partitioning and it is considered that a modern decor using pastel colour schemes adds to the working efficiency of the office. Similar care is exercised in the choice of office furniture and equipment suitably designed and sited to ensure maximum comfort and ease of working. The smooth running of the office is further facilitated nowadays by modern telephone, intercom, and dictating systems.

Appropriate lighting, adequate heating and ventilation, together with efficient cleaning services all have a material bearing on the output of work.

Records and Stationery

Insurance Offices are well ahead in the adoption of modern devices for facilitating the keeping of records.

The requirements of Insurers vary within wide limits according to the classes of business transacted, but all or most of the following stationery and record books are required:

a Proposal forms.

b Policy forms.

c Letter headings.

d Description books (also known as policy registers) containing details of all policies issued.

e Renewal records (sometimes termed renewal registers), renewal notices and receipts; also, alphabetical index of policyholders.

f Endorsement forms and the necessary books of entry.

g Claim forms, registers, and incidental books.

h Classification registers and various indexing records.

i Declinature book in which details are entered of any business declined.

j Revision book in which to insert details of any alterations to be made to existing policies at the next renewal date.

k Books of account.

l Statutory books.

Sometimes these records are kept on the loose-leaf system, or cards may be used when an Office is mechanized. Most Companies now use a computer installation so that many of their records are maintained on magnetic tape. The adoption of a good system in the preservation of records and filing is vital so that there is no delay when information is required.

Mechanization

The modern Insurance Office is often highly mechanized and this development has been in the best interests of all concerned. It results in a reduction of time spent on routine work, reduces the margin of error, and makes for economy of effort generally.

Typewriters. The typewriter is an essential part of the equipment of all offices; in some instances, the electric typewriter is used. Dictating machines are sometimes used, because they eliminate the time spent in taking dictation, and the matter may be dictated whenever convenient, whether or not the typist is available.

Accounting machines. Many Insurers have mechanized their accounting. The ledger sheets are on the loose-leaf principle so that they can be easily adapted to machine accounting. Adding machines and machines which will also subtract and multiply are used in the actuarial, fire, guarantee, and other departments.

Mechanization of renewals. In the old days, all renewal notices and receipts were written by hand, but many Companies have now installed one or other of the types of addressing machines, so that this considerable volume of work is now done from embossed plates, thereby saving time and eliminating errors.

Computers. The computer has taken over much of the routine work formerly done manually or by other types of machine. In a modern computer system large volumes of data can be stored and can be assessed at electronic speeds. These facilities, combined with the use of terminals at branches and head office departments, give those locations almost immediate access to the large files held within the computer system. Modern developments in computer-based systems both in the USA and in Europe are designed to create what might be termed a computer-based information system. By this means it is possible to offer an information service which can deal with the majority of enquiries which would formerly have required reference to and perusal of paper files and index cards. The system is also capable of providing management with the information which they require to perform their functions more effectively.

Other machines. It would be impossible within the present chapter to deal with the various other kinds of machines and apparatus in general use, but among them may be mentioned postal frankers, letter openers, duplicating and printing machines, photostat micro-photographic machines, folding machines, and card punching machines.

Services of Independent Experts

All Insurers engage the services of independent experts. Each Company has its own solicitors to deal with matters affecting its legal constitution, and the services of lawyers are likewise necessary when proceedings are taken against the Insured by third parties, as often happens in the accident department, particularly in connection with running down claims. A Company must also have auditors for the purpose of auditing its accounts.

Adjusters are invariably instructed in order to deal with large fire claims, and the same firms (but not necessarily the same individual adjusters) may also assess heavy theft, 'all risks,' and similar claims.

Certain of the large motor Insurers have full-time qualified engineers on their own staff. Others seek the services of independent consulting engineers. Such engineers deal with damage claims ('own damage' and third party) and render advice on any matters within their specialized field.

Life Assurance Companies usually have their own medical officers with accommodation at Head Office premises (and at some branches) for examinations to be made. Proposers in the provinces are as a rule examined by local medical practitioners approved by the Company. Medical reports are also frequently required in connection with all types of accident claims. The services of veterinary surgeons are vital to the livestock Underwriter.

Some Insurers place their advertising in the hands of a specialist firm which will also deal with the Company's selling literature generally. Even if this is not done, all printing and other stationery and office supplies may be centralized under the care of one responsible official, to ensure standardization and economy.

How Lloyd's Operates

It was once said of Lloyd's, 'individually we are underwriters, but collectively we are Lloyd's.' This is true, for Lloyd's today is, on a massive scale, precisely what it was in the 17th century—a building in which, by payment of a subscription (then the price of a cup of coffee, and now an amount decided by the Committee), men of substance may congregate to invite offers from those who are anxious to insure against certain risks. The complexities of handling a premium income of hundreds of millions of pounds per annum have resulted in a build-up of organization to deal with it, but the fundamental principle is constant.

A Committee of sixteen watches over the activities at Lloyd's. Its members are elected by and from the members of Lloyd's for a term of four years. They select from their own ranks a chairman and a deputy chairman. Among their responsibilities are the election of new members, arbitration in salvage disputes, and the smooth running of the Policy Signing Office, the Claims Offices, the Recoveries Department, the Foreign Legislation Department and the Agency System. More will be said about some of these features later.

How Risks are Placed

Underwriters do not deal with the public direct. Insurances must be placed through a Lloyd's broker (a firm which has satisfied the Committee of its financial and ethical soundness), who advises a client of the contract most suitable to his needs and then seeks to obtain it at the best rate.

The broker approaches an underwriter in 'The Room' who is a recognized leader in the particular branch of insurance concerned. The underwriter agrees the conditions and rate with the broker in the light of the particulars shown on the 'slip' submitted by the broker. The underwriter initials the slip to show the extent of his acceptance. If he accepts less than 100 per cent of the risk, the broker must negotiate with other underwriters until the risk is fully covered. Underwriters usually operate in syndicates, for convenience. An underwriter, whether operating alone or in a syndicate, is a person who has proved his integrity and financial standing and has furnished security which may be used in the event of his trading yielding a loss. Each underwriter is personally responsible to the limit of his means to the policyholder for his share of any loss arising under the policy. For this reason the strictest possible rules are applied to candidates for membership.

The slip of paper on which the underwriters have written their initials and percentages is the document from which the broker then prepares the policy. At one time it would have had to be checked and signed by the clerks of each underwriter on the slip; today a central organization, Lloyd's Policy Signing Office, mentioned already, fulfils this function. It passes over twenty million advices a year to syndicates, informing them of policies signed or endorsed on their behalf. Syndicates, and brokers also, are given the debit and credit balances on their accounts, and final settlement between them is made through the central office.

The Agency System

There is a network of some 1,500 agents operating throughout the world, and they contribute to the accuracy of Lloyd's astonishing intelligence system. They also survey claims and negotiate not only on behalf of Lloyd's underwriters but also for the international marine insurance world.

Marine and Non-marine

As a rule underwriters do not deal with both marine and non-marine business. In fact, they are separated in 'The Room', the marine underwriters being seated in their 'boxes' (with their clerks) on the ground floor and the non-marine underwriters in the gallery.

Organization of an Insurance Broker's Office

The organization of an insurance broker's office must have three separate but inter-related objectives:

1 to allow sufficient time to see existing clients to discuss new business or problems arising in respect of existing business;

2 to keep in touch with the market, which in London consists of Companies and Lloyd's, so that they may know where and how to obtain insurance on terms most suitable to their clients' requirements; and

3 to set up a qualified staff to deal promptly and efficiently with all routine matters, i.e., correspondence, issue of policies, issue of renewals, accounts, surveys and claims.

In addition to these office requirements, the properly organized broking house will devote much thought to the acquisition of new business, for which in a large office a separate outside department will be set up.

At the head of the organization stand the chairman and his fellow directors, who decide the general policy of the firm, its methods of approach to Insurers, its contacts with its own insuring public, and the maintenance of its standing and reputation in the insurance world.

There are, of course, considerable differences in the set-up of brokers' offices, according to the size of the business, for clearly a broker with a small business working entirely by himself, with perhaps a clerk or two and a typist, will arrange his business affairs differently from firms with perhaps half a dozen directors, a large business at home and abroad and a staff of several hundred employees.

Such large firms find it convenient to set up departments for each separate section of their business, and there are such departments for marine, non-marine, life and aviation business respectively. This is to write in broad terms, for everything depends on the size of the business. Thus, sometimes, aviation goes in with marine; again, non-marine may be divided between fire and accident, or life may not be big enough for a separate department. These are all matters for the firm to arrange according to its convenience. Each department is self-sufficient, dealing with its own policies, its surveys (where required), its claims and its renewals. Accounts, however, are almost invariably centred in an accounts department responsible for all accounting and production of the firm's annual balance sheet.

When necessary, a separate department is formed for American business, an important matter because of the many technicalities of that branch of broking. Such a department may be divided into different sections according to class.

Some firms devote special attention to reinsurance broking, a business with a technique of its own. There are, indeed, a few firms who carry on this branch exclusively, although, as a rule, the big direct brokers have set up reinsurance departments.

The staff of a large, fully equipped broking firm is thoroughly organized, with experienced departmental managers and all grades of staff to assist them, and the organization is as extensive and as detailed as that of any other insurance organization. This is perhaps the more important for those brokers who are at Lloyd's, since they have to prepare policies, collect premiums, deal with claims and generally carry out all the detailed work ordinarily done by the insurance companies.

11 Associated Action: Insurers' Services

Within the insurance world there are many different kinds of associations. There is no uniform pattern, and this is because such associations have grown up from time to time as the need has arisen, while their functions are diverse. Some of these associations are housed in one building—Aldermary House, Queen Street, London, EC4—but others are located in various places in London and elsewhere.

Associated Action

These associations are dealt with under four headings, as follows:

1 Companies' and Underwriters' associations.

2 Associations of intermediaries.

3 Associations of persons employed in insurance.

4 Other associations.

This classification is not completely satisfactory, because there is inevitably some overlapping, but it makes possible a description of the principal associations within each category.

1 Companies' and Underwriters' Associations

These associations do not accept insurance business, but are designed to promote, advance and protect the interests of their members and to disseminate current information and intelligence. They are a recognized medium of approach to and from Government departments, and they consider and at times express views on proposed legislation affecting Companies and Underwriters.

The day-to-day affairs of each association (and the same applies to some of the associations under the other headings) are entrusted to a paid executive and staff, but the policy-making decisions are dealt with by committees on which senior officials of the member-Insurers and Underwriters serve. A huge volume of voluntary work in the general interests of the business is in this way undertaken and at times this is unusually exacting, as happened when compulsory third party insurance for motor vehicles was first introduced in 1931, necessitating many changes in motor insurance practice. A more recent example arises out of the entry of the UK into the EEC. A very large number of senior insurance people are involved in frequent visits to Brussels and Paris where detailed and time-demanding work is currently taking place in the effort to harmonize insurance law and practice within the Community.

Some of the associations have dealt with rating and the formulation of tariffs to be observed by their members, although these functions are not so prominent today.

The British Insurance Association is dealt with first, because it is the central association for so many Companies as a whole. Associations concerned with separate classes of business are studied next, followed by the international associations.

British Insurance Association

This Association was formed in 1917, and it speaks for almost all the British Insurance Companies, including British Commonwealth Companies which transact business in Great Britain. It is, in fact, the trade association of Insurance Companies generally, irrespective of the types of insurance business transacted. At the date of writing, there are some 300 members who transact around 95 per cent of the worldwide business of the British insurance company market.

In recent years, the Association has expanded its activities considerably, particularly in insurance public relations. The object is to improve the public understanding of insurance, and this it has done by conducting a public relations programme and maintaining an information service about insurance, designed to meet the needs of the Press, broadcasting services, research workers and others. Other activities include the following:

1 Preparation and submission of evidence to Royal Commissions,

notably in recent years that on Civil Liability for Personal Injury and also the Wilson Committee to Review the Functioning of Financial Institutions.

2 The control of garage repairs costs by means of a Garage Pricing Scheme in some of the larger cities, under which members encourage their Insured to have damaged vehicles repaired by approved garages.

3 The operating of a Motor Repair Research Centre in co-operation with Lloyd's to gain basic technical information on the anatomy of motor repairs and of standard repair times.

4 The formation of a University Liaison Panel to strengthen and coordinate the ever-increasing and valuable liaison with universities and also with the major business schools.

5 The preparation of statistics of the premiums and investments of member Companies.

6 The production of films, such as 'The Square Deal', 'In the Dark', and 'The Stable Door.'

7 The preparation of suitable notes of interest to teachers in insurance.

8 Public relations activities through advertising campaigns, the provision of spokesmen on radio and television programmes and a series of broadsheets designed to encourage a dialogue between politicians and the insurance industry with special reference to the investment performance of the industry and its overseas earnings.

The Association is closely concerned with investment and taxation problems, and valuable work is done by the Investment Protection Committee.

MARINE ASSOCIATIONS

There are three main[1] associations of marine Underwriters in the United Kingdom. These are: Lloyd's Underwriters' Association, The Institute of London Underwriters and The Liverpool Underwriters' Association. They work in co-operation because there are many common problems. They are in constant touch with similar organizations throughout the world, and their members represent the

1 There are also the Association of Marine Underwriters and Brokers in Glasgow, and the Manchester Marine Insurance Association.

Associations on many national and international committees and bodies.

In addition to the usual services described above, these Associations support steps taken to save life and property at sea, including improvements to lighthouses, ports and harbours.

Lloyd's Underwriters' Association was formed in 1909 and has a membership of approximately 70. Each year 15 members of the Association are elected by ballot to form the committee, which meets regularly for the discussion of the various underwriting and general administrative problems which arise in Lloyd's marine market. The results of their deliberations are usually embodied in the form of a recommendation which is submitted to all members of the Association for ratification. (The chairman and deputy chairmen of Lloyd's are *ex officio* members of the committee.)

The Association acts in close liaison with The Institute of London Underwriters and The Liverpool Underwriters' Association.

The Institute of London Underwriters was formed in 1884. The foundation members consisted of 20 companies, but now the total membership is well over 100 companies. It is, in fact, an association of marine insurance companies operating in London, but its work extends far beyond this, as illustrated by the Joint Committees referred to below.

An important step forward was taken in 1939 when combined ILU policy forms were introduced and a policy department formed to deal with the signing of combined policies on behalf of all members of the Institute, on similar lines to Lloyd's Policy Signing Office. This was a major labour-saving device. The department also deals with the checking of additional premiums and returns and has recently commenced dealing with claims.

The latest development is a Central Accounting Scheme between all members of the Institute and brokers, involving the supply of daily journals, monthly ledgers, and settlement statements for all items passing through the books of the Institute. It is hoped ultimately to extend settlement, which at present is between individual Companies and brokers, to central settlement through the Institute.

The Liverpool Underwriters' Association is the oldest in the United Kingdom; it was established in 1802. Initially, its membership comprised brokers acting for underwriting syndicates made up of Liverpool shipowners and merchants. These, however, were gradually replaced following the formation of the marine insurance companies, the first of which was floated in 1860.

In 1865 the Association began to survey iron ships, and from 1862 it published for 23 years its own *Register of Iron Vessels* until amalgamation with *Lloyd's Register* (see p. 225).

There is a considerable marine insurance market in Liverpool, and membership of the Association now comprises the head offices of the Liverpool marine insurance companies, marine branch offices, and brokers in that market. Its member companies are acknowledged to be the pioneers in the development of marine insurance overseas, and today they control, from Liverpool, a large portfolio of overseas business.

This Association is well known throughout the world for its compilation of casualty statistics.

Joint committees. All the associations mentioned above participate in many important committees, which deliberate upon problems that are common both to the Lloyd's and company marine markets, and The Institute of London Underwriters act as Secretaries to these Joint Committees. Among these are the Joint Hull, the Joint Cargo, and the Technical and Clauses Committees. The 'Institute Clauses,' as they are called, are drafted and kept up to date by the latter Committee, and they are used throughout the British market and in many overseas countries. The clauses book (published by Witherby) is a monumental work, which has grown in complexity in post-war years, with frequent clause revisions.

FIRE ASSOCIATIONS

Fire Offices' Committee

The Fire Offices' Committee is the title of an association of fire Insurance Companies who have agreed voluntarily to act collectively on various aspects of fire insurance business. The members of the Committee are known as the 'Tariff Companies.' The Fire Offices' Committee (Foreign), which is concerned with overseas business, and a number of other committees and organizations dealing with specific overseas territories or general questions affecting overseas business are dealt with by the same administration.

The Committee formally adopted a constitution in 1868, although a number of tariffs and local rating agreements existed earlier. The jurisdiction of the Committee covers the U.K. and Eire.

The establishment of the Committee on an official basis was profoundly influenced by the great Tooley Street fire of 1861, as a result of which the fire tariff system was greatly strengthened. A number of kindred organizations are administered by the Committee, e.g., the London Wharf and Warehouse Committee and the Consequential Loss Committee.

In addition to a large number of tariffs for the principal trades and occupations, the Committee has formulated, for the use of its members, 'General Rules for the Regulation of Fire Insurance Business' and 'Rules Governing Reinsurance Business (Facultative Reinsurance Transactions).' A standard fire policy was adopted in 1922, and a standard consequential loss policy and specification were adopted in 1939.

In 1972 the Monopolies Commission reported on the supply of fire insurance on property in the United Kingdom and recommended that tariff agreements should be terminated. Most Insurers disagreed with the findings of the Commission in this respect and tariffs have been retained for commercial and industrial risks although they were discontinued for household insurances. Apart from tariffs the Report contains much useful information about the functions of the Fire Offices' Committee.

One of the Committee's main aims is to encourage reduction in fire hazard, not only by penalizing under the tariffs features which constitute additional fire hazards, but also by providing allowances for favourable underwriting features.

A considerable part of the Committee's work is of a technical nature. Some fifty items of rules and recommendations have been prepared and made available to the public, ranging from rules for the installation of automatic sprinklers, fire alarm systems, and the like, to recommended precautions for the protection of factory canteens, the installation and maintenance of grain dryers and the protection of computer installations.

The members of the Fire Offices' Committee inaugurated, in consultation with H.M. Government, the Joint Fire Research Organization, now the Fire Testing Station based at Elstree—a unique form of partnership between government and industry until its dissolution in 1976. (See p. 35.) They were also responsible for the establishment of the Fire Protection Association and the Fire Insurers Research and Testing Organization.

Lloyd's Underwriters' Non-marine Association

This Association was formed in 1910 and deals with matters generally affecting the business of fire and non-marine insurance at Lloyd's.

With the growth of this type of business at Lloyd's at that time, the need for an association to look after non-marine underwriters' interests was considered advisable.

LIFE ASSOCIATIONS

Industrial Life Offices' Association

The Association was founded in 1901 to promote the principles, practice and business of industrial assurance; its membership comprises proprietary Companies, collecting friendly Societies and mutual Offices. Most member-Offices also transact ordinary life assurance, and many undertake general insurance business. Industrial assurance is under the supervision of the Industrial Assurance Commissioner, to whom the Association gives all possible assistance.

The ILOA first concerned itself with public relations in the late 1940s, when the business was threatened with nationalization; since the early 1950s the Association's public relations effort has been directed both nationally and locally towards winning prestige and goodwill by encouraging the fullest possible understanding of industrial assurance (or home service insurance, as it is now termed) among all sectors of the public.

The Life Offices' Association and the Associated Scottish Life Offices

There are no tariffs in life assurance; the business is highly competitive. Nevertheless, there is a wide field of important interests common to all Offices, such as legislation, taxation and the reputation of the business as a whole, which call for an agreed policy and sometimes concerted action. Recognition of this community of interest led in 1889 to the formation of The Life Offices' Association, which has now established a Standing Committee with its elder sister-organization, the Associated Scottish Life Offices, formed in 1841.

These bodies are concerned with ordinary branch assurance only, and their work is largely parallel to that of the Industrial Life Offices' Association with which, naturally, they have much in common. The three bodies publish joint statistics annually. Public relations, designed to foster greater public understanding of life assurance and its underlying principles, constitutes a function of fast-growing importance.

ACCIDENT AND AVIATION ASSOCIATIONS

Accident Offices Association

The AOA was founded in 1906 at a time when the accident insurance market needed a strong lead, particularly in the field of Workmen's Compensation. For many years the Association has occupied a commanding place in the accident insurance market. Since the introduction of compulsory third party motor insurance, and particularly since 1945, there have been an increasing number of occasions when it has been necessary for all accident Insurers to consider common problems. This co-operation has been achieved under the auspices of the AOA through the Motor and Employers' Liability Conferences, which are informal bodies comprising accident Insurers and Lloyd's, and which can speak for the UK motor and employers' liability markets generally.

The Accident Offices Association (Overseas) corresponds to the Fire Offices' Committee (Foreign), and it is concerned with the considerable portfolio of tariff accident insurance business transacted overseas by its members.

One of the principal functions of the AOA was to formulate minimum terms for certain classes of accident insurance, but in 1968 it discontinued this function.

The offices of the Motor Insurers' Bureau are located at the same address as those of the AOA (in Aldermary House, Queen Street, London, EC4), and the Bureau acts for the motor insurance market as a whole. The Engineering Offices Association works closely in conjunction with the AOA.

Lloyd's Motor Underwriters' Association

Motor insurance is such an important section of the non-marine market, with its own specialized problems, that a separate association was found to be necessary in 1931, soon after the introduction of compulsory third party motor insurance. While this Association deals with matters generally affecting the business of motor insurance at Lloyd's, it does not underwrite insurances.

Mutual Insurance Companies' Association

Mutual Insurance Companies differ in their constitution from proprietary Offices, and it was necessary for them to present their special viewpoint before the Beveridge Committee on Social Insurance and

Allied Services, which was set up in 1941. It was for this reason that the Association (MICA) was formed, and it takes its part at all meetings on market issues necessitating discussion through the joint consultative machinery; it is represented on a number of BIA Committees. It is included under accident associations because it is principally concerned with employers' liability insurance and motor insurance.

Federation of Plate Glass Insurance Societies

The Federation was established in 1920 for the interchange of information and combined action for the benefit of mutual Insurance Societies concerned with the insurance of glass.

Aviation Insurance Offices' Association

The post-war growth of aviation insurance made desirable the formation of a Company aviation Underwriters' association in 1950. It is an association of aviation Insurance Companies in order *inter alia* to encourage uniformity of action in relation to the principles and practice of aviation underwriting, and to co-operate with other insurance associations.

Lloyd's Aviation Underwriters' Association

This Association came into being in 1935 and deals with all matters generally affecting the business of aviation insurance at Lloyd's. Membership is open to Underwriters not only of specialist aviation syndicates but also those of any syndicate which underwrites this class of business.

Reinsurance Offices Association

This Association was formed in 1969 on the initiative of the leading professional Reinsurers. The objects of the Association are 'to bring together companies transacting reinsurance business, to facilitate and encourage co-operation between such companies on technical matters of general interest, and the study and development of reinsurance.'

The Association is not concerned with tariffs or with binding agreements between members. It is designed to be a forum for discussion of reinsurance matters and problems, with a view to raising technical standards in reinsurance generally.

INTERNATIONAL BODIES

International Union of Aviation Insurers

This Association was formed in 1934 in order to constitute an official body which should be able to speak and negotiate on behalf of aviation insurance interests, to provide a central office for the circulation of information among members, to co-operate for the better regulation and conduct of aviation insurance, and generally to do all such things as might be beneficial to the development and conduct of this branch of insurance.

Those eligible for membership (on a world-wide basis) are registered Insurance Companies authorized by law to carry on aviation insurance business, insurance pools consisting of groups of insurance interests authorized to carry on such business, and other aviation insurance bodies or groups considered to have special qualifications for membership.

In view of its wide field of membership, and bearing in mind the fully international aspect of aviation in all its branches, especially in matters of international law, the Association forms a valuable means of liaison with various international official organizations, such as ICAO (International Civil Aviation Organization) and IATA (International Air Transport Association).

Among its other activities the Association, on behalf of its members, has submitted observations and recommendations to the appropriate authorities in respect of existing and projected Conventions and Agreements affecting aviation Insurers, and its co-operation is being increasingly sought in such matters.

International Union of Marine Insurance

The International Union of Marine Insurance was formed in 1874, and the founder members were German, Austrian, Russian and Swedish marine Underwriters. The objects were to represent, safeguard and develop marine insurance interests. British and French Underwriters were not officially connected with the Union until 1925. The meetings of the Union were suspended during World War Two and whereas, before that war, representation was by individual Companies and Underwriters, the Articles of Association were amended after the war and now provide for membership on a national or market marine insurance association basis. Each delegation to the conference consists of the chairman, deputy chairman and secretary of the member association. The annual meeting enables Underwriters of many lands to get to know one another and to try to understand each other's point of view. Meetings of the council are restricted to the official delegates, but there is usually an open meeting following the council meetings which accredited Underwriters, in addition to the official delegates, may attend. Brokers are not admitted to any meetings of the Union. Current problems are discussed, and in recent years papers have been read, for instance, on nuclear energy as it affects marine insurance.

2 Associations of Intermediaries

British Insurance Brokers' Association

It is estimated that there are in the region of 10,000 broking firms in the United Kingdom. Over the years perhaps a third of this number joined one of several organizations designed to raise the standards of professional conduct among insurance brokers. Until 1 January 1977 there were four such associations when they all agreed to merge in what is now the British Insurance Brokers' Association (BIBA). Its purpose is to enable the Insurance Broking Industry to speak with a single voice in discussions with the Government, other insurance organisations, trade associations, the media and general public; and at the same time protect the consumer.

The Association provides a technical service to its members and its technical committees cover such subjects as legislation, insurance education and training, personnel management, public relations, life and pensions, motor and reinsurance business and include the United Kingdom Insurance Brokers' European Committee and the United Kingdom Credit Insurance Brokers' Committee.

An important aspect of BIBA work is to ensure that consumers are better informed on the role and functions of Insurance Brokers and that consumers fully understand the advantages of obtaining insurance protection through them.

All the major broking firms and some medium sized and smaller firms are in membership with BIBA. However, by far the larger number of firms, mostly small ones, have not sought membership.

Insurance Brokers Registration Council

As a result of consultations between the BIBA and the Department of Trade a private member's Bill was presented to the House of

Commons to provide for the registration of insurance brokers so as to ensure that, for the protection of the public, the competence and conduct of practising insurance brokers are of a sufficiently high standard and that their financial resources are adequate. The Bill became law on 29 July 1977 when the Insurance Brokers (Registration) Act, 1977, received the Royal Assent.

Section 1 of the Act provides for the setting up of an Insurance Brokers Registration Council to carry out the powers and duties conferred on them by the Act. This Council was duly constituted on 1 December 1977.

Section 2 of the Act requires the IBRC to set up and maintain a register containing the names, addresses and qualifications of brokers who satisfy the requirements for registration.

Section 3 sets out the conditions for registration. Insurance brokers with a recognized professional qualification and a practice qualification in insurance business to which the section applies and who are of good character are to be entitled to registration. Insurance brokers with no recognized professional qualification but with a practice qualification in insurance business to which the section applies and who are of good character, are also to be entitled to registration. The section provides similar entitlements for persons employed by partnerships and bodies corporate practising as insurance brokers who have adequate practical experience. In addition, insurance brokers accepted by the Committee of Lloyd's are to be entitled to registration. The section also deals with the future admission to the register of persons with professional qualifications, both within and outside the United Kingdom.

Except in the case of insurance brokers accepted by the Committee of Lloyd's, the entitlement to registration is conditional upon the Insurance Brokers Registration Council being satisfied about the financial resources of applicants, their independence from Insurers and the impartiality of their advice.

The section also confers a right of appeal to the High Court, the Court of Session or the High Court of Justice in Northern Ireland against the refusal of the Council to admit a person to the register.

Other sections deal with the regulation of conduct and disciplinary procedures while an important provision is contained in Sect. 22 which makes it a punishable offence for persons and bodies corporate not on the register to describe themselves as insurance brokers or to use any style, title or description which includes the expression 'insurance broker' or related expressions such as 'assurance broker', 'reinsurance broker' and 'reassurance broker'. When this section of the Act is in force those firms which choose not to register or which are ineligible for registration will need to use other descriptive titles such as insurance consultants, insurance advisers, insurance specialists and the like.

The Society of Pension Consultants

The Society of Pension Consultants was formed in 1958 as a society affiliated to the Corporation of Insurance Brokers now merged in the BIBA.

There are two classes of membership: Member, and Associate Member. In order to qualify as a Member, an applicant is required to have been for a period of not less than five consecutive years directly concerned, through its own specialized staff of not less than three persons, with the installation of, the giving of advice on, and the provision of continuous service on, pension schemes or funds. An insurance broker or pension consultant who is not eligible for election as a Member may become an Associate Member.

Almost all the leading insurance brokers concerned with pension business are members of the Society, and they are responsible for about 60 per cent of the pension business premium income of the life offices.

The Corporation of Insurance Agents

In 1906 a body known as The Association of Insurance Brokers and Agents was founded, and the two branches were linked until 1919, when The Corporation of Insurance Agents became a separate organization, although administered from the same address as the CIB and by the same secretariat until 1958. There was then a complete separation of work and secretariat.

The Corporation was envisaged as an organization for those who undertake insurance agency as an adjunct to their main profession or occupation, and this basis has been generally maintained. The present council may be regarded as a representative cross-section of the membership as a whole, consisting as it does of chartered surveyors, auctioneers, chartered accountants, chartered architects and solicitors. The services required by members are summed up in the Memorandum—'. . . to collect and disseminate to members information in regard to all matters relating to Insurance or to the practice, duties and obligations of Insurance Agents. . . .' From time to time the Corporation has felt it necessary to make a policy declaration in the interests of members; for example, the opposition to 'own case' agencies and the allowance of commissions direct to the insured.

3 Associations of Persons Employed in Insurance

Actuarial Bodies[1]

The Institute of Actuaries, whose home is at Staple Inn Hall in London, was formed in 1848 and received a Royal Charter in 1884. Its Scottish counterpart, the Faculty of Actuaries in Scotland, whose Hall is in St. Andrew Square, Edinburgh, was constituted in 1856, but obtained its Royal Charter before the Institute, in 1868. Both the Institute and Faculty combine the functions of professional examining bodies and learned societies, sessional meetings being held during the period October to April each year.

The examinations of the two bodies are of a high standard. The Institute has two categories of members, Associates and Fellows, but the Faculty normally confers Fellowship only. In addition, the Institute now issues a special certificate in investment to those who, though not qualifying as actuaries, pass the relevant parts of its examinations.

For the purposes of providing tuition in respect of all except the Preliminary Parts of their examinations, the Councils of the Institute and Faculty have set up a joint tuition organization, known as the Actuarial Tuition Service. This operates under its own secretary and staff from Staple Inn, but tuition is provided by practising members of the Institute and Faculty in the form of correspondence courses and oral classes for both sets of examinations. In order further to assist, the Councils of the two professional bodies have appointed local representatives in some of the larger cities in the UK to advise students about the educational activities of the Actuarial Tuition Service and professional education generally.

Meeting and discussion among students is encouraged through the Students' Societies of the Institute and Faculty, which meet regularly in London and Edinburgh during the session. Papers are normally presented in advance of the meetings to facilitate the proceedings, which take part in an informal atmosphere, no record being made and the Press not being present.

1 Actuarial bodies have been included in this third sub-section, but some 25 per cent of the active membership of the Institute of Actuaries is employed in fields other than insurance.

Association and discussion between members of the Institute and Faculty is further encouraged by the existence of a number of dining clubs. The most senior club of the Institute, the Actuaries' Club, ante-dates the Institute itself. Of the other clubs, the Argonauts is of particular interest, in that it represents the spread of the actuarial profession into fields other than life assurance, pension funds and the like.

The Chartered Insurance Institute

The first Insurance Institute was formed in Manchester in 1873. Institutes were later established in other centres, until in 1897 they formed the Federation of Insurance Institutes of Great Britain and Ireland. In 1912 a Royal Charter was granted, and today The Chartered Insurance Institute has a membership of over 50,000, with 85 local institutes, six associated institutes in Ireland, and 42 affiliated institutes overseas.

It is primarily an educational body providing tuition and training through its Postal Tuition Service and the College of Insurance, and holding diploma examinations—and also certain certificate examinations—which are of a high standard.

Much of the work of the Institute is undertaken by voluntary effort on the part of its members, and in recent years many insurance men and women have given unstintingly of their time and energies over a period of two or more years to the devising of a new educational policy which has been geared to the needs of the business in the eighties and beyond.

The Institute, which is one of the few professional bodies to enjoy the patronage of Her Majesty the Queen, also caters for social activities, while the benevolent aim is implemented by a sister-organization, the Insurance Charities (see below).

The Insurance Charities

The Institute sponsors the Insurance Benevolent Fund, which is a charitable fund for orphans of insurance men and for ex-insurance men and their dependants who have fallen on hard times. The Fund is administered by the Insurance Charities, which function as a separate unit with its own constitution and governing council.

Staff Associations

Insurers are first-class employers. Salaries are good and so are the conditions of service, with, as a rule, pensions of up to two-thirds' salary at age 60 or 65 (55 or 60 for women), provision for widows and orphans, specially favourable terms for staff life assurance and house purchase, and other 'fringe' benefits.

Many employees in insurance are organized for the purpose of consultation with managements about salaries and working conditions and have generally adopted the pattern of staff associations or 'in-house' unions which in recent years have formed themselves into the 'Confederation of Employee Organizations'.

Some employees belong to the Association of Scientific Technical and Managerial Staffs, affiliated to the TUC, and some to the Banking, Insurance and Finance Union.

The field staffs of industrial life Assurance Offices also have staff associations which come together for some purposes in the National Federation of Insurance Workers, and yet other industrial assurance field staffs are members of the National Amalgamated Union of Life Assurance Workers.

4 Other Associations

Association of Average Adjusters

This Association, founded in 1869, is a private association of practising average adjusters dealing with the promotion of correct principles in the adjustment of marine claims, uniformity of practice among adjusters and the maintenance of good professional conduct. As such, it is not of interest to the general public. The average adjuster is a highly skilled person who must have a sound knowledge of marine insurance and of marine and commercial law generally.

The Association's examinations are private and are confined rigidly to persons who intend to carry on business exclusively as average adjusters, either solely or in partnership, with a provision that, if in partnership, all members of the firm shall be members of the Association.

The Chartered Institute of Loss Adjusters

It is an established practice of insurers to instruct independent firms of loss adjusters to deal with serious material and consequential loss claims. They investigate the circumstances in which the fire or other insured peril occurred, establish that a valid claim within the terms of the policy has arisen, and by negotiation reach agreement with the Insured on the measure of the loss and of Insurers' liability (if any), when they report to the Insurers giving their recommendation as to payment. The adjusters' duties extend to the apportionment of losses, the handling and disposing of damaged goods to Insurers' best advantage, the collection of evidence to support repudiation of a claim, if this is necessary, or for the prosecution or rebuttal of third-party claims, and generally to dealing with all matters that arise when claims are made.

It became clear that it would be to the advantage of all concerned if there could be friendly co-operation among the individual firms of adjusters, and in 1941 the Association of Fire Loss Adjusters was formed. The widening scope of the duties of its members led to a realization that the word 'Fire' was too limiting, and on the granting of a royal charter (in 1961) the Association was renamed The Chartered Institute of Loss Adjusters. (Many theft claims are dealt with by adjusters.)

The objects of the Institute, as laid down in its charter, include the securing of the observance of strict professional conduct, the co-ordination of the activities of its members for the better execution of their work, and, by providing the necessary facilities, the establishing of high standards of education and knowledge.

Fire Loss Association

This association of male personnel currently engaged in fire claims work with Insurance Companies was formed in 1964. Its main object is to provide opportunities for fire loss staff to meet and to provide a medium through which information on market practice can be exchanged.

Fire Mark Circle

Fire marks are today of interest only to collectors, and the objects of the Circle are the encouragement and advancement of knowledge of and interest in fire marks, by the interchange of views and news and in any other manner thought fit.

Fire Protection Association

The circumstances in which this Association was formed in 1946 are described on p. 36.

The objects of the Association are:

To advance the science of fire protection.
To disseminate advice on fire protection and allied subjects.

To investigate the causes and spread of fire.
To publish codes of practice relating to fire protection.
To collate and analyse statistics.
To propagate knowledge in connection with fire protection.
To co-operate with Government departments and other bodies interested in fire protection.

Many first-class publications are produced, including a quarterly journal and bulletins as well as technical booklets, in which valuable information is to be found on many features of fire protection.

Any interested bodies or persons can become Associate Members on payment of an annual subscription, and the Association also operates a free advisory service. It is glad to answer any requests for technical advice on fire protection and prevention.

The council, which is responsible for the work of the Association, is composed of representatives of the fire offices which are members of the FOC, and from commerce and industry. Government departments also nominate assessors to sit with the council.

Lloyd's Register of Shipping

Lloyd's Register of Shipping, which dates from 1760 and was reconstituted in 1834, was the pioneer of ship-classification societies. It is a non-profit-making body and 'exists for the purpose of obtaining for the use of merchants, shipowners and underwriters a faithful and accurate classification of mercantile shipping, and for the government of which rules and regulations have been from time to time adopted.' The superintendence of the affairs of the Society is under the direction of a general committee composed of merchants, shipowners and underwriters, and shipbuilders and/or engineers who may be elected by the general committee.

Ships and their machinery classed with the Society are surveyed annually and periodically by the Society's surveyors, and in this way trustworthy information is available to underwriters about the ships that they are requested to insure.

Motor Insurers' Bureau

The Cassel Committee in 1937 recommended that a central fund be established to make provision for persons injured in motor-vehicle road accidents who were unable to recover the damages to which they were entitled. In 1946 the whole of the motor insurance market voluntarily implemented this recommendation by the formation of the Motor Insurers' Bureau, so that no road-accident victim would be prejudiced by reason of ineffective motor insurance or absence of such insurance.

One-Fifty Association

This Association has, as its objects, the advancement of knowledge of and interest in loss of profits insurance, and the interchange of views upon this subject. The Association meets periodically for lectures and discussion.

Salvage Associations

The Salvage Association was formed in 1856, and incorporated by royal charter in 1867. Its full title describes its functions: 'The Association for the protection of commercial interests as respects wrecked and damaged property.' The Salvage Association does not own or operate any salvage plant or vessels, but works through salvage contractors. It is a non-profit-making undertaking financed solely from fees. The Liverpool and Glasgow Salvage Association, formed in 1857, is similar in all respects to the (London) Salvage Association, except that it does, in fact, own and operate salvage vessels and equipment.

They are both world-wide organizations, run by marine Underwriters, providing expert technical assistance where maritime salvage is concerned.

Salvage Corps

As stated on p. 36, there are three salvage corps—the Glasgow Rate and Salvage Association, the Fire Salvage Association of Liverpool, Ltd., and the London Salvage Corps.

They are maintained by fire Insurers and their work results in reducing to a minimum the loss and damage caused by fire. A modern fire engine can pump water at the rate of 1,000 g.p.m., and water used to extinguish fires often itself causes considerable damage, sometimes greatly exceeding that caused by burning alone. The salvage men, with their waterproof sheets, can minimize this type of damage, and they attend fires, together with the public fire services, in order to prevent or mitigate as far as is practicable any damage which might be caused by water to extinguish fires, smoke, heat, steam, debris, inclement weather entering damaged premises and delay in dealing with salvable contents. Apart from the prevention of water damage these measures include ventilation to clear smoke, heat and steam, drying out premises, drying furniture, oiling machinery, first-aid repairs to damaged buildings, deodorizing to remove the smell of smoke, and searching debris for valuables.

Insurance Industry Training Council

The Insurance Industry Training Council was established in August, 1968. Its objects are:

1 To make recommendations to employers with regard to the nature and length of training for persons employed in insurance, the further education to be associated with such training, and the standards to be attained.

2 To encourage the provision of adequate facilities for training in insurance and associated further education.

3 To take such further steps as the Council may deem desirable for the furtherance of the foregoing purposes.

In an era when rapid developments are taking place in the field of training and the further education associated with it, the time seemed ripe for a central advisory body representative of employers, employees and The Chartered Insurance Institute to ensure that the effective work of training and education which Insurers have long been doing is developed to the fullest extent throughout the industry. Unlike a statutory Training Board, the Council does not have power to introduce any form of levy or grant system on insurance employers, and at present the secretarial work entailed is carried out by the CII.

Since its inception the Council has issued guides for the training of clerical and professional staff and for the development of supervisory and management skills. Most insurance employers have adopted or adapted the recommendations contained in the guides, thus providing modern systematic training for their staffs.

Miscellaneous

Other associations include the Association of Burglary Insurance Surveyors, the Incorporated Association of Architects and Surveyors (Fire Surveyors' Section), the Insurance Debating Society, the Insurance Choir and the Insurance Orchestral Society of London, the Institute of Automobile Assessors, and associations covering many sports and pastimes.

Services Rendered by Insurers

The primary purpose of insurance is to mitigate the financial difficulties caused by the happening of untoward events, so that the unfortunate few are compensated from a common fund to which the many have contributed.

In addition to this obvious service rendered by insurance, there are other services which are often overlooked by the public.

Selection and Rating of Risks

Insurers 'underwrite' the various risks that are proposed for insurance, and this is in the public interest. For example, if a motorist with a bad accident record is required to bear the first amount of each and every loss, that will tend to make him more careful than he would otherwise be, because every accident will touch his own pocket. The system of check and method of supervision must be investigated by Insurers before acceptance of a commercial fidelity guarantee, and recommendations are made so that defalcations are less likely; indeed, Insurers try to ensure that the system is such that it is almost impossible to flout it. In fire insurance favourable features are rewarded by appropriate rebates of premium, e.g., discounts for fire-extinguishing appliances, and bad features are penalized.

Selection and rating of risks are closely connected with the inspection services by property insurance surveyors and the engineer-surveyors of the engineering companies. Recommendations are made to reduce the risk of fire or accident, and the engineer-surveyor enables the Insured who is responsible for plant, e.g., boilers in factories, to comply with statutory requirements, such as those of the Factories Act, 1961, and the Health and Safety at Work etc. Act, 1974.

Specialized Experience

Insurers in the course of their business accumulate a fund of specialized experience and this is freely placed at the disposal of the Government and the community generally. When Royal Commissions are set up or Departmental Committees appointed, Insurers frequently give evidence and thus play an important part in any contemplated legislation or other changes affecting matters of which they have special knowledge.

A major activity of insurers in recent years has been the provision of evidence and statistics to the Royal Commission on Civil Liability and Compensation for Personal Injury which culminated in the Pearson Report in March 1978. Similarly, much specialized work has gone into the preparation of evidence to the Committee to Review the Functioning of Financial Institutions. Submissions have been made on the provision of finance for industry and trade and subsequently on a comprehensive coverage of UK insurance companies' main activities.

Ancillary Services of Central Bodies

The various central bodies or associations (see pp. 208–17) have a far wider influence than is realized; they play an essential role in the life of the nation. For instance, the Fire Protection Association undoubtedly reduces the risk of fire through its publications and advisory service, and the salvage corps must save Insurers thousands of pounds, which is in the public interest. The work of the Motor Insurers' Bureau also deserves special mention (see p. 225).

Contribution to Fire Brigades

Fire brigades were originally formed and maintained by fire Insurance Offices. In London, Insurers formed a fire brigade for general use from the bodies which they had earlier maintained for the protection of the property that they insured. Eventually, this brigade was taken over by the Metropolitan Board of Works, but even to this day fire Insurers contribute towards the upkeep of the Greater London Council fire brigade on the basis of £35 for every £1,000,000 of sums insured on property which they insure in the area formerly administered by the London County Council.

Financial Features

People are encouraged to save, in the national interest, and the life Assurance Companies perform an important service in this respect. In view of high taxation, substantial saving by the individual is not easy, and life assurance premiums represent many small savings which are canalized through the companies and invested in various ways.

All Insurers build up large funds—they are essential to their business and they are not profits—which have to be invested. Today, Insurers tend to invest over a wider field than formerly, in both long-term and short-term investments.

12 Financial and Related Considerations

Insurers, by reason of the magnitude of their business alone, play an important part in the financial system. In 1978 the total premium income of members of the British Insurance Association (representing about 95 per cent of the companies) was some £11,989m., and in addition there was the considerable business transacted by Lloyd's underwriters.

Reserves

Marine

Marine insurance business necessitates special arrangements in relation to reserves, because heavy general average, particular average or collision claims cannot be immediately settled, requiring possibly twelve months or more to complete. In the same way, with cargo going all over the world it is not always possible immediately to advise Insurers of the exact extent of claims. Indeed, claims may not be notified for some considerable time after the happening of the loss or damage.

In the circumstances, it is not possible to ascertain the final result at the end of each year of account. Some Insurers work on a two-year basis and others on a three-year basis. At the end of the second (or third) year, all claims which have been notified are carefully considered and estimates revised as may be necessary. To the total figure thus computed a loading is added in order to provide for any claims yet to be received, and the whole is transferred to a suspense account, so that any late claims are debited to that account.

There is no necessity to make any reserve for unexpired risk (see p. 232), because there is, in effect, no such risk, as the books are not closed within twelve months of the date of acceptance of a risk.

Life

Under life assurance policies, the premiums received are gradually accumulated to form a fund out of which claims are paid, and a claim is inevitable under almost every life policy, sooner or later. In a sense, therefore, Assurers hold the premiums paid as trustees for their policyholders.

The bases in the calculation of life assurance premiums differ from those for other branches of assurance. The life assurance risk is an increasing risk and three main factors enter into the calculation to cover that risk—mortality, interest, and expense loading.

The risk covered under whole life and term assurances is that of death, and the cost of that risk each year may be ascertained from a mortality table which measures the probability of death occurring year by year. Theoretically, premiums should increase annually with the age of the assured life, but in practice the rates would become prohibitive at advanced ages. In consequence, an average level premium system has been devised whereby more is paid in the early years than is required to meet the risk run, so that, in theory, a reserve may be built up to meet the deficit in the premiums in later years required to meet the enhanced risk. This reserve is deemed to earn interest, the benefit of which is given to the policyholder by use of an interest basis as a discounting factor in assessing the premium payable. The calculations are such that the reserves of all life policies of a similar class at any time together with all future premiums anticipated from that group will, with interest, be exactly sufficient to meet the total sums assured that will still have to be paid.

Additional loading is imposed to cover expenses of management, and any variation in experience from the premium bases adopted will mean either a profit or a loss on the life assurance underwriting account. It follows that the life assurance fund is the premium income invested at interest, less claims paid, agency commission, expenses, and other payments. This life fund is often spoken of as the 'reserves,' but, strictly speaking, the reserves of a life Office represent the net liability under its policies. A valuation is made periodically, when each policy is valued, and if it is found that the funds exceed the total liability, it is said that there is a surplus, while if the fund is less than the liability, there is said to be a deficiency.[1] Bonuses under with-profits policies are paid according to the divisible surplus revealed by means of the valuation.

1 The market value of assets in which the fund is invested and existing investment contingency reserves must be considered as a basis for these assumptions.

Fire and Accident

The essential reserves are those for unexpired risk (see below) and for outstanding claims (see p. 233). In addition, most Companies make a practice of strengthening the departmental funds by creating special reserves of an arbitrary figure which are usually added to from time to time. These special reserves are held against future years which may show an exceptionally unfavourable experience.

Hidden Reserves

Hidden reserves refer to reserves which are not apparent from the published figures. They can be constituted either by the undervaluation of assets or by the over-estimation of liabilities. By way of illustration, a Company may (*a*) under-value its buildings and securities for balance sheet purposes, (*b*) base its valuation calculations, for life assurance, on an unnecessarily heavy mortality table, or on an artificially low rate of interest in the valuation, or (*c*) load the reserve for outstanding claims. It is mainly on account of these hidden reserves that it is impracticable to make an accurate comparison of the financial position of various Companies.

Reserve for Unexpired Risk

Although many fire policies fall due for renewal at one of the four quarter-days, other fire and accident policies may be effected at any time and, as they are annual contracts, they will not fall due within any one accounting year. Insurers must close their books on a specified date, which is usually 31 December. At that time it is clear that the premiums received during the twelve months will include premiums for certain risks which have still to run.

The method for dealing with unexpired premium and unexpired risk is laid down in Statutory Instrument 1978 No. 721—The Insurance Companies (Accounts and Forms) Regulations, 1978. This method, known as the 24ths method, is not defined in the Statutory Instrument or by the Department of Trade, but it is generally interpreted as meaning that premium income is divided according to the month in which it has arisen and all the premium income of the individual month is assumed to have arisen at the mid-point of that month. For premium income arising in January, one-half of a month will be unexpired at the end of the year, i.e., 1/24th of premium for January will be unearned. For February the figure will be 3/24ths, and so on throughout the year up to 23/24ths of the December premiums. The unearned premiums are calculated in respect of each month's business and aggregated to give the total unearned premiums at the year end.

The foregoing method is based on the assumption that claims are evenly spread over the year, but takes no account of expenses of management and commission which are usually incurred at the inception and renewal of a risk. It is therefore permissible for the premium which is brought into the calculation to be discounted in respect of these expenses, usually at a rate of 20 per cent.

With the help of computers, some Companies can use more sophisticated methods than the 24ths method in making provision for unexpired risk. This is acceptable to the Department of Trade, but if the method adopted is less accurate than the 24ths method, the reason for its adoption must be stated and justified in the Company's returns to the Department of Trade.

Reserve for Outstanding Claims

In fire and accident insurance, it is necessary to make a reserve at the end of each year of insurance in respect of further estimated liability for outstanding claims. Each claim is reviewed and an estimate placed thereon. To this amount is added a further estimate for claims which may have arisen but have not been reported to the Insurers. These are referred to as IBNR claims, i.e. incurred but not reported. Special returns have to be made to the Department of Trade for outstanding claims under personal accident policies in the form set out in the Insurance Companies Act, 1974.

Where there is a fairly steady account, then instead of estimating the further liability under each claim, the average cost system may be adopted. A sample is taken as, for instance, the number and cost of claims in, say, three months, and the average obtained. This is applied to the total number of claims outstanding at the end of the year. Great care has to be exercised in the adoption of this system; it is not widely used in this country, but a general estimate has to be used for inward treaty acceptances. The system is applicable only where there is a large volume of claims and individual assessment is difficult.

There are also the general additional reserves of the Company to provide against any serious unforeseen contingency (see p. 232).

Investments

The importance of a sound investment policy cannot be over-emphasized because of the considerable funds which are necessarily in the hands of Insurers and which are essential to their business. Profit from investments is a vital source of income, and as a guiding rule it will be recognized that Insurers so control their investment policy as to secure the highest rate of interest consistent with maintaining the value of the capital invested and the requisite convertibility, as and when required.

Life assurance policies are in the nature of permanent contracts and long term securities are therefore suitable for the greater part of the life assurance fund. Different considerations, however, are present in connection with marine, fire, and accident insurances because it is impossible to foresee the occurrence of heavy catastrophes, resulting in an unexpected drain upon the funds. For the latter purpose, therefore, it is essential that securities should be readily convertible.

In any event, investments should be well spread in order to smooth out market fluctuation, and Insurers therefore need to watch the market closely. Investments, of course, are not limited to Stock Exchange securities, as will be evident from a glance at any company's balance sheet. Insurers grant mortgages, purchase freehold and leasehold ground rents, and, indeed, are always prepared to find new avenues for the investment of their funds as long as the capital is secure and the general conditions satisfactory.

Overseas Earnings

Insurance (and reinsurance) is not a national but an international business, and insurance is a valuable invisible export which affects the balance of payments, as do other services. The overseas earnings of British Insurers in recent years are known to average £909m. per annum.

British Insurers have always led the world and they have built up a reputation for a promise to pay. They are strongly represented in the Commonwealth countries, on the Continent, in the USA and elsewhere.

Statistics

Statistics play a very important part in the business of insurance. The layman may think that rates are fixed by chance, but this is entirely wrong and Insurers have to incur time and effort in order to ascertain whether or not the rates charged are adequate.

In *insurances of the person* statistics are of great importance in life assurance and are dealt with in the highly specialized actuarial departments of the Companies in conjunction with the valuation of the assets by the investment departments. Periodical valuations of liabilities under assurance contracts in force and of assets, at least once in every five years, enable life Companies to ascertain *inter alia* whether existing tables of rates are adequate. In addition to the periodical valuation, a special valuation may be made as and when necessary. (Personal accident risks (e.g., fatal injury, permanent total (partial) disablement, temporary total (partial) disablement) are analysed according to the policy benefits.)

In *property insurance* each separate type of risk is usually given a classification and the sums insured and premiums received for each section of the business classified in this way are ascertained and totalled. Losses are similarly classified, so that, after making allowance for commission and other expenses it is possible to ascertain whether rates require revision.

In *marine insurance* there is such a wide variety of risks and different types of policies that the keeping of statistics is by no means an easy task. Nevertheless, it is vital to do this, for in no class of business is it so essential that the experience should be available.

It is necessary to have entirely different methods of keeping records for cargo and hull business, for, while the risk on the former runs off comparatively quickly, the hulls of vessels are usually insured for periods of twelve months, and several years often elapse before the extent of Underwriters' liability in respect of losses is known.

In cargo insurance, records must be kept of the claims experience of the various accounts on the Underwriter's books. Claims should be analysed according to their nature, e.g., marine perils, theft, breakage, leakage. As tariffs are unusual, it is only by constant comparison of premiums and claims over a long period that Underwriters can accurately rate the risks involved.

Hull business is usually classified (*a*) by fleets and (*b*) by certain well-defined groups of vessels, such as liners, coasters, tramps, tankers, and yachts. Further, types of casualties (fire, strandings, and collisions) should be segregated in respect of each group in order to give the Underwriter a correct view of the running of the account. This enables him to increase or restrict his acceptances according to the experience shown by his statistics.

As to the methods used by individual Companies and Underwriters, these of necessity vary considerably with the personal wishes of those in charge, and there is no standard system.

Insurance Public Relations

Every bona fide business wants to enjoy the goodwill of its customers. In a very large business, such as insurance, the customers make up a major part of the population, and may be called the public at large. To have public support and approval for one's business makes it easier to expand, and to follow the policies that it is desired to pursue. To operate without this support, or in an atmosphere of suspicion or ill-will, may lead to a loss of business, lowering of staff morale, and, at the worst, to interference by other bodies.

Insurers have built up over the years a reputation for a promise to pay and they have therefore earned considerable public goodwill, but special attention must be given to insurance public relations because insurance is such a technical business that there is always the risk of unfortunate misunderstandings. Even an outline knowledge of insurance necessitates some grasp of law and finance, but these are subjects outside the range of the ordinary man so that, for instance, he thinks a policy should be conditionless or that Insurers' funds are profits.

It follows that insurance public relations activities are particularly important among those who are unfamiliar with the concept of insurance, and who possibly make their first contact with it through ownership of a motor cycle or motor car.

Planned Effort of Public Relations

The art of fostering business goodwill is as old as the market place itself. But only in comparatively recent times has industry generally made a conscious effort to inform the outside world of its objects in order to gain public appreciation and, particularly, customers' patronage. Thus has grown up the practice of public relations, which has been defined by the Institute of Public Relations as 'the deliberate, planned and sustained effort to establish and maintain mutual understanding between an organization and its public.' Insurance has entered the public relations field even later than industry generally—mainly since the last war—because it is now too dangerous to allow any serious misconceptions to remain uncorrected. Whose task is it to try to promote the public relations of the insurance business? The answer is: everybody in insurance, whether he be a new entrant or a chief executive. The British Insurance Association (see p. 209), the specialist life associations and Lloyd's carry out public relations work on behalf of the business as a whole, but their efforts can carry little weight if they are not supported by the work of everyone engaged in insurance.

Public relations cannot whitewash or hide an industry's deficiencies; at least, it could not do so for very long. Hence, public relations depends on everyone doing as good a job as he is capable of performing. Every time an insurance man writes a letter, answers the telephone, or deals with an inquiry from a member of the public, he has an opportunity to improve or mar his Company's public relations. If he is concerned with the issue of a policy to a new proposer, he can foster good relations by ensuring that the prospective policyholder has adequate protection for his needs. If he is concerned with settling claims, he has the duty of handling them promptly and fairly, so the policyholder feels that he has had value from his insurance. Above all, public relations is fortified by an attitude of mind which puts the customer first.

Role of Managements

Although everyone in insurance has an opportunity to improve the industry's public relations, it is clear that each management has the duty of giving a lead. This is because only the management can decide that the insurance policies it sells provide value for money, that claims are dealt with promptly and generously, and that all members of the staff are trained to give their best. An insurance management will earn good public relations if it gives its customers a square deal, provides the best possible service, and seeks to keep its customers informed, through advertising or other media of communication.

In many industries, including insurance, there is a growing tendency to employ specialist public relations officers to advise managements on public relations techniques.

Conclusion

Public relations is an aspect of insurance management which calls for the co-operation of everyone in the industry. But it is more than a one-way flow of ideas by which Insurers can impress their views on other people. The flow of ideas must and does work both ways. A good public relations policy will ensure that an Insurer will carefully consider any criticisms from policyholders and, if it thinks them justified, will alter its practice so that the criticism cannot recur.

In this and many other ways, public relations can be used to build up confidence between the insurance industry and its public, and make life more rewarding for everyone engaged in that industry.

Bibliography

As this book is concerned with the elements of insurance generally, it necessarily covers a wide field. The student should therefore select from the following books additional reading according to the sections of insurance in which he is specially interested.

Insurances of the Person

The Principles and Practice of Life Assurance (Bacon & New). Buckley Press.

Property and Pecuniary Insurances

The Principles of Marine Insurance (Turner). Stone & Cox.
Institute Handbook on Marine Contracts (Institute of London Underwriters). Witherby & Co.
Lloyd's Calendar (published annually).
Fire Insurance Theory and Practice (Smith & Francis). Stone & Cox.
Fire and Motor Insurance (Ivamy). Butterworth.
The Principles and Practice of Accident Insurance (Dinsdale). Buckley Press.
Burglary Protection and Insurance Surveys (Bûgg). Stone & Cox.
Fidelity Guarantee and Contingency Insurance (Howard & Dinsdale). Stone & Cox.
Motor Insurance: theory and practice (Cannar). Witherby.

Insurances of Liability

Employers' Liability at Common Law (Munkman). Butterworth.
Professional Indemnity Insurance (Madge). Butterworth.

Miscellaneous

Insurance (Cockerell). English Universities Press.
Specimen Proposal Forms and Glossaries (Dinsdale). Stone & Cox.
The Law of Insurance (Colinvaux). Sweet & Maxwell.
Insurance Law (Macgillivray). Sweet & Maxwell.
Reinsurance for the Beginner (Bellerose). Witherby.
Reinsurance (R.L. Carter). Kluwer Publishing.
General Principles of Insurance Law Ivamy). Butterworth.
The Insurance Directory and Yearbook—Post Magazine Almanack.
(published annually).
Journal of the Chartered Insurance Institute.
Handbook of Insurance (Carter). Kluwer-Harrap.

Glossary of Insurance Terms

Abandonment	Surrender by the Insured of all proprietary rights in the subject-matter of insurance. It is then for the Insurers to decide whether to take over such subject-matter.
Accommodation line	An insurance which on its intrinsic merits is unacceptable, but is taken to preserve goodwill or to oblige a connection.
Actuary	A specialist who applies the mathematical doctrine of probabilities to the subject of vital statistics from which life assurance, annuity, and analogous undertakings derive their principles of operation. (Many actuaries are engaged in fields of activity unconnected with insurance.)
Adjuster	A person who assesses losses, hence the term 'average adjuster'; the term is primarily used in marine insurance. Fire loss adjusters have formed an association known as the Association of Fire Loss Adjusters.
Agent (general)	A person who acts on behalf of another (the principal).
Agent (industrial assurance)	An industrial assurance agent is in a different category; he is a full-time employee of an Insurance Company.
Agent (insurance)	A person who introduces business for which he receives commission. He may act for the Insurer or for the Insured or for both.
Agreement	A legal contract.
Arbitration	An alternative to litigation for the settlement of disputes. Differences may be referred to a single arbitrator, or to two arbitrators and an umpire, the

umpire giving a decision if the arbitrators cannot agree.

Articles of Association
The regulations of a Company incorporated under the Companies Acts.

Assignment
The transfer of rights under a contract.

Assurance
This term has the same meaning as Insurance (*q.v.*), but it is generally used in reference to life assurance.

Assured
In marine and life assurance, it is usual to refer to the Assured, but it has the same meaning as Insured (*q.v.*).

Assurer
This term has the same meaning as Insurer (*q.v.*), but Assurer is generally used in reference to life assurance.

Attestation clause
The signing clause. The words declaring the execution of the policy.

Average
a The distribution of an expense or sacrifice.

b In fire insurance, the *pro rata* average clause lays down that the Insurers are liable only for such proportion of the loss as the sum insured bears to the total value at risk.

c In marine insurance:
  i Particular average: partial loss or damage by a peril insured against which is not general average and is not shared generally.
  ii General average: liability for contributions to sacrifice of ship or cargo and expenditure.

d In life assurance, an under-average life is one suffering from some physical defect or disability; a sub-standard life.

Bailee
A person to whom goods are entrusted for a specific purpose; he may be a gratuitous bailee or a bailee for reward.

Bonus
A reduction in premium to reward some specially favourable feature of the risk, e.g., no-claim bonus (termed no-claim discount in motor insurance). In life assurance, it is the method of distribution of profits to the holders of with-profits policies by an addition to the sum assured.

Bordereau(x)
The term used in reinsurance for list(s) of risks,

premiums, and losses, supplied by the ceding Office to the Reinsurer.

Broker A person or firm exercising professional skill and concerned with the placing of insurance business.

Case Law That part of the law which is found in the decisions of the Judges as reported in the various series of law reports.

Catastrophe risk The possibility of an exceptionally heavy loss, e.g., the San Francisco earthquake and fire, 1906.

Cede To give; an Insurer cedes reinsurances to a Reinsurer.

Cession The surplus amount which is given off by a ceding Company to the Reinsurer.

Claim A demand by the Insured for payment under his policy.

Co-insurer 1 A large insurance is sometimes scheduled, that is to say, it is divided among a number of Insurers and they are termed Co-insurers.
2 The term is sometimes used where the Insured is required to bear part of each and every loss; for example, in credit insurance the Insured may be required to bear as much as 50 per cent of each and every loss.
Strictly speaking, however, the term Co-insurer should be limited to (1) above because a policy-holder is in no sense an Insurer.

Commission The remuneration paid to an agent for the introduction of business, usually in the form of a percentage of the premium.
(*See also* 'Overriding Commission' and 'Profit Commission.')

Common Law The law which has been founded upon immemorial usage, established custom, and legal decisions, as distinct from Statute Law.

Condition A part of a contract which must be complied with by one party or the other. A condition governs the validity of the contract. (*See also* Warranty.)

Contract of insurance An agreement between the Insurer and one or more parties, called the Insured, whereby the Insurer undertakes in return for the payment of a certain consideration, called the premium, to pay to the Insured a certain sum of money or to grant certain compensation on the happening of a specified event.

Contribution The division of a loss between Insurers where two or more cover the same Insured and the same risk. Contribution arises from the principle of indemnity and ensures equitable distribution of losses as between Insurers.

Cover note A document issued by Insurers giving temporary cover pending the issue of a formal policy.

Declaration A statement signed by the Insured, certifying the accuracy of information that he has given. Normally, such a declaration appears at the foot of accident and life proposal forms. In fire insurance, declarations refer to periodical returns of the value of stock under declaration policies for the purpose of premium adjustment.

Deposit *a* The payment of a portion of a premium pending completion of the contract.
b The term also refers to sums of money which may have to be deposited with a Government before permission is granted to transact insurance business.

Discharge A form of receipt given by a claimant, acknowledging that he has no further claim in respect of the happening concerned.

Discount A reduction in premium in respect of some favourable feature of the risk, e.g., discount for fire extinguishing appliances or for freedom from claims. Where customary, as in marine insurance, it may originate from a reward for prompt payment of premium.

Endorsement A memorandum added to a policy embodying some alteration to the terms of the policy.

Equity The system of law formerly administered by the Lord Chancellor.

Exception A peril or contingency specifically excluded from the terms of the policy.

Excess The first portion of a loss, being an agreed or fixed sum, which the Insured (usually in consideration of a reduction of premium) agrees to bear. This term is to be distinguished from Franchise (*q.v.*).

Excess of loss	A form of reinsurance in which the Reinsurer agrees to bear the loss over and above a fixed figure.
Facultative reinsurance	Reinsurance of individual risks; the reinsurance is offered to a Reinsurer who may accept or decline, as he is not bound by a reinsurance treaty.
First loss insurance	An insurance for an amount known to be less than the full value of the Insured's interest in the property at risk.
Flat rate	An all-round rate as distinct from differential rating. (The term is sometimes incorrectly used to refer to a fixed premium.)
Franchise	A relief to Insurers of each and every loss which does not exceed a specified amount. If the limit is reached, the loss is paid in full. Thus, with a £5 franchise, an Insured who suffers a loss of £4 has no claim, while one who suffers a loss of £9 receives £9. This term is to be distinguished from Excess (*q.v.*).
Freight	*a* Charge for the transportation of goods by water. *b* Hire of ship for transportation of goods.
Good faith	Lack of fraudulent acts or intentions. In general, all contracts are subject to good faith. Compare with Utmost Good Faith (*q.v.*).
Indemnity	Security against financial loss. A policy of indemnity is designed to place the Insured in the same financial position as he was immediately before the happening of the event insured against.
Insurable interest	A legal or equitable financial interest in property or in the happening of some event.
Insurance	A means whereby the losses of the few are distributed over the many.
Insured (Assured in Marine and Life)	A person with an insurable interest, who stands to benefit from a policy of insurance.
Insurer	An individual or corporate body granting policies of insurance.
Investments	Property, stocks, and shares. Money invested to earn interest.
Limit of indemnity	The maximum figure for which the Insurer is liable

under a policy of insurance. The term is normally used to denote the maximum sum for which Insurers are liable under a public liability indemnity.

Line

Used in reinsurance to denote the retention of the ceding Office.

Loss

A claim under a policy. The financial loss caused to the Insured by the happening of the event insured against.

Margin of solvency

By the provisions of the Insurance Companies Act, 1974, the total assets of an Insurance Company must exceed its total liabilities (other than share capital) by a relevant amount, known as the margin of solvency.

Memorandum of Association

A form setting out the objects and powers of a Company incorporated under the Companies Acts.

Onus of proof

The obligation on a party to a contract of proving a certain allegation in connection with that contract and relied on by the party on whom the burden of proving it rests. For example, if the Insurers allege lack of good faith by the Insured in the negotiations preceding the issue of a policy, the responsibility is theirs to produce sufficient evidence to justify the allegation. On the other hand, it is the obligation of the Insured to prove that a loss has been caused by an insured peril.

Operative clause

The clause in a policy which (subject to the policy conditions) sets out the various responsibilities of the Insurer.

Overriding commission

Commission payable in addition to the original commission.

Peril

A contingency, or fortuitous happening, which may be covered or excluded by a policy of insurance.

Policy

The document containing written evidence of the contract between the Insurers and the Insured.

Pool

A combination of Insurers in a specific class of business in which they agree to share premiums and losses.

Premium

The monetary consideration paid by the Insured

to the Insurers for the insurance granted by the policy.

Profit commission
A share of the profits derived from the business.

Proposal form
The form on which a proposal is made to an Insurer.

Proximate cause
The active, efficient cause that sets in motion a train of events which brings about a result without the intervention of any force started and working actively from a new and independent source.

Quarter-days
The days arrived at by dividing the year into four parts and on which rents and other periodical payments are customarily made. English quarter-days are Ladyday—25th March; Midsummer—24th June; Michaelmas—29th September, Christmas—25th December. Scottish quarter-days are Candlemas—2nd February; Whitsunday—15th May; Lammas—1st August; Martinmass—11th November.

Quota share
A form of reinsurance in which the ceding Office gives a fixed proportion of all its business of one or more classes to the Reinsurer.

Rate
The sum charged for each unit by which the premium is calculated. It is usually £100 of sum insured, but may be *per capita* or other unit.

Receipt
An acknowledgment of the payment of money.

Recital clause
The commencement of a policy setting out the names of the Insurers and the Insured and the statement that the latter has made application for the contract of insurance.

Recoupment
Recovery of what has been expended.

Reinsurance
An agreement made between the ceding Company and the Reinsurer, whereby the ceding Office agrees to cede and the Reinsurer agrees to accept a certain fixed share of a risk upon terms as set out in the agreement.

Reinsurer
An Insurer who accepts insurance from another Insurer.

Renewal
The continuation of a policy beyond its original term.

Retrocession
A Reinsurer may decide not to hold for his own

account the full amount ceded to him by an Insurer, and he therefore, in turn, reinsures or retrocedes part of the cession.

Return (or refund)   The paying back to the Insured of a portion of the premium he has paid, either because of cancellation of all or part of the risk or because of some decrease in hazard.

Rider   A corollary; something which naturally arises from a decision previously made. In marine insurance a rider is an 'endorsement.'

Salvage   Property which is saved from a misfortune; a reward for salvage services paid under contract.

Special peril   An extra risk added to a policy not originally designed to cover that risk (e.g., the risk of bursting or overflowing of water tanks, apparatus, or pipes, added to a fire policy).

Statute   An Act of Parliament.

Stop loss reinsurance   This is an adaptation of an excess of loss treaty. The loss ratio of the ceding Company for a particular class of business is 'stopped' at an agreed percentage of the premium income, so that the Reinsurer is responsible for the balance.

Subrogation   The right which one person has of standing in the place of another and availing himself of the rights and remedies of that other, whether already enforced or not.

Sum insured   The limit of liability of the Insurers under a policy.

Surplus   The amount given off by way of reinsurance after the direct Insurer has decided upon his own retention.

Tort   A breach of a personal duty owed to a third party. The injured person has a right of damages from the wrongdoer.

Treaty reinsurance   Reinsurance effected under contract between Insurers and Reinsurers whereby the latter accept, without option, reinsurances within the terms of the contract.

Underwriter   An Insurer. Normally applied to Lloyd's Underwriters. The term is also used to describe an official of an Insurance Company who has the power to accept risks.

Utmost good faith	A duty imposed on both parties to an insurance contract. It is of greater force than ordinary good faith. The legal duty implies full disclosure of all facts material to the contract during negotiations for the contract. This duty, in effect, may be maintained throughout the existence of the contract by virtue of policy conditions.
Valuation	A list of property with values allocated to each item as the basis of insurance.
Valued policy	A contract under which the Insurers agree to pay the sum(s) stated in the event of *total* loss without the usual allowance for depreciation or appreciation. In marine insurance a valued policy is a contract where the value is conclusive in the absence of fraud and represents the maximum liability of the Insurer.
Warranty	A condition which must be complied with literally. Infringement of a warranty precludes the Insured from recovering under his policy, although the loss may not have been affected by the warranty. In insurance, a warranty has the same effect as a condition in the ordinary law of contract.

Glossary of Special Terms

A fortiori	much more; with stronger reason.
Ab initio	from the beginning.
Actio personalis moritur cum persona	a personal action dies with the person (an old Common Law rule that has now been largely superseded by Statute Law).
Actus Dei nemini facit injuriam	the Act of God prejudices no one.
Ad hoc	for a special purpose.
Ad idem	of the same mind; agreed.
Ad valorem	according to the value.
Aliunde	from elsewhere (e.g., indemnification *aliunde*).
Assecuratus non quaerit lucrum sed agit ne in damno sit	the Insured does not seek to make a profit, but takes steps to secure himself against loss.
Ats. (ad sectam)	at the suit of.
Bona fide	in good faith.
Causa proxima non remota spectatur	the immediate, not the remote, cause is to be considered.
Caveat emptor	let the buyer beware.
Cestui que trust (pl. cestuis que trust)	the beneficiary under a trust.
Ceteris paribus	other things being equal.
Chose in action	a personal right of property, which can be enforced only by action, e.g., a debt.
Consensus ad idem	in perfect agreement.
Cum testamento annexo	with the will annexed.
Damnum	loss or damage.
Damnum absque injuria	loss without wrong.
Damnum sine injuria esse potest	there may be damage or loss inflicted without any act being done which the law deems an injury.

De die in diem	from day to day.
De facto	as a matter of fact.
De jure	as a matter of law.
De minimis non curat lex	the law does not concern itself with trifles.
De novo	anew.
Delegatus non potest delegare	a delegate cannot delegate (an agent may not delegate his authority).
Duress	actual or threatened violence, or imprisonment.
Ejusdem generis	of the same kind.
Ex delicto	arising out of wrongs.
Ex gratia	as of favour.
Ex hypothesi	from the hypothesis.
Ex nudo pacto non oritur actio	out of a bare promise no action can arise.
Ex parte	on the one side; an action by one party in the absence of another.
Ex turpi causa non oritur actio	an action does not arise from a base cause.
Exempli gratia (e.g.)	for example.
Factum est	it is done.
Feme covert	a married woman.
Feme sole	an unmarried woman.
Force majeure	superior power.
Habeas corpus	(lit.) you shall have the body—a writ to a jailer to produce the body of one detained in person and to state the reasons for such detention.
Ibidem (ibid.)	in the same place.
Id est (i.e.)	that is.
Ignorantia juris quod quisque scire tenetur non excusat	ignorance of the law which everybody is supposed to know does not afford excuse.
In camera	not in open court.
In esse	in actual being.
In extenso	at full length.
In re	in the matter of.
In statu quo	in the former position.
In transitu	on the way; in passing.
Infra	below.
Inter alia	among other matters.
Intra vires	within the powers of.

Inter vivos	during life; between living persons.
Lex loci	the law of the place.
Lex mercatoria	mercantile law.
Lex non scripta	the unwritten, or Common Law.
Lex scripta	the written law, i.e., Statute Law.
Locus in quo	the place in which.
Mala fide	in bad faith.
Mutatis mutandis	the necessary changes being made.
Nemine contradicente (nem. con.)	without opposition.
Nemo dat quod non habet	no one can give what is not his.
Novus actus interveniens	a new act intervening.
Obiter	by the way.
Obiter dictum	a saying by the way (as in a judgment without creating a precedent).
Pari passu	with equal step, i.e., ranking equally.
Passim	in various places; here and there.
Pendente lite	while litigation is pending.
Per capita	by heads; by the number of individuals.
Per se	by itself.
Per stirpes	by the number of families.
Pro hac vice	for this occasion.
Pro tanto	for so much.
Qua	in the capacity of.
Quantum	amount.
Quantum meruit	as much as he has earned.
Qui facit per alium facit per se	he who acts through another is deemed to act in persom
Quid pro quo	something in return for something (lit. 'what for what'); a mutual consideration.
Ratio decidendi	the reason or ground of a judicial decision.
Res ipsa loquitur	the thing speaks for itself.
Res judicata pro veritate accipitur	a thing adjudicated is received as the truth.
Respondeat superior	let the principal answer.
Scienter	knowingly (e.g., that the owner of an animal knows of its dangerous propensities).
Sine die	without fixing a day.
Sub judice	under consideration.
Sui generis	of its own kind.

Sui juris	without disability.
Supra	above.
Uberrima fides	utmost good faith.
Uberrimae fidei	of the utmost good faith.
Ultra vires	beyond the legal power.
Versus (v.)	against.
Videlicet (viz.)	namely; that is to say.
Vis major	irresistible force (Act of God).
Viva voce	by word of mouth (oral testimony).
Volenti non fit injuria	that to which a man consents cannot be considered an injury.

Index